Wrinklefree jQuery and HTML5

A cutthroat guide to honing your jQuery and JavaScript skills, while learning how to use cutting edge HTML5 APIs.

Matthew Keas

Wrinklefree jQuery and HTML5

A cutthroat guide to honing your jQuery and JavaScript skills, while learning how to use cutting edge HTML5 APIs.

Matthew Keas

This book is for sale at http://leanpub.com/wrinklefree-jquery-and-html5

This version was published on 2013-11-18

ISBN 978-1-304-63536-5

This is a Leanpub book. Leanpub empowers authors and publishers with the Lean Publishing process. Lean Publishing is the act of publishing an in-progress ebook using lightweight tools and many iterations to get reader feedback, pivot until you have the right book and build traction once you do.

©2013 Matthew Keas

Tweet This Book!

Please help Matthew Keas by spreading the word about this book on Twitter!

The suggested tweet for this book is:

Wrinklefree jQuery and HTML5, just got mine! :D #wrinklefreejs
https://leanpub.com/wrinklefree-jquery-and-html5

The suggested hashtag for this book is #wrinklefreejs.

Find out what other people are saying about the book by clicking on this link to search for this hashtag on Twitter:

https://twitter.com/search?q=#wrinklefreejs

Also By Matthew Keas
Wrinklefree JS for Hipsters

For Rebecca and Pip - Thank you for putting up with the numerous 2am bedtimes and the sleepless nights. I love you both.

Contents

1 Dynamic HTML5 Forms 1
   The cat registration form 2
   Basic Support 7
   JavaScript templates: a primer 8
   Importing external scripts as templates 9
   JavaScript object representation of our fictional Cat Form 11
   jQuery events and delegates 12
   Examples on the Web 14
   Summary 15

2 Geolocation API 17
   HTML5 Geolocation on the Web 17
   Geolocation API Support 18
   An Introduction 18
   Handling Errors 19
   The Coordinates Object 20
   Higher Accuracy Readings with Mobile Devices 21
   Example Project - "Dog Sitters Unite!" 22
   Building jQuery Plugins 23
   Boots' Supporters Club – Beginning the jQuery plugin 25
   Summary 30

3 HTML5 Local Storage 31
   The Local Key-Value Store 32
   HTML5 Local Storage Support 32
   Local Storage – An Introduction 33
   Listening for Changes Made to the Local Storage 34
   Limitations of HTML5 Local Storage 35
   Putting it all together 36
   The Problem 36
   The Project 36
   The Code 37
   Summary 50

CONTENTS

4 Reading Files with jQuery and HTML5 File API 51
    Testing Browser Support 53
    The Three Musketeers (of the File API) 53
    Alternative methods for selection – dragging and dropping 56
    Reading File Contents with the FileReader API 60
    Monitoring Progress 68
    Review from this Chapter 69

5 Webcam Access with jQuery 71
    Why WebRTC is Important 72
    Defining WebRTC Formally 72
    Browser Support for WebRTC 73
    When Not to Use WebRTC 74
    Lossy Versus Lossless Codecs 74
    The Open Web Platform is the Perfect Blend of Technologies 74
    Streaming Screen Capture 75
    Examples of WebRTC in Action 75
    Tools of the Trade 77
    The Details of `getUserMedia()` 78
    WebRTC and HTML5 Canvas 80
    The HTML 80
    The jQuery / JavaScript 82
    Determining Support 82
    Defining the Options for `getUserMedia()` 83
    Grabbing a screenshot 85
    Putting It All Together 87
    Summary 91

6 Web Workers 93
    Examples of Web Workers 95
    Browser Support 98
    Detecting Support 99
    Running Examples 101
    Threads 102
    When Not To Use Web Workers 104
    Defining Web Workers Formally 104
    Limitations of Web Workers 105
    The Properties of Web Workers 105
    Spawning a new Web Worker 106
    Communicating with a Web Worker 109
    Terminating a Web Worker 114
    Shared Web Workers 114
    Capturing Errors from Web Workers 116

	Using Web Workers in our Own Web Applications	116
	Using Web Workers with Libraries	117
	Summary	121

7 jQuery and WebSockets – Low Latency Networking in JavaScript 123
    The Benefits of WebSockets 126
    When to Use or Not Use WebSockets 127
    Examples of WebSockets in Use 128
    Browsers Currently Supporting WebSockets 132
    Server Side WebSocket Frameworks 133
    The WebSocket API - Getting Started 135
    Same Origin Policy and WebSockets 137
    Encapsulating WebSockets with ws 137
    Coding our example application - Boots' Return! 139
    Summary 149

8 HTML5 Audio, Video and jQuery 151
    Examples of HTML5 Audio and Video 151
    Browsers Currently Supporting HTML Video and Audio 155
    Audio File Support 158
    Video File Support 158
    HTML5 Audio and Video Attributes 159
    HTML5 Audio and jQuery 159
    HTML5 Video and jQuery 167
    Reader Challenge 175
    The canplay Event 175
    HTML5 Video and SVG 176
    The Fullscreen API 178
    Summary 181

9 HTML5 Canvas 183
    Examples 184
    Browser Support for HTML5 Canvas 185
    Canvas - The Basics 185
    Why To Choose Canvas 186
    Simple Drawing 187
    Working With Paths 190
    Bezier Curves 191
    The Coordinate System 194
    Images 195
    Text 195
    Gradients 196
    Mixing With jQuery 200

Summary	214
10 WebGL	**217**
Examples	217
Which Browsers Currently Support WebGL?	224
WebGL - The Basics	225
Details	231
Getting out of Clipspace	233
Setting Variables in the Shaders	236
Drawing Images with WebGL	239
A Final Word on the Variable Types in Shaders	245
Summary	246

1 Dynamic HTML5 Forms

HTML5 introduces many fantastic form features. However, a limited number of browsers support these today. Thus, we as web developers must accommodate with graceful degradation – if a browser doesn't support a software feature, do we write code to handle the feature in a different manner, or do away with it entirely?

Moreover, as we learn to write plugins and immersive JavaScript applications, fine-tuning the overall design and architecture becomes more difficult – and more important. My answers are working answers, but not always the best answers.

The paradigms learned here will set the foundation in which you can construct your own coding techniques and general approaches, not just follow a recipe.

In this chapter, the reader will learn how to manage form persistence, rendering, validation, and ajax submission with jQuery. We will finish the chapter with an example project on rendering and updating views with data-binding, interacting with editable content, setting default text for inputs, and other HTML5 form features like validation, email and web address fields, and ajax form submission.

Demonstrating mastery in these core sections will provide a knowledge framework to writing your own jQuery that can manage other HTML5 and web-platform features.

Another challenge that we face in preparing this chapter is to keep it within a reasonable length. As enthusiastic as we may be in giving you a complete tour of a jQuery/HTML5 approach, we will take short-cuts wherever possible to keep things simple.

You can download the entire sample code from this book's Github page [http://github.com/matthiasak/wrinklefree-jquery-and-html5][1].

To summarize, by the end of this chapter you will:

- Understand generic attributes of new HTML5 input fields, such as email, date, number, and range
- Understand placeholders
- Autofocusing fields without using `$.select()` or `$.focus()`
- Setting required input fields
- Building custom input validation with regular expressions

Additionally, for those readers who are new to some of these topics below, will have had practice with:

---

[1] http://github.com/matthiasak/wrinklefree-jquery-and-html5

- jQuery templating
- jQuery events
- Submitting forms via AJAX

The cat registration form

Note: The following code and project is all based on a fictional brief. It entails a problem, and follows up with a thought process on designing a solution, not just the solution itself.

We have a cat, named Banjo, and would like to sign him up for a Cat-sitter service online.

Hello Banjo

While most basic pieces of forms involve inserting HTML for a simple form submission (think of a contact form), there are many things we can do to enhance the experience with HTML5 and jQuery.

Using simple jQuery, we can modify the different HTML5 attributes of the form. Let us start with a scenario:

The Cat-sitter asks for some information about Banjo:

- Cat's Name
- Cat's Email (yes, **Banjo** has an email account)

- Cat's Breed
- Cat's Date of Birth
- Number of mice caught today
- Cat's Blog (yes, that too!)

When entering this information, we expect to be able to see some features working on the page to help prevent from sending incorrect information.

Here is a simple barebones HTML (with CSS and jQuery linked) for such a page:

```
1   <html>
2   <head>
3           <title>Example 1 - Forms</title>
4           <script src="http://code.jquery.com/jquery-1.9.2.min.js"></script>
5           <link href="./styles.css" rel='stylesheet'>
6   </head>
7   <body>
8           <div class="container">
9                   <h1>My Cat's Registration Form</h1>
10                  <div class="ten columns offset-by-three">
11                          <form class="CatForm">
12                                  <label for="Name">My Cat's Name</label>
13                                  <input name="Name"
14                                          type="text"
15                                          placeholder="Banjo the Almighty"
16                                          autofocus
17                                          required>
18                                  <label for="Email">My Cat's Email</label>
19                                  <input name="Email"
20                                          type="email"
21                                          placeholder="mycat@gmail.com"
22                                          required
23                                          mulitple>
24                                  <label for="Breed">My Cat's Breed</label>
25                                  <input name="Breed"
26                                          type="text"
27                                          pattern="(Orange Tabby|Scottish Fold)"
28                                          placeholder="Type of Cat's Breed"
29                                          required>
30                                  <label for="DOB">My Cat's Date of birth</label>
31                                  <input name="DOB" type="date">
32                                  <label for="Mice">Number of mice caught today</label>
```

```
33                              <input name="Mice" type="number" value="0" required>
34                              <label for="Site">My cat's blog</label>
35                              <input name="Site" type="url"
36                                     placeholder="http://www.thecatsmeow.org"
37                                     required>
38                              <hr>
39                              <h4> My Cat's To-Do List </h4>
40                              <ul name="todolist" contenteditable="true">
41                                      <li> Get a treat. </li>
42                                      <li> Bathe in sunlight coming through the window. </li
43                                      <li> Have a staring contest with self in mirror. </li>
44                              </ul>
45                      </form>
46              </div>
47      </div>
48 </body>
49 </html>
```

A few quick things that you will note as you glance over this code:

1. `placeholder` is an attribute which sets default text. If a form is submitted with placeholder text in-place, then the value will be sent up as empty. Not supported in Internet Explorer 9 or less.
2. `autofocus` is an HTML5 attribute which automatically sets the focus the page to this exact element. Thus, just like when you visit Google, without tapping/clicking/selecting any items on the page, the element with this attribute will be highlighted and prompted on page-load.
3. `required` is an attribute which disables the form from submitting, and for most HTML5-compliant browsers will display an error message if a required element is not given a value.
4. `multiple` is an attribute which specifies the ability to have more than one value sent up to the server. The server will receive an array of values instead of a comma-delimited list of text.
5. `contenteditable` is an attribute available for almost any type of element, where the element is selectable and editable by the user, even if it is not a form element.

This code produces the following screenshot, quick and easy.

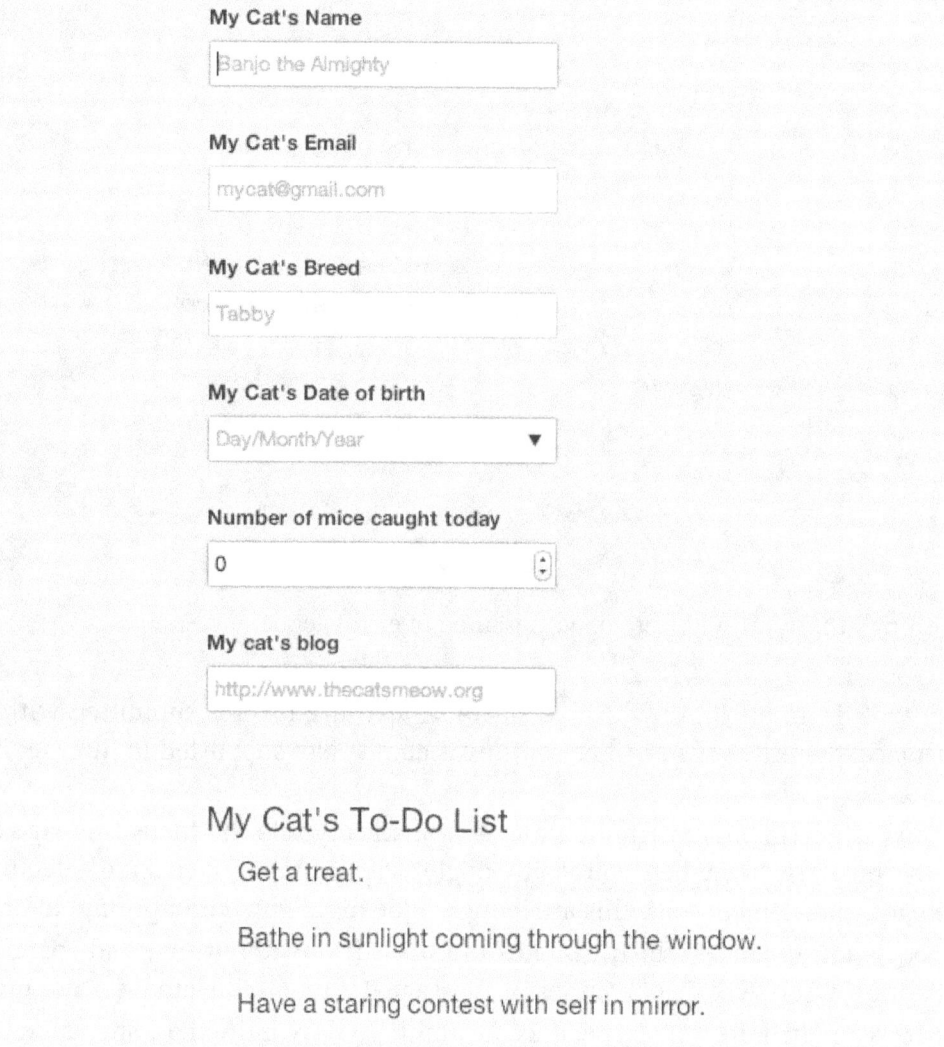

First Screenshot

Already, this code provides a few features from HTML5:

- Built-in HTML5 Email and HTML5 Date inputs without the need for jQuery UI widgets (or similar libraries)
- HTML5 form validation, that tests for correctness of fields
- HTML5 placeholder text that displays when the field is empty
- An HTML5 editable list for adding / removing from the cat's todo list

After being in contact with The Cat-sitter, he has hired you (yes, you!) to build a jQuery plugin that can build any form like the above with a provided list of fields, the field types, and field requirements to be displayed on the screen. To top it off, our very HTML5 friendly Cat Registration Form will:

- Be dynamically rendered with a templating engine
- Submit form data via AJAX for the best user experience.

Basic Support

HTML5 Form Validation is supported under these browsers:

Form Validation Support

HTML5 has baked in clientside form validation, and polyfills can enable this for legacy browsers as well. Using the defined HTML5 API for constraint validation may be a more maintainable direction than using a jQuery Validation plugin, depending on your team. When detecting this feature, be aware of Safari's half baked support. It does support form validation, but won't highlight invalid fields or present error messages.

Some *polyfills* (third-party scripts and includes which can replace functionality for graceful-degradation of browser support) for HTML5 Form features are:

1. https://github.com/ryanseddon/H5F[2]
2. http://afarkas.github.io/webshim/demos/[3]

Instructions for these are outside the scope of this book, however flip me a message @matthiasak[4] and I will be happy to help!

---

[2]https://github.com/ryanseddon/H5F
[3]http://afarkas.github.io/webshim/demos/
[4]https://twitter.com/matthiasak

JavaScript templates: a primer

One particular feature I would like to demonstrate is templating. Whilst templating isn't a JavaScript *feature* per sé, it is a powerful organizational tool that can help us separate and glue together concerns in an application (logic and presentation).

Templating simply allows us to provide a basic HTML structure, and for multiple datum can produce different results. For instance, an example would be printing someone's latest tweets.

Tweet

Simple enough as it is, this little snapshot is actually full of information and components. The presentation itself stays the same, but the data can be different per tweet.

Let's take a deeper look.

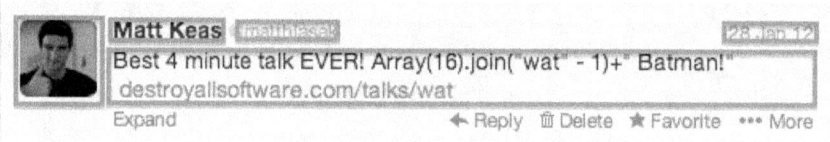

Annotated Tweet

Now, I can spot some more integral and repeatable pieces of a tweet:

1. A profile image source
2. The name
3. The twitter handle
4. The date
5. The message text itself

Instead of typing twenty different versions of this HTML, templating instead helps us by *filling in* the variables we pass to it for a specified template.

Let's take a look at this further with the Mustache templating library.

> Mustache is one of many templating libraries. Each library is unique in its value proposition - some are faster, some have some logic built into them, and some are only a few kilobytes in size. What matters is that the library you choose fits the requirements with which you need it to fulfill.

Mustache templates have built-in functionality that processes an input object and produce HTML from:

- A string containing markup, and
- An object or array with values to send to the view.

You can learn more about Mustache here: https://github.com/janl/mustache.js[5].

If you download and include this file https://raw.github.com/janl/mustache.js/master/mustache.js[6] in your page with a `<script>` tag (`<script src="mustache.js"></script>`), then the Mustache library will be available to use in the code.

One particular favorite of mine is the *Content Delivery Network* CDN.js [http://cdnjs.com/][7]:

```
<script src="//cdnjs.cloudflare.com/ajax/libs/mustache.js/0.7.2/mustache.min.js"\
></script>
```

A simple example is all we need! Let's print out a basic form with a mustache template.

```
var view = {
    title: "Banjo's Registration Form",
    age: function () {
        return 2 + 4;
    }
};

var output = Mustache.render("<h1>{{title}}</h1><form><input type='number' name='\
age' value='{{age}}'></form>", view);
```

Templating with Mustache, and most other JavaScript templating libraries, will reduce the complexity of nested HTML and force the developer and designer to think about reducing the number unnecessary DOM elements. This can have a positive impact on the speed and presentation of your website or web-app.

Importing external scripts as templates

Alternatively, we don't need to store a template's presentation as a string in JavaScript. Instead, we can store the template in a *named script tag*, allowing us to edit the template and import it from the `<head>` of the document:

---

[5] https://github.com/janl/mustache.js
[6] https://raw.github.com/janl/mustache.js/master/mustache.js
[7] http://cdnjs.com/

```
 1  <script type="text/template" id="CatFormTemplate">
 2      <h1>{{title}}</h1>
 3      <div class="ten columns offset-by-three">
 4          <form class="CatForm">
 5              {{#fields}}
 6                  <label for="{{name}}">{{label}}</label>
 7                  <input name="{{name}}"
 8                         type="{{type}}"
 9                         {{#placeholder}} placeholder="{{placeholder}}" {{/placeholder}}
10                         {{#value}} value="{{value}}" {{/value}}
11                         {{#autofocus}} autofocus {{/autofocus}}
12                         {{#required}} required {{/required}}
13                         {{#pattern}} pattern="{{pattern}}" {{/pattern}}>
14              {{/fields}}
15              <hr>
16              <h4> {{ToDoListTitle}} </h4>
17              <ul name="todolist" contenteditable="true">
18                  {{#ToDoListItems}}
19                      <li>{{text}}</li>
20                  {{/ToDoListItems}}
21              </ul>
22              <hr>
23              <button>Submit</button>
24          </form>
25      </div>
26  </script>
```

Mustache lets us define basic HTML – this is clear. However, I have defined a few *interpolating sections*, such as {{#fields}} and {{#ToDoListItems}}.

Let's take a look at {{#fields}}. This section repeats **for each item in the fields attribute**. This code would read out in simple English as *"for each field, render a label for that field's name, and render an input field with all the attributes set on this field."* There are tests for each property of a field we wish to render. If that property exists, then we render an attribute to the output HTML string. For example, if the autofocus attribute of a field is *truthy* (not null, an empty string, or 0), then the {{#autofocus}}...{{/autofocus}} block gets rendered as HTML with the autofocus variable placed into the HTML.

```
Example output:
---------------

<label for="test">Test</label>
<input name="test" autofocus>
```

JavaScript object representation of our fictional Cat Form

So we have the presentation and logic for the template setup. What we need next is the context to provide the template. This will be an object with a structure that loosely fits the input for this template.

Here is some example data:

```
<script>
    var formData = {
        title: 'Banjo\'s Registration Form for Shots',
        fields : [
            {name: 'Name', label: 'My Cat\'s Name', autofocus: 1, required: 1, type
', value: 'Banjo Kazooie'},
            {name: 'Breed', label: 'My Cat\'s Breed', required: 1, type: 'text', v
range Tabby', pattern: '(Orange Tabby|Scottish Fold)'}
        ],
        ToDoListTitle: 'My Cat\'s Typical Schedule',
        ToDoListItems: [
            {text:'Scratch a post'},
            {text:'Bathe in sunlight on window sill'},
            {text:'Chase a laser pointer'}
        ]
    };
    var CatForm = Mustache.compile($('#CatFormTemplate').html());
    var formHTML = CatForm(formData);
</script>
```

There we go! The `formHTML` variable now contains the HTML of the template as a string. If we so choose, we can add this string to the DOM:

```
$('body').append(formHTML);
```

We can even append the `formHTML` to a popup or modal window.

So, let's have a look at what our CatForm app currently looks like:

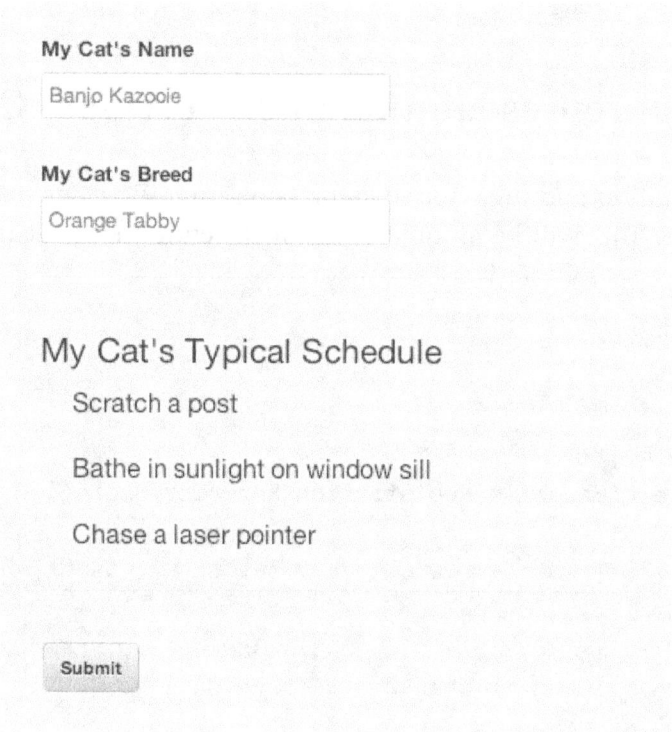

Dadadadadada CatForm!

However, we still haven't managed to submit the form via AJAX, and thus any interaction with the `<button>` element in the form will post back to the server and refresh the page, which is not the user experience wanted by the Cat-sitter service. What we want is to not force the page to refresh after the submit button is clicked.

jQuery events and delegates

Listening for events is a simple and standard functionality of jQuery. jQuery provides a wonderful abstraction layer that allows a standardized method for handling, triggering, and blocking events. We can even disable default events, such as letting the browser HTTP POST our Cat Form back to the server when the submit button is clicked.

The next step is to capture all submit events from our CatForm and post the data to a supplied URL.

The most efficient and cleanest solution to coding this is to use a jQuery delegate. While we can use the `$.delegate()` function, as supplied here http://api.jquery.com/delegate/[8], the latest builds

---

[8] http://api.jquery.com/delegate/

of jQuery as of this writing has a universal $.on() function that calls $.delegate() or $.click() for us "automagically." See http://api.jquery.com/on/[9].

jQuery delegates allow us to specify a proxy, essentially, that handles events for elements within it. This provides us with a multi-faceted improvement. The browser does not have to create multiple events and attach them to multiple elements in the DOM, and the delegate can accept events for items not yet existing within the DOM (which is not possible by using $.click() directly on an element before it exists within the DOM.

Here is how we listen for form submissions from CatForm without needing CatForm HTML within the DOM.

```
$(function(){
    $('.container')
    .on('click', 'button', function(){
        var $this = $(this);
        $this.parents('form').trigger('submit');
    })
    .on('submit', '.CatForm', function(e){
        e.preventDefault();
        var $this = $(this),
        data = $this.serialize(),
        url = $this.attr('action');
        $.post(url, data).success(function(){
            // do something when it finishes
        });
    });
});
```

We have added a click handler for the button element. This handler will force the <form> element to trigger the submit event, instead of the <button> itself.

Afterwards, we listen for submit events within $('.container') from any element that has the class CatForm and provide a handler. This handler will collect all the data of the <form> element with $this.serialize(), and POST it to the URL specified in the form via AJAX - asynchronously.

As a small note, e.preventDefault() is included because the default action (<form> submit event) can trigger a page refresh. We are blocking this and instead providing our own action.

Let us finish the application with a few additions to the code by adding the action to the <form> in the template, and to the context object.

---

[9]http://api.jquery.com/on/

```
1   Template:
2   -----------
3
4   <form class="CatForm" action="{{action}}">
5           // .. rest of the template
6   </form>
```

```
1   Data:
2   -----------
3
4   var formData = {
5           title: 'Banjo\'s Registration Form for Shots',
6           action: "",
7           // .. rest of the data
8   };
```

This form will be printed out now with the proper `action`. As a requirement (and possible reader practice), the `action` must be either an empty string (in which case the `<form>` will POST back to the same URL the page is loaded on), or a valid URL.

If the `<form>` fails to validate based on the specified requirements in `formData`, then the `submit` event will never be triggered, thus the AJAX code will never be trigger by the `$('.container').on('submit', '.CatForm', function(e){...})` handler.

> It is also my duty to say this: Validation should be done on the server as well as the client, no matter the case. Client-side validation creates better experiences by improving feedback loops. Server-side validation protects the real application from all possible attack vectors, which could be other websites or even the command-line / terminal from a cracker's personal computer.

Examples on the Web

One particular library I have found to be well-done is http://www.matiasmancini.com.ar/jquery-plugin-ajax-form-validation-html5.html[10]. This jQuery plugin allows you to call `$('#myform').html5form();` on an existing `<form>` element in the DOM.

This will let browsers lacking HTML5 Form Validation support interpret different form features, such as the `placeholder` attribute.

---

[10]http://www.matiasmancini.com.ar/jquery-plugin-ajax-form-validation-html5.html

```
1    <input type="text" placeholder="Full Name"/>
```

Summary

That finishes our CatForm application! As a wrap-up, in this chapter we have:

1. Rendered email and date inputs without the need for jQuery widgets
2. Specified placeholders, autofocusing, and multiple & required inputs
3. handled arbitrary regex as validation for inputs
4. Dynamically rendered an entire form from metadata passed in a JSON object with the use of JavaScript templating
5. Delegated event handlers for the form
6. Configured the form to send its data via AJAX instead of refreshing the page

In the next chapter, we will cover the HTML5 Geolocation API – which gives us the power to collect users' location.

2 Geolocation API

The Geolocation API specifies a number of wonderful features, letting a user share his or her location with trusted web sites. A user's latitude and longitude are available to JavaScript on the page, which can in turn decide to send this location to a server and provide *fancy-shmancy* services like recommending nearby restaurants and serving up coupons from local businesses.

Browser vendors slowly began adding Geolocation features to their browsers, however they were vendor specific and not widely supported. Fortunately, around the same time that HTML5 was finalized, the W3C also helped finalize a Geolocation API. Thank goodness!

You've Got Maps!

In this chapter, we will cover:

1. Basic use of the Geolocation API
2. Support of the API
3. Handling errors
4. Increasing the accuracy of Geolocation data
5. Writing a jQuery plugin which uses the Geolocation API

HTML5 Geolocation on the Web

- http://html5demos.com/geo[1]

---

[1] http://html5demos.com/geo

- Google Maps [https://developers.google.com/maps/documentation/javascript/examples/map-geolocation][2]

Geolocation API Support

The Geolocation API is supported by these browsers and environments:

- Internet Explorer 9+
- Firefox 3.5+
- Safari 5+
- Chrome 5+
- Opera 10.6+
- iOS 3.0+
- Android 2.0+

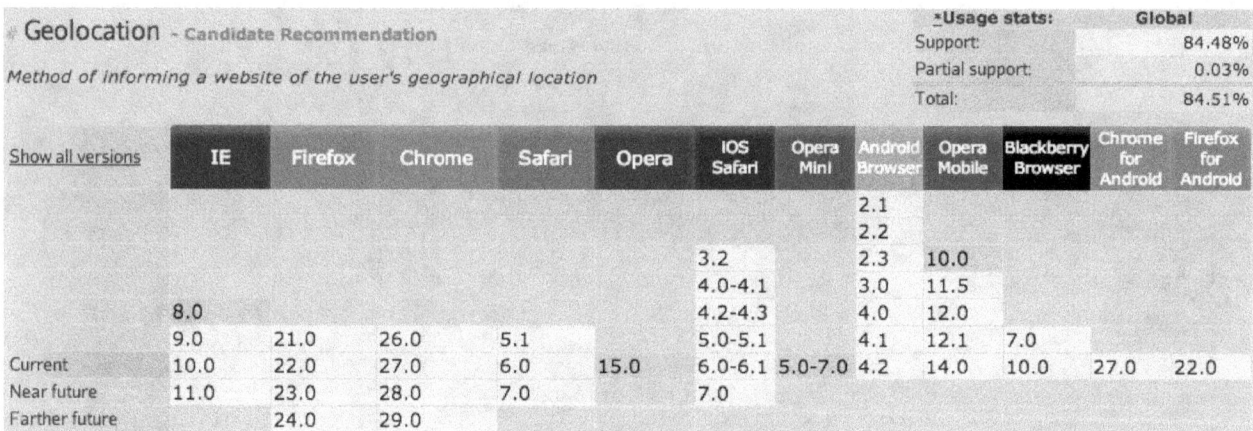

Geolocation Support

An Introduction

The Geolocation API centers around one global object:

```
navigator.geolocation
```

The simplest use of the geolocation API looks a little like this:

---

[2]https://developers.google.com/maps/documentation/javascript/examples/map-geolocation

```
1  function get_location(){
2      navigator.geolocation.getCurrentPosition(callback_function, error_handler, posit\
3  ionOptions);
4  }
```

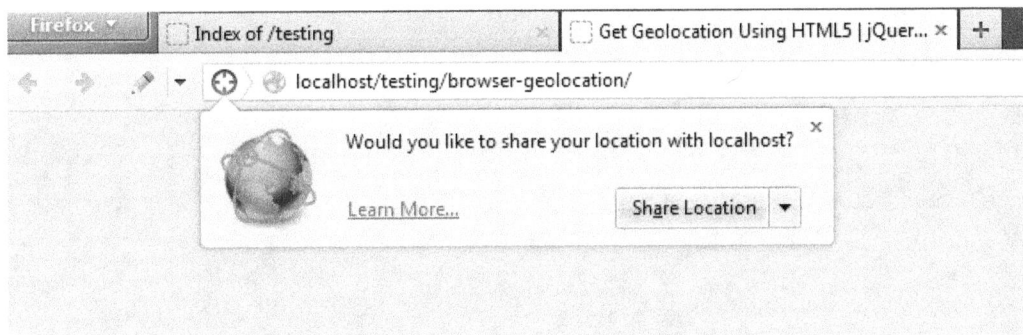

This code will actually prompt the user to Allow access to his or her location.

Geolocation support is *opt-in*, such that you should be prompted to either *allow* or *disallow* use of your location by the browser you are using.

If you choose to *disallow* access to your location, then `getCurrentPosition()` should receive an error handler as an argument, too.

Handling Errors

Our code above needs a handler for the success or failure of accessing a user's location. Here, we can define an error handler, which will receive an error object.

Two particular attributes I try to pay attention to:

1. The `code` attribute holds a specified W3C code for the type of error that was thrown.
2. The `message` attribute holds a slightly more semantic error string for the error thrown.

Let's take a look at how we can stet to handle these errors:

```
1   function error_function(positionError){
2       var code = positionError.code,
3           message = positionError.message;
4       switch(code){
5           case 1: /// PERMISSION DENIED
6           case 2: /// POSITION UNAVAILABLE
7           case 3: /// TIMEOUT
8       }
9   }
10
11  function callback_function(){
12      …
13  }
14
15  function get_location(){
16      navigator.geolocation.getCurrentPosition(callback_function, error_function);
17  }
```

The Coordinates Object

The `heading` and `speed` should be supplied if the current session has yielded previous geolocation results.

The `coords` object is accessible underneath the `position` object provided by `getCurrentPosition()`

Only three of the `coords` object's properties will always be available (The rest may be `null`):

1. latitude,
2. longitude,
3. and accuracy

```
▼ [Geoposition]
  ▼ 0: Geoposition
    ▼ coords: Coordinates
        accuracy: 49
        altitude: null
        altitudeAccuracy: null
        heading: null
        latitude: 29.7328074
        longitude: -95.4025884
        speed: null
      ▶ __proto__: Coordinates
        timestamp: 1373765672081
      ▶ __proto__: Geoposition
        length: 1
      ▶ __proto__: Array[0]
```

The `coords` object, from Chrome's debugging console.

```
1  function callback_function(position){
2      var latitude = position.coords.latitude,
3          longitude = position.coords.longitude,
4          altitude = position.coords.altitude,
5          accuracy = position.coords.accuracy,
6          altitudeAccuracy = position.coords.altitudeAccuracy,
7          heading = position.coords.heading,
8          speed = position.coords.speed,
9          timestamp = position.timestamp;
10 }
```

Thus, depending on support and previous requests to *getCurrentPosition()*, a developer may be able to make informed decisions on the accuracy on movement of a user's position. **Now that's hot.**

Higher Accuracy Readings with Mobile Devices

So, being a quick witted programmer, you may have thought about how a smartphone might access this functionality. Currently, mobile devices might use three different methods to provide geolocation data:

1. Mobile devices can have a GPS radio, which provides a widely-varying range of accuracy.
2. Mobile devices can use the built-in Wifi chipset, where Geolocation capabilities can stem from geolocating an IP address.
3. Mobile devices can be located by triangulation from cellphone towers.

So how do cell/smart/feature phones supply their location to the browser?

The answer is: mobile devices use the developer's choice! (Hot, again.)

How do I choose which method to take, and why should I not choose GPS at every turn?

Each of the options will differ on power-requirements (Wifi chips use less power than GPS chips) and accuracy (GPS chips will more frequently have greater accuracy than triangulation).

How do I select which method to take?

These options are triggered by supplying the third argument to the `getCurrentPosition()` function, the `PositionOptions` object.

```
1  var positionOptions = {
2       enableHighAccuracy: true, // true or false
3       timeout: 5000, // in milliseconds
4       maximumAge: 30000 // in milliseconds
5  };
6
7  function get_location(){
8       navigator.geolocation.getCurrentPosition(callback_function, error_function, posi\
9  tionOptions);
10 }
```

Some things to note about providing `positionOptions`:

- If **enableHighAccuracy** is "truthy" (is a number != 0, is an object, or is a non-empty string), and the device/browser supports it, then a higher accuracy `location` will be provided by `getCurrentPosition()`.
- The `timeout` property defines how long to wait to retrieve a position. This countdown does not begin until after the user provides permission to calculate his or her position.
- The `maximumAge` property defines how "fresh" a location must be. If a cached location is provided by the browser, `getCurrentPosition` will check that the location was retrieved at least some X milliseconds ago.

As an example, let's say I request access to my phone's location on my own web application. If I provide a `maximumAge` attribute to the `positionOptions`, then one of two things will happen: 1. The browser will give me a fresh Geolocation (determined by the Browser/OS/Platform). 2. The platform isn't ready to give me a brand new location, so it provides me with the latest location, if it is *"fresh"*. I wrote the application to access my location, and set the `maximumAge` to 30000ms (or 30 seconds). If 45 seconds later the application makes a second call for my location, then the Geolocation API will need to get a new position from my phone.

Savvy? If you are still having some trouble understanding how this all works together, have no fear. I'm going to create another example project which will glue these concepts together.

Example Project - "Dog Sitters Unite!"

> **Note:** The following code and project is all based on a fictional brief. It entails a problem, and follows up with a thought process on designing a solution, not just the solution itself.

The owner of the Cat-Sitter Service from *Chapter 1: jQuery and HTML5 Forms* has created somewhat of a buzz about different cats in the neighborhood. Our neighbor, Jeremy, decided to hire us to put together a little feature to get people excited about dogs, too!

Jeremy's Saint Bernard, Boots, would love to have more attention than the Orange Tabby cat – Banjo – who lives down the street.

The objective will be to create a webpage for the newly-formed "Boots' Supporters Club". This webpage needs to record the number and location of the users who want to show their support for Boots. The end result will record the location and quantity of people who want to rally behind support for dogs.

We will create a small web page which will:

- Test for Geolocation API support
- Establish an ability to grab the location periodically
- Handle errors from `getCurrentPosition()` gracefully
- Write a jQuery plugin
- Update a list of locations of dog enthusiasts and print the list on the page

Now, before we build our application, let's walk through how to build a jQuery plugin.

Building jQuery Plugins

Once you have become comfortable with using jQuery, the next step is to add to it. jQuery, being as developer focused as it can be, has supplied methods for JavaScript developers like us to modify it without butchering the jQuery source code.

> Knowing how jQuery works is the key to writing really *fast*, *efficient*, and *memory-friendly* code. I highly recommend looking at the jQuery source to figure out how jQuery does some of the features it provides. You can find the latest jQuery source at https://github.com/jquery/jquery[3]

Extending jQuery with plugins and methods is a very powerful technique which can save our peers (and more importantly, ourselves) time and agony. We can incur less heartache (and more *win*) by abstracting written functions into logically separated pillars. These pillars are plugins.

Let's jump into code quickly so we can get up to speed with an example.

Modifying the jQuery Variable (or Not Really)

We start by adding a new property to the *jQuery.fn* attribute.

---

[3] https://github.com/jquery/jquery

```
1  jQuery.fn.myPlugin = function(){
2      // awesome plugin stuff here
3  }
```

That's all we have to do define accessible functions from jQuery selections. We can then use the them as normal:

```
1  jQuery('#someElement').myPlugin();
```

Of course, this does nothing right now, but that is the next step. But first, where is the lovely dollar sign ($) that we all know and love? We can make use of the dollar sign from jQuery just as easily:

```
1  (function($){
2      $.fn.myPlugin = function(){
3          //--> `this` is a jQuery object, $('#someElement')
4          this.text('Hello World!');
5          return this;
6      }
7  })(jQuery);
```

A word about `return this;` from line 5:

As per jQuery Plugin Development guidelines, we have to return the `this` at the end of a plugin function, to support chaining and maintain reference.

But what about working with multiple elements in the jQuery selection?

We can do that, too. As a matter of fact, it isn't very difficult to iterate over multiple `<div>`s (or other elements).

Let's write a jQuery plugin that will return the tallest HTML element from a jQuery selection:

```
1   $(function(){
2       $.fn.tallestElement = function(){
3           var $max = $();
4           this.each(function(index, el){
5               var $el = this;
6               if(!$max || $el.height() > $max.height()){
7                   $max = $el;
8               } else if($el.height() == $max.height()){
9                   $max.add($el);
10              }
11          });
12          return $max;
13      };
14  });
```

Now the `tallestElement` function is accessible from jQuery selections. The following code makes the tallest `<div>` on the page have the text `"I'm tall!"`:

```
1   $('div').tallestElements().text("I'm tall!");
```

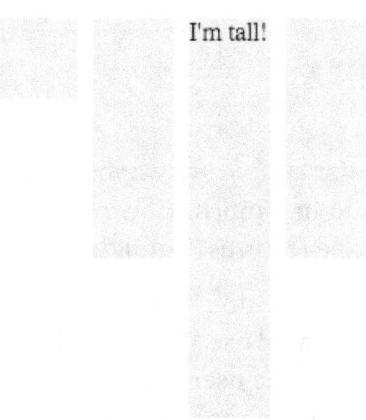

That is one tall `<div>`

There are some very small details you should be sure to understand:

- We can create an empty jQuery object, just as on line 4.
- Then we loop over all the elements in the query (e.g. $('div')).
- In the loop, we compare this element's height to the $max height.
- We return a jQuery object ($max) to allow chaining of jQuery functions.

Simple! That is my short introduction to jQuery plugins. Now let's move on to the showcase.

Boots' Supporters Club – Beginning the jQuery plugin

Let us start by building a jQuery plugin that will test for Geolocation API support in our device.

```
1   $(function(){
2       $.fn.bootsy = function(){
3           // simple test for Geolocation object
4           if(!navigator || !navigator.geolocation || !navigator.geolocation.getCurrentPos
5   ition) {
6               return;
7           }
8
9           // else we have geolocation support, print out something into
```

```
10                  // jQuery elements provided
11
12                  this.each(function(index, el){
13                          el.text('Hooray! We have Geolocation support! Boots the Saint Bernard wi
14  e this!');
15                  });
16              };
17  });
```

It is best to use tools such as Modernizr [http://www.modernizr.com/][4] which will provide feature-detection APIs, but this plugin will do in a pinch. However feature-detection libraries and services provide the ability to gracefully degrade features (through polyfills and fallbacks) in our applications.

For instance, if we were to build an application which would use HTML5 Local Storage to persist data related to our web application, we could use Modernizr [http://www.modernizr.com/][5] to detect support for this from a user's browser. If the user's browser doesn't support HTML5 Local Storage, then we can detect this issue without making the JavaScript thread *crash*.

Here is a simple and quick way to use **Modernizr** to detect support for the Geolocation API:

```
1   function get_location() {
2       if (Modernizr.geolocation) {
3           navigator.geolocation.getCurrentPosition( ... );
4       } else {
5           // no native support; maybe try a fallback?
6       }
7   }
```

Now that we have a simple plugin to detect the geolocation functionality, we can test it out!

```
1   <!DOCTYPE html>
2   <html>
3       <head>
4           <title>Example 2 - A big, lovable Saint Bernard named Boots</title>
5           <script src="http://code.jquery.com/jquery-1.10.2.min.js"></script>
6           <link href="/styles.css" rel='stylesheet'>
7           <script src="http://cdnjs.cloudflare.com/ajax/libs/mustache.js/0.7.2/mustache.m\
8   in.js"></script>
9       </head>
10      <body>
```

---

[4] http://www.modernizr.com/
[5] http://www.modernizr.com/

```
11              <div></div>
12              <script>
13              $(function(){
14                      $('div').bootsy();
15              });
16              </script>
17        </body>
18 </html>
```

So, we have a jQuery plugin now that accesses the HTML5 Geolocation object. If geolocation is successful, we print out a success message.

In the next steps, we will:

- Establish an ability to grab the location periodically, with an interval defined by options passed to the jQuery plugin.
- Handle errors from `getCurrentPosition()` gracefully, and print errors to the HTML elements involved.
- Update a list of locations the current user has submitted and print the list on the page.

Let's work forward here, starting with grabbing the location. We can even process arguments which can overwrite default error message text, and supply an optional `interval` attribute which specifies the recurring time window to grab the location of the user every X seconds.

```
1  $(function(){
2          // simple test for Geolocation
3          if(!navigator || !navigator.geolocation || !navigator.geolocation.getCurrentPosi\
4  tion) {
5                  return;
6          }
7
8          $.fn.bootsy = function(options){
9                  var defaults = {
10                         interval: 0, // interval in seconds, not milliseconds
11                         permission_denied: 'Permission denied, human!',
12                         position_unavailable: 'Can\'t get the position, human!',
13                         timeout: 'Timed out! :('
14                 };
15                 var positionOptions = {
16                 enableHighAccuracy: true, // true or false
17                 timeout: 5000, // in milliseconds
18                 maximumAge: 30000 // in milliseconds
```

```
19          };
20
21          options = $.extend(defaults, options);
22
23          // else we have geolocation support, print out something into
24          // jQuery elements provided
25          this.each(function(index, el){
26                  el.text('Hooray! We have Geolocation support! Boots the Saint Bernard will love
27  this!');
28          });
29
30          var $this = this;
31          var error_function = function(positionError){
32                  var code = positionError.code
33                      , message = positionError.message;
34                  switch(code){
35                          case 1: /// PERMISSION DENIED
36                                  $this.each(function(el){
37                                          el.text(options.permission_denied);
38                                  });
39                                  break;
40                          case 2: /// POSITION UNAVAILABLE
41                                  $this.each(function(el){
42                                          el.text(options.position_unavailable);
43                                  });
44                                  break;
45                          case 3: /// TIMEOUT
46                                  $this.each(function(el){
47                                          el.text(options.timeout);
48                                  });
49                                  break;
50                  }
51          }
52
53          var callback_function = function(position){
54                  var latitude = position.coords.latitude,
55                      longitude = position.coords.longitude,
56                      altitude = position.coords.altitude,
57                      accuracy = position.coords.accuracy,
58                      altitudeAccuracy = position.coords.altitudeAccuracy,
59                      heading = position.coords.heading,
60                      speed = position.coords.speed,
```

```
61                    timestamp = position.timestamp;
62
63            $this.each(function(index, el){
64                    el.text('We have located you at ' + latitude + ', ' + longitude + ' --
65  Date(timestamp).toLocaleString());
66            });
67        }
68
69        var get_location = function(){
70            navigator.geolocation.getCurrentPosition(callback_function, error_function, po
71  itionOptions);
72        }
73
74        if(options.interval) {
75            setInterval(function() {
76                get_location();
77            }, options.interval * 1000);
78        } else {
79            get_location();
80        }
81  });
```

Whew! Now that is a lot more verbose! Aren't we awesome? Now we can make use of this plugin like so:

```
1   <!DOCTYPE html>
2   <html>
3       <head>
4           <title>Example 2 - A big, lovable Saint Bernard named Boots</title>
5           <script src="http://code.jquery.com/jquery-1.8.3.min.js"></script>
6           <link href="/styles.css" rel='stylesheet'>
7           <script src="http://cdnjs.cloudflare.com/ajax/libs/mustache.js/0.7.0/mustache.
8   in.js"></script>
9       </head>
10      <body>
11          <div></div>
12          <script>
13              $(function(){
14                  $('div').bootsy({
15                      interval: 60,
16                      permission_denied: 'Sorry, but you CAN\'T TOUCH THIS.'
17                  });
```

```
18                    });
19                </script>
20        </body>
21  </html>
```

Hotness. We have made use of our awesome jQuery plugin, and supplied a 60 second interval and a new error message when permission is denied.

Summary

That's all for this chapter! Here is a recap of the topics and paradigms we covered:

- We learned the inner workings of the HTML5 Geolocation API
- We tested for Geolocation API support
- We Handled errors from `getCurrentPosition()` *gracefully*
- We learned how to write a jQuery plugin
- We learned how to combine the power of jQuery and the HTML5 Geolocation API!

In the next chapter, we will cover the nuances of HTML5 Local Storage, and how we can store persistent data in the browser – without cookies.

3 HTML5 Local Storage

Browser vendors slowly began adding different library support to each software environment which provides the ability to persist data between sessions and page reloads. This is an extremely powerful ability that allows web applications developers to cache and persist all sorts of awesome stuff. For example:

- Cache and access music and sound files for audio-based web applications and games
- Store local databases of products, to-do lists, or even information on local places and venues when traveling away from our handy mobile networks
- Store images for an HTML5 Canvas-powered image editing application

That is a just a really tiny subset of possible applications that were once only possible under the context of native applications. Normally, a native application's operating system provides a deep abstraction layer for getting and setting application-specific data like preferences or local database models. Whilst web applications historically had none of these luxuries, there was one Web 1.0 feature that allowed application developers to store some data with the browser – in the form of cookies.

Cookies, controversially, had a few downsides:

- Cookies are included in every HTTP Request, slowing down the application by needlessly and repeatedly transmitting the same data.
- Cookies are also sent over-the-wire on the same protocol that the site is sent, so if a site is not hosted completely over SSL, then security breaches can occur.
- Cookies are very limited in size – about 4KB in all – which is, under many circumstances, not worth the weight of the data.

What we really desire is the ability to store a lot of data, on the client only, that not only can persist between page refreshes and isn't sent across the wire each request, but is a secure place to store data.

Enter HTML5 Local Storage. Most beneficially, once stored on the client, any and all data is cached and quickly accessible, so it is entirely possible to work with an entirely localized set of data and files versus making any network calls, which is a really powerful ability that reduces the disadvantages of web-versus-native application development.

The official W3C specification for HTML5 Local Storage is under Web Storage, at http://dev.w3.org/html5/webstc

---

[1]http://dev.w3.org/html5/webstorage/

Want to run the example code for this chapter? Grab and install the latest version of Node.js[2]. After installing, you can run a simple web server by opening the Chapter 3 code directory and using node to run the server:

`node my/directory/wrinklefree-jquery/ch3/server.js`

Afterwards, simply open a browser to `localhost:8888`.

The Local Key-Value Store

HTML5 Local Storage is a local database of sorts. It is a key-value datastore that persists across requests and page reloads. Just like many NoSQL technologies, the core functionality lets the developer store any scalar JavaScript data type (strings, numbers, or booleans) in quick and simple fashion, addressable by a key string. All data is then stored as a string, so if necessary, use `parseInt()` and `parseFloat()` to process numbers. Booleans, will be stored as strings, as well – `"true"` or `"false"`.

HTML5 Local Storage Support

HTML5 Local Storage is supported by the following browsers and environments. Note that it is supported all by even Internet Explorer 8!

- Internet Explorer 8+
- Firefox 3.5+
- Safari 4+
- Chrome 4+
- Opera 10.5+
- iOS 2.0+
- Android 2.0+

---

[2] http://nodejs.org

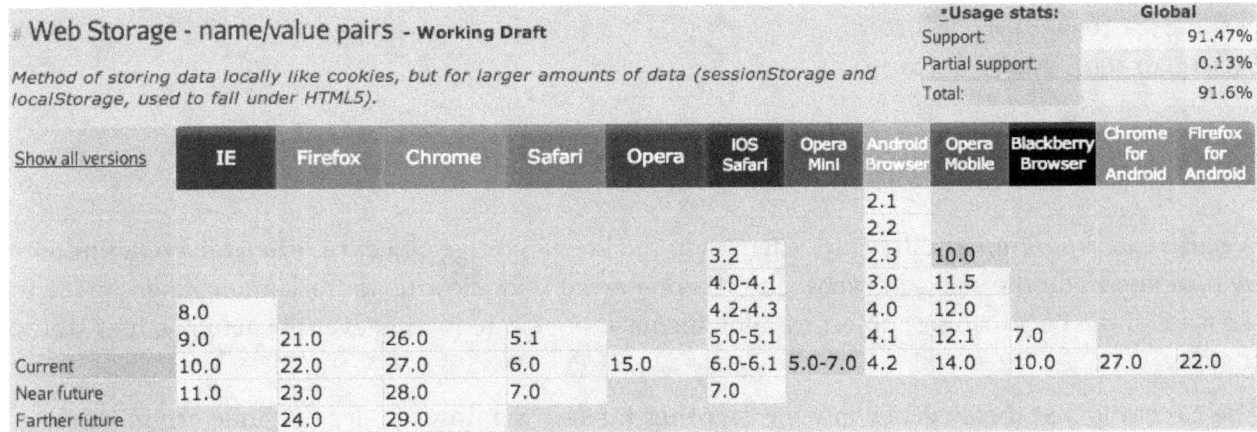

WebStorage Support

Local Storage – An Introduction

HTML5 Local Storage centers around one global object:

```
window.localStorage
```

The core functionality is based around a few functions that the supporting browsers provide:

- `localStorage.getItem('someItem')`
- `localStorage.setItem('someItem', 'string to be written to someItem')`
- `localStorage.removeItem('someItem')`

Some things of note:

- When calling `getItem( ... )` without an input, an error will not be thrown. Instead, null will be returned.
- When calling `setItem( ... )` with a key that already exists, the data currently stored at that key will simply be overwritten.
- When calling `removeItem( ... )` without an input, no errors will be thrown. Instead, nothing will happen.

Also, we can make use of Local Storage by simply accessing it as a persistent keyed array, instead of using the functions provided:

```
1  var bar = localStorage['foo'];
2  localStorage['foo'] = bar;
```

Listening for Changes Made to the Local Storage

We also can programmatically track changes to the Local Storage object **in other tabs or windows** by listening in on the `storage` event. The `storage` event will allow us to track any changes made to the state of the Local Storage object by allowing us to hook into it whenever the actual values stored change.

The caveat is that these events only fire on **other tabs or windows** under the same origin (scheme, domain, port number), so don't be surprised if the `storage` event doesn't fire on the same page.

In other words, the event will not trigger whenever calls `setItem()`, `removeItem()`, or `clear()` result in no change to the Local Storage object.

We can listen for `storage` events by making use of `addEventListener()`. Internet Explorer 8 doesn't support But we can also use a fallback for older browsers - `attachEvent()`:

```
1  if(window.addEventListener){
2          window.addEventListener("storage", handler, false);
3  } else {
4          window.attachEvent("onstorage", handler);
5  }
```

We can then handle the event with our handler function, where the `e` is a StorageEvent object, except in older Internet Explorer versions, where we need to grab `window.event`:

```
1   function handler(e){
2           var event = e || window.event;
3
4           // "string" -- key name that was added/removed/modified
5           var key = event.key;
6
7           // the previous value, _null_ if new value
8           var oldValue = event.oldValue;
9
10          // the new value, _null_ if removed
11          var newValue = event.newValue;
12
13          // the url of the page that triggered this change
14          // some older browsers use uri, newer browsers use url
15          var url = event.url || event.uri;
16  }
```

As you may see, we can access four properties from the event:

- `event.key`
- `event.oldValue`
- `event.newValue`
- `event.uri` or `event.url`, depending on browser

Limitations of HTML5 Local Storage

Each origin may store a minimum of 5MB of data in Local Storage by default. This means that if we were to browse to http://www.whatwg.org/specs/web-apps/current-work/multipage/[3], then our origin is http://www.whatwg.org[4], which includes the scheme (http), the domain (www.whatwg.org), and the port (80 by default).

> 5MB is equivalent to 5x1024KB = 5x1024x1000B. JavaScript characters are stored as 16bit UCS-2. If each character is 16bits, and 16bits = 2B, then 5x1024x500 characters can fit under Local Storage. That means, 2,560,000 characters or about 512,000 words. For reference, Homer's Iliad contains only 358,020 words. The Odyssey contains 117,319 words.
>
> That is a lot of space!

Thus, http://www.whatwg.org[5] can store 5MB of strings (Local Storage stores everything as a string), so there are some things to consider, such as storing numbers. Storing n powers of 2 in Local Storage will take up considerably more space than it would normally. Storing `[1, 2, 4, 8, 16, 32, …]` will take up far less space than `["1", "2", "4", "8", "16", "32", …]`.

So, as far as we can see, Local Storage is really fast, but there are storage space limitations, and as of the time of this writing there is no means to ask for more capacity from a user.

How will I know when I've hit the limit, you say? There's an app for that! Or rather, the storage API will throw an error: `"QUOTA_EXCEEDED_ERR"`. We can catch this error and decide what to do then (Notify the user? Crash like a bomb went off?):

---

[3] http://www.whatwg.org/specs/web-apps/current-work/multipage/
[4] http://www.whatwg.org/
[5] http://www.whatwg.org/

```
1  try{
2      localStorage.setItem(key, JSON.stringify( someObject));
3  } catch(e){
4      if( e.name === "QUOTA_EXCEEDED_ERR"){
5          alert("Oh no! We ran out of room!");
6      }
7  }
```

Putting it all together

It's time to put the reading above to use and wrap this HTML5 Local Storage stuff up with a bow! So let's start an example project and go from there.

The Problem

In the last chapter on HTML5 Geolocation, we began to setup a site which recorded and submitted users' locations. Well, Jeremy has since gone and hired bunch of other developers to work on the site and add more features.

Unfortunately, those other developers didn't read **Wrinklefree jQuery and HTML5**, so they aren't as awesome as you! They have added on thirty more scripts that are loaded into the pages on the site, as well as three more CSS files, for the sum of 1MB more of data that must be loaded and cached by the browser.

Due to this, Jeremy has requested that you help him speed up his website again! Naturally, the mission is yours Agent, should you choose to accept it.

The Project

So you've decided to help Jeremy again, and you are armed with some knowledge of HTML5 Local Storage. How can we manage to speed up Jeremy's site?

Let's get creative and use HTML5 Local Storage to inject cached JavaScript and CSS files into the browser page!

By using HTML5, and piggybacking onto the API provided by jQuery, we can manage to load and cache files in HTML5 Local Storage if we can, and gracefully fail if we cannot.

To load files via jQuery, we can simply make use of jQuery's `$.ajax()` method, and its helper functions: `$.getScript()` or `$.get()`. By using jQuery to handle the network requests, we don't have to worry about *Cross-Origin Resource Sharing*.

Cross-Origin Resource Sharing

Cross domain AJAX requests transgress the browser's security model called the *Same Origin Policy*. This policy states that, among many other things, scripts originating from different *origins* cannot access the browser's page without certain restrictions.

AJAX requests, such as those made with the XMLHttpRequest object (handled by jQuery for us), are also subject to the policy, and thus if we try to load a resource from another domain, we are unable to access the *contents* of a script or CSS file due to the *Same Origin Policy*.

One technique for relaxing the *Same Origin Policy* is *Cross-Origin Resource Sharing* (also handled by jQuery). This allows us to use our scripts to access the contents of files from other *origins*.

Continuing on, the only drawback to CORS is that any server of *different origin* (e.g. not our server) where we pull the files from must implement the CORS protocol to allow our *origin* to use it. Otherwise, we must simply fallback to injecting a script tag into our page and letting those scripts run, like many script loaders do today. However, our project will not be able to cache those files into HTML5 Local Storage.

So, are you ready to start coding?

The Code

Let's start by scaffolding a class that we can use to access the Local Storage object.

```
$(function(){
    $.setStorage = function(key, data){
        try {
            localStorage.setItem(key, JSON.stringify(data));
            return true;
        } catch(e) {
            return false;
        }
    };
});
```

This is a simple enough piece to start. This code will allow us to call $.setStorage('foo', {foo: 'bar'}), where the object {foo: 'bar'} will be saved as a string in Local Storage (and fail without breaking execution).

We can also write some functions to load the stored data and also to clear it.

```javascript
// definition code for our Class
window.jqLocalStorage = function(){
        this.head = document.head || document.getElementsByTagName('head')[0];
}

$.existsInStorage = function(key){
        var data = $.parseJSON(localStorage.getItem(key) || 'false');
        return data;
}

$.clearStorage = function(){
        try{
                for(var i in localStorage){
                        localStorage.removeItem(i);
                }
        } catch(e){
                ...
        }
};
```

Next, we want to create functions to load script and stylesheet content (remote, local, or CORS supported).

```javascript
jqLocalStorage.prototype.loadScriptContentAndCacheIt = function (url){
        var self = this;
        return $.get(url, null, null, 'script').then(function(data, success, Promise){
                self.injectScriptTagByText(data);
                $.setStorage(url, data);
        });
};

jqLocalStorage.prototype.loadStyleContentAndCacheIt = function (url){
        var self = this;
        return $.get(url).then(function(data, success, Promise){
                self.injectStyleTagByText(data);
                $.setStorage(url, data);
        });
};
```

And, of course, the respective functionality to inject it.

```
jqLocalStorage.prototype.injectScriptTagByText = function (text){
    var script = document.createElement('script');
    script.defer = true;
    script.text = text;
    this.head.appendChild(script);
}

jqLocalStorage.prototype.injectStyleTagByText = function (text){
    $('head').append('<style>'+text+'</style>');
}
```

So now we have the functions to put our cached scripts and styles onto the page! You'll notice that the function to inject a script is done without jQuery. This is because we want to be sure Internet Explorer and other older browser engines will properly interpret the script's text properties and execute it.

We also want to handle the ability to load external, non-CORS scripts and stylesheets. We can do this by making use of simple techniques used by most script loaders today. Script tags will just need to be inserted into the DOM with a src attribute set, and link tags will be injected with href attributes.

```
jqLocalStorage.prototype.injectScriptTagBySrc = function (url, dfd){
    var script = document.createElement('script');
    script.defer = true;
    script.src = url;
    script.onload = script.onreadystatechange = function(){
        dfd.resolve();
    };
    this.head.appendChild(script);
}

jqLocalStorage.prototype.injectStyleTagBySrc = function (url, fn){
    var style = document.createElement('link');
    style.href = url;
    this.head.appendChild(style);
}
```

Tying all of this functionality together, we will need to define a few helper functions first before creating the final piece of our project. First off we need some functions to distinguish between a local or CORS file and remote file, as well as a regex test if a file is a CSS file.

```
1  jqLocalStorage.prototype.isLocal = function(url){
2      var hasHttp = url.indexOf('http://') != -1,
3          hasHttps = url.indexOf('https://') != -1,
4          hasSlashSlash = url.indexOf('//') != -1;
5      return !hasHttp && !hasHttps && !hasSlashSlash;
6  }
7
8  jqLocalStorage.prototype.isCSS = function (url){
9      var isCSS = url.indexOf('.css') != -1;
10     return isCSS;
11 }
```

Great! The `isLocal()` function is a bit of a hack, but it allows for us to interpret if a file is served from the same domain. The `isCSS()` function simply tests a url for a '.css' substring.

So, we can begin finalizing our API by setting up the function to load an array of files.

```
1  $.cacheFiles = function (files){
2      var arr = [],
3          jqls = new jqLocalStorage();
4
5      for(var i in files){
6          arr.push(jqls.handle_file(files[i]));
7      }
8
9      return $.when.apply($, arr)
10 };
```

This code will iterate over an array of files that look like this:

```
1  {
2      url: '...',
3      CORS: true/false
4  }
```

We then just need application logic to implement the decision tree in determining:

1. The type of file
2. and the type of file-loading mechanism

```javascript
jqLocalStorage.prototype.handle_file = function (file){
    if(!file || !file.url) return;

    var url = file.url,
        isCORS = file.CORS,
        isLocal = this.isLocal(url),
        data,
        dfd = $.Deferred();

    if(!this.isCSS(url)){
        if(isLocal){
            data = $.existsInStorage(url);
            if(data){
                this.injectScriptTagByText(data);
                dfd.resolve();
            } else {
                $.when(this.loadScriptContentAndCacheIt(url)).then(function(){
                    dfd.resolve();
                });
            }
        } else {
            this.injectScriptTagBySrc(url, dfd);
        }
    } else {
        if(isLocal){
            data = $.existsInStorage(url);
            if(data){
                this.injectStyleTagByText(data);
                dfd.resolve();
            } else {
                $.when(this.loadStyleContentAndCacheIt(url)).then(function(){
                    dfd.resolve();
                });
            }
        } else {
            this.injectStyleTagBySrc(url);
            dfd.resolve();
        }
    }
    return dfd.promise();
}
```

You will notice that the `$.cacheFiles()` function that we defined returns a jQuery when(), which is, in fact, a jQuery Promise object. By making use of the prototypal `call()` function the all Function objects implement, we can read in an arbitrary list of files in the array passed as input to `$.cacheFiles()`, and convert an array of Promise objects into an argument list for `$.when()`. The resulting call to `$.when()` will result in something similar to this:

```
return $.when(promise1, promise2, ...);
```

By using promise objects, we have the ability to run callback functions once all of the files being loaded have completed loading from network or Local Storage and are inserted into the page. Due to this functionality, our API will let us know when it is acceptable to run any code that depends on the loaded resources to look or execute without errors.

An example use case of this feature would be to load a script dynamically that provides a function to play music once we've determined that a user's browser supports this feature. We can load this script file and then run some code after it is available on the page.

```
$.cacheFiles([{url:"/music.js"}]).then(function(){
    // do something with our music
    music.play()
});
```

This is a powerful feature that not only will let us control how many scripts are loaded onto a page, but the fact the Local Storage can cache and insert content onto the page faster than the roundtrip time it takes to check if a script is cached will drastically reduce loading times of resources!

Just to put the final reasoning into place, let's load test this functionality. As a simple test, we will load 5 JavaScript files and 3 CSS files.

The JavaScript files will be local files for:

- Raphael.js – an SVG library (graphics)
- Angular.js – an MVC framework competitor
- lodash.js – a wonderful utility library and dependency for Backbone.js
- Backbone.js – another MVC framework
- D3.js – an SVG and HTML5 graphing framework
- Fine Uploader – a standalone comprehensive file uploader

The CSS files will be:

- styles.css – the same css file used for our previous chapters
- normalize.css – a modern HTML5-ready alternative to CSS resets
- font awesome – an iconic font that includes tons of great application icons

Our basic page structure is going to look something like this:

```
1   <html>
2       <head>
3           <title>Example 3 - Optimizing with Local Storage</title>
4           <script src="http://code.jquery.com/jquery-1.10.2.min.js"></script>
5           <script src="/03_01.js"></script>
6       </head>
7       <body>
8           <div class="container">
9               <div class="ten columns offset-by-three">
10                  <h1>Test Form</h1>
11                  <form class="CatForm" action="#">
12                      <label for="test">Test</label>
13                      <input name="test" type="text" placeholder="test" auto
14                      <hr>
15                      <button>Submit</button>
16                  </form>
17              </div>
18          </div>
19      </body>
20  </html>
```

As we can see, the previous markup creates a basic and minimal page structure with some random content on the page. Here's what the page looks like without loading anything with our new Local Storage project:

Test Form

Test [test]

[Submit]

An Unstyled Form

The page is very basic and unstyled. Here's a snapshot of the network requests from Chrome to my local server:

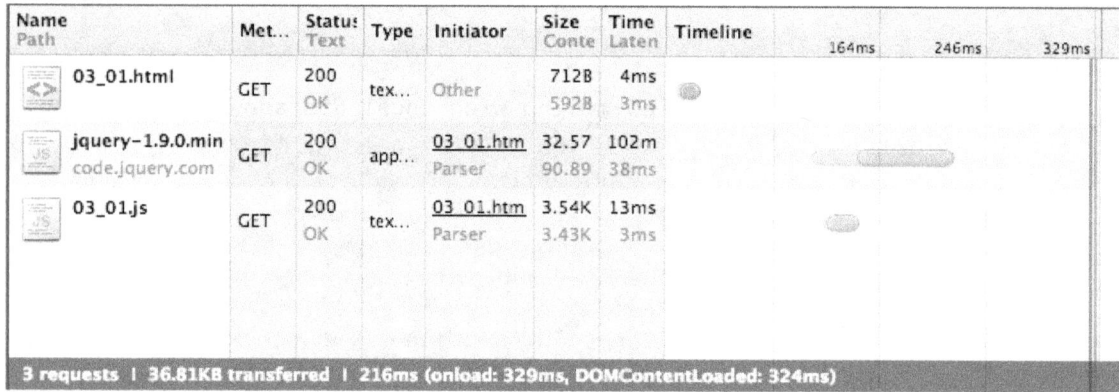

The Network Requests for the Basic Page

Every browser loads a webpage by first making a request for that HTML file. Once this completes, the browser will read through the HTML, and find the attached resources for the page and immediately begin loading the page.

Note :

The screenshot says `jquery-1.9.0.min.js`, which is the version of jQuery used when creating these screenshots. The version of jQuery has been updated in the code in this chapter and this book's code samples online.

Let's add in the styles and scripts to the HTML first to get a basic idea of how long it would take to load this page (from my local server, thus a relatively fast page load).

```
1  <html>
2      <head>
3          <title>Example 3 - Optimizing with Local Storage</title>
4          <script src="http://code.jquery.com/jquery-1.10.2.min.js"></script>
5          <script src="/03_01.js"></script>
6          <script src="/vendor/raphael-min.js"></script>
7          <script src="/vendor/angular.min.js"></script>
8          <script src="/vendor/lodash.min.js"></script>
9          <script src="/vendor/backbone-min.js"></script>
10         <script src="/vendor/d3.v3.min.js"></script>
11         <script src="/vendor/fineuploader.min.js"></script>
12         <link href="styles.css">
13         <link href="/vendor/normalize.css">
14         <link href="/vendor/font-awesome.min.css">
15     </head>
16     <body>
17         <div class="container">
18             <div class="ten columns offset-by-three">
```

```
19                        <h1>Test Form</h1>
20                        <form class="CatForm" action="#">
21                            <label for="test">Test</label>
22                            <input name="test" type="text" placeholder="test" auto
23                            <hr>
24                            <button>Submit</button>
25                        </form>
26                  </div>
27            </div>
28      </body>
29 </html>
```

This page load from `localhost://` looks something like this:

Loading Scripts over the Wire

Cool! So now we have a control with which to test our experiment. Let's switch our code over to use the jQuery-ified function that we wrote:

```html
 1  <html>
 2      <head>
 3          <title>Example 3 - Optimizing with Local Storage</title>
 4          <script src="http://code.jquery.com/jquery-1.10.2.min.js"></script>
 5          <script src="/03_01.js"></script>
 6      </head>
 7      <body>
 8          <div class="container">
 9              <div class="ten columns offset-by-three">
10                  <h1>Test Form</h1>
11                  <form class="CatForm" action="#">
12                      <label for="test">Test</label>
13                      <input name="test" type="text" placeholder="test" autofo
14                      <hr>
15                      <button>Submit</button>
16                  </form>
17              </div>
18          </div>
19          <script>
20              var files = [
21                  {url: "/vendor/raphael-min.js"},
22                  {url: "/vendor/angular.min.js"},
23                  {url: "/vendor/lodash.min.js"},
24                  {url: "/vendor/backbone-min.js"},
25                  {url: "/vendor/d3.v3.min.js"},
26                  {url: "/vendor/fineuploader.min.js"},
27                  {url: "/styles.css"},
28                  {url: "/vendor/normalize.css"},
29                  {url: "/vendor/font-awesome.min.css"}
30              ]
31              $.cacheFiles(files);
32          </script>
33      </body>
34  </html>
```

By switching from conventional resource loading to our jQuery loading plugin, the number of network requests will drop. The resulting page looks like this:

A Styled Form - with CSS Loaded via jQuery

However, instead of nine separate network requests, we make only three!

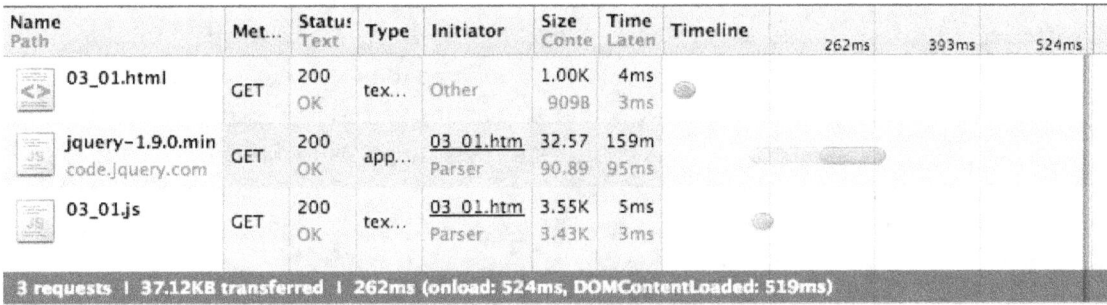

3 Requests, The Rest Were Cached by Local Storage

Note that while we have minimized data to be loaded, there is very miniscule gains in network load times due to the files being served from a local server.

To quantify the real-world differences, let's test the benefit from a CDN, such as http://cdnjs.com[6]. This will force our webpage to load scripts from a website. Even though this will still take very little time to load the external files (because http://cdnjs.com[7] is extremely fast), I will prove that we can cut times even from the tiny round-trip cost incurred from an HTTP request.

---

[6]http://cdnjs.com/
[7]http://cdnjs.com/

```
1   <html>
2       <head>
3           <title>Example 3 - Optimizing with Local Storage</title>
4           <script src="http://code.jquery.com/jquery-1.10.2.min.js"></script>
5           <script src="/03_01.js"></script>
6           <script src="//cdnjs.cloudflare.com/ajax/libs/raphael/2.1.0/raphael-min.js"></s
7   cript>
8           <script src="//cdnjs.cloudflare.com/ajax/libs/angular.js/1.1.1/angular.min.js">
9   </script>
10          <script src="//cdnjs.cloudflare.com/ajax/libs/lodash.js/1.0.0-rc.3/lodash.min.j
11  s"></script>
12          <script src="//cdnjs.cloudflare.com/ajax/libs/backbone.js/0.9.10/backbone-min.j
13  s"></script>
14          <script src="//cdnjs.cloudflare.com/ajax/libs/d3/3.0.1/d3.v3.min.js"></script>
15          <script src="//cdnjs.cloudflare.com/ajax/libs/file-uploader/3.1.1/fineuploader.
16  min.js"></script>
17          <link rel="stylesheet" href="/styles.css">
18          <link rel="stylesheet" href="vendor/normalize.css">
19          <link rel="stylesheet" href="vendor/font-awesome.min.css">
20      </head>
21      <body>
22          <div class="container">
23              <div class="ten columns offset-by-three">
24                  <h1>Test Form</h1>
25                  <form class="CatForm" action="#">
26                      <label for="test">Test</label>
27                      <input name="test" type="text" placeholder="test" autofo
28                      <hr>
29                      <button>Submit</button>
30                  </form>
31              </div>
32          </div>
33      </body>
34  </html>
```

So, by loading most of our styles and scripts from http://cdnjs.com[8], we have the opportunity to measure a 'fast' website with:

- really low latency and
- very high bandwidth file distribution

---

[8] http://cdnjs.com

The results, on the other hand, prove how powerful Local Storage can be. Let's compare the timings between loading scripts http://cdnjs.com[9] and caching them with Local Storage:

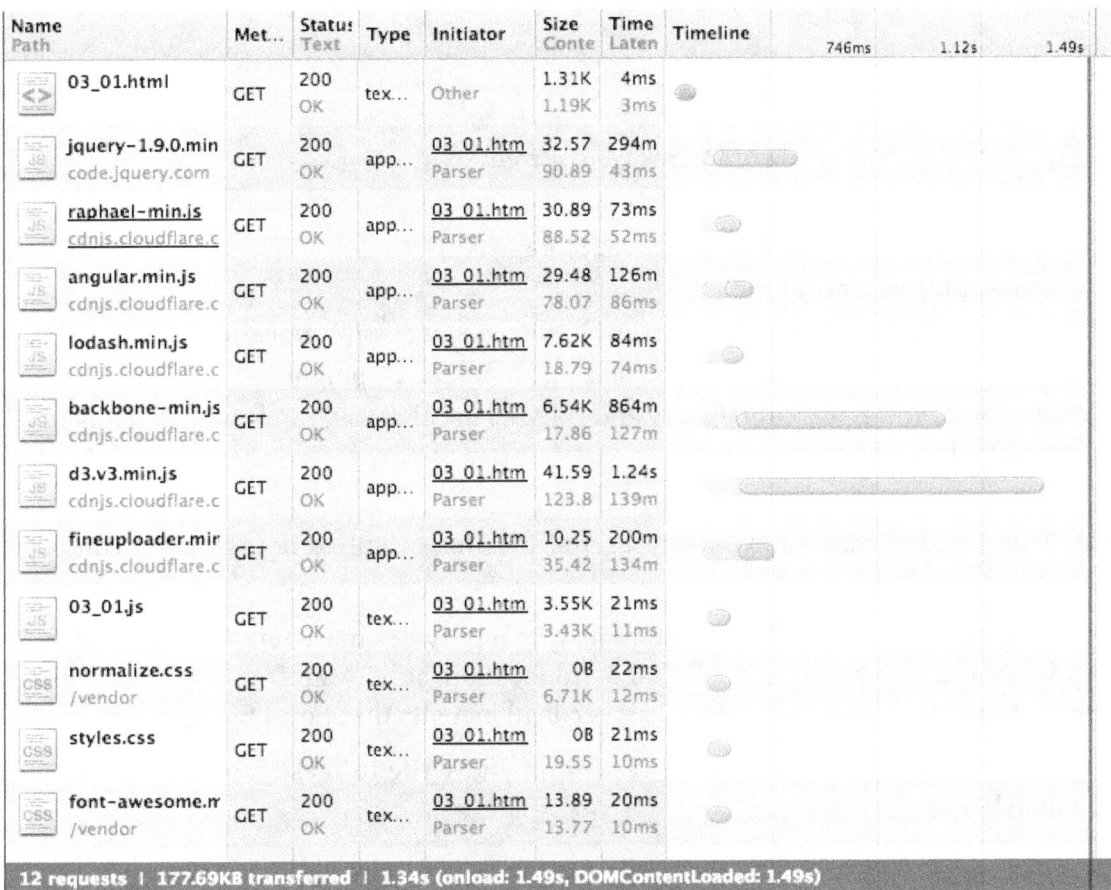

Loading Scripts from http://cdnjs.com

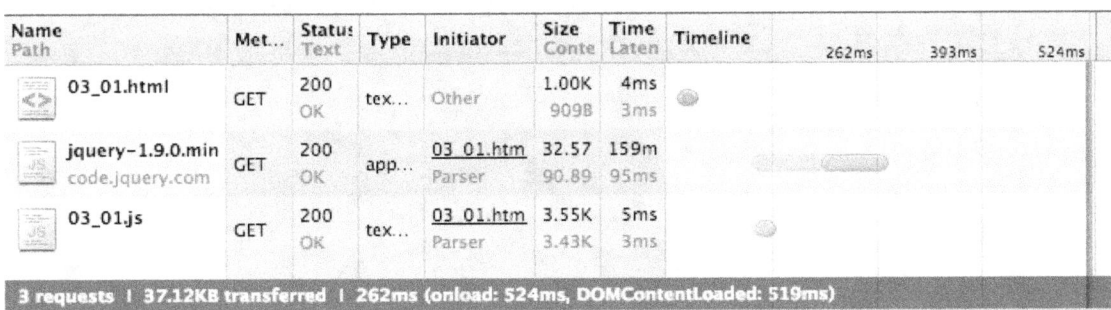

3 Requests, The Rest Were Cached by Local Storage

Yikes! Using an external script source resulted in significantly higher load times. Unfortunately, this is just how the internet works. If you browse to a website `http://example.com`, then your browser probably loaded a CSS and JavaScript file from either `example.com` or some CDN.

---

[9]http://cdnjs.com

Preventing these network requests with HTML5 Local Storage can drastically improve page load times instead of only relying on browser caching mechanisms.

Summary

Here is a recap of the topics and paradigms we covered:

- The inner workings of the HTML5 Local Storage API
- How to test for support of the API
- Handle errors from `getItem()`, `setItem()`, and `removeItem()` gracefully
- How to load and cache resources and add this to a jQuery plugin
- How to combine the power of jQuery and HTML5 Local Storage and coincidentally drastically improve page-load times

While HTML5 Local Storage is extremely useful, it is important to note a few technologies not covered in this book (yet?).

One such technology is HTML5 Session Storage, which provides more long-term persistent storage than Local Storage. The other is the HTML5 ApplicationCache Manifest, which provides offline browsing on top of the speed and reduced server-load benefits that Local Storage provides.

In the next chapter, we will learn how to read from and write to files on our computers with the HTML5 File APIs.

4 Reading Files with jQuery and HTML5 File API

The HTML5 standard brings us a plethora of methods for web application developers to access and store files on users' local file systems, and not just the developer's servers. Ultimately, developers are now able to interact with local files through the HTML5 File API.

This specification makes available several interfaces for accessing a user's filesystem, however the only ones I care about are:

- File - Provides only the ability to read a file's metadata, such as the name, file size, mimetype, and a reference to the file handle
- FileList - Provides the same as File, only it is an array-like sequence of File objects
- Blob - Provides the ability to slice a file into byte arrays / ranges

With the API, we get a *file handle*, just like in native applications. Once the *file handle* is attained, a developer can utilize the FileReader API to asynchronously read a file, just as one would make an XMLHttpRequest.

What browsers support these APIs?

Show all versions	IE	Firefox	Chrome	Safari	Opera	iOS Safari	Opera Mini	Android Browser	Opera Mobile	Blackberry Browser	Chrome for Android	Firefox for Android
								2.1				
								2.2				
						3.2		2.3	10.0			
						4.0-4.1		3.0	11.5			
	8.0		26.0			4.2-4.3		4.0	12.0			
	9.0	21.0	27.0	5.1		5.0-5.1		4.1	12.1	7.0		
Current	10.0	22.0	28.0	6.0	15.0	6.0-6.1	5.0-7.0	4.2	14.0	10.0	27.0	22.0
Near future	11.0	23.0	29.0	7.0		7.0						
Farther future		24.0										

File API - Working Draft
Method of manipulating file objects in web applications client-side, as well as programmatically selecting them and accessing their data.

*Usage stats:
Support: 69.93%
Partial support: 5%
Total: 74.93%
Global

File API Support

FileReader API - Working Draft

Method of reading the contents of a File or Blob object into memory

Usage stats: Global Support: 73.56%

Show all versions	IE	Firefox	Chrome	Safari	Opera	iOS Safari	Opera Mini	Android Browser	Opera Mobile	Blackberry Browser	Chrome for Android	Firefox for Android
								2.1				
								2.2				
						3.2		2.3	10.0			
						4.0-4.1		3.0	11.5			
	8.0		26.0			4.2-4.3		4.0	12.0			
	9.0	21.0	27.0	5.1		5.0-5.1		4.1	12.1	7.0		
Current	10.0	22.0	28.0	6.0	15.0	6.0-6.1	5.0-7.0	4.2	14.0	10.0	27.0	22.0
Near future	11.0	23.0	29.0	7.0		7.0						
Farther future		24.0										

File Reader API Support

Blob URLs - Working Draft

Method of creating URL handles to the specified File or Blob object.

Usage stats: Global Support: 72.34%

Show all versions	IE	Firefox	Chrome	Safari	Opera	iOS Safari	Opera Mini	Android Browser	Opera Mobile	Blackberry Browser	Chrome for Android	Firefox for Android
								2.1				
								2.2				
						3.2		2.3	10.0			
						4.0-4.1		3.0	11.5			
	8.0		26.0			4.2-4.3		4.0 webkit	12.0			
	9.0	21.0	27.0	5.1		5.0-5.1		4.1 webkit	12.1	7.0		
Current	10.0	22.0	28.0	6.0 webkit	15.0	6.0-6.1 webkit	5.0-7.0	4.2 webkit	14.0 webkit	10.0 webkit	27.0 webkit	22.0
Near future	11.0	23.0	29.0	7.0 webkit		7.0 webkit						
Farther future		24.0										

Blob URLs Support

Want to run the example code for this chapter? Grab and install the latest version of Node.js[1]. After installing, you can run a simple web server by opening the Chapter 4 code directory and using node to run the server:

```
node my/directory/wrinklefree-jquery/ch4/server.js
```

Afterwards, simply open a browser to `localhost:8888`.

Alternatively, if you are running all examples in Google Chrome, you can run Chrome with this command line argument:

```
chrome --allow-file-access-from-files
```

Let's start with an introduction to these APIs and how they are used.

---
[1] http://nodejs.org

Testing Browser Support

The developer will need to know if the File APIs are supported in a user's browser. We can test this with a simple collection of test statements, which I have put within a function that extends jQuery.

```
$.filer = function(){
    // check for various File API support
    var hasFile = !!window.File,
        hasFileList = !!window.FileList,
        hasBlob = !!window.Blob,
        hasFileReader = !!window.FileReader;
    if(!hasFile || !hasBlob || !hasFileList || !hasFileReader){
        console.error('You don\'t have the required support for this feature. Please update your browser.');
        return false;
    }
    return true;
}
```

This `$.filer()` function will test for some variables which will tell us if the File API is available in the current browser.

The Three Musketeers (of the File API)

Our humble File API has three major data structures: File, FileList, and Blob.

We can utilize any of these – whichever fits our requirements. Using a `File` is as direct as adding an `<input>` tag with `type="file"`. For instance:

```
<input type="file" name="file"/>
```

This HTML would handle working with a single file. In order to handle multiple files, I've added `multiple` as an attribute to the `<input>` element:

```
<input type="file" name="files" multiple/>
```

FileList is just a collection of the previously mentioned File objects.

A Blob, on the other hand, is handled through the JavaScript APIs exclusively.

Reading Files

The absolute minimalist approach to reading files with the FileReader API is to use the HTML5 File `<input>` field in a form on a page:

```
<input type="file" name="files" multiple>
<div class="output"></div>
```

This will handle multiple files as a FileList, not just a single File. Now we handle the change event, triggered when files are selected for input:

```
$('input[type=file]').on('change', filesSelected);
```

When the change event fires on the file input, our `filesSelected()` function will receive an event with a list of files. This list is a FileList.

```
function filesSelected(e){
        var files = e.target.files //FileList object
            , output = [];

        for(var i = 0, f; f = files[i]; i++){
                output.push(
                        '<li>'
                        , f.name.wrapSpans()
                        , (f.type || 'no file type').wrapSpans()
                        , (f.size + ' bytes').wrapSpans()
                        , (f.lastModifiedDate ? f.lastModifiedDate.toLocaleString() : 'new file'
Spans()
                        , '</li>'
                );
        }

        $('.output').html('<ul>'+output.join(' ')+'</ul>');
}
```

The first demo in Chapter 4 supplied in the sample code (https://github.com/matthiasak/wrinklefree-jquery-and-html5)[2] demonstrates the previous code. I have also included a screenshot for handling a single file, to show how Google Chrome visually states a single file <input> and an <input> with the multiple attribute.

---

[2]https://github.com/matthiasak/wrinklefree-jquery-and-html5

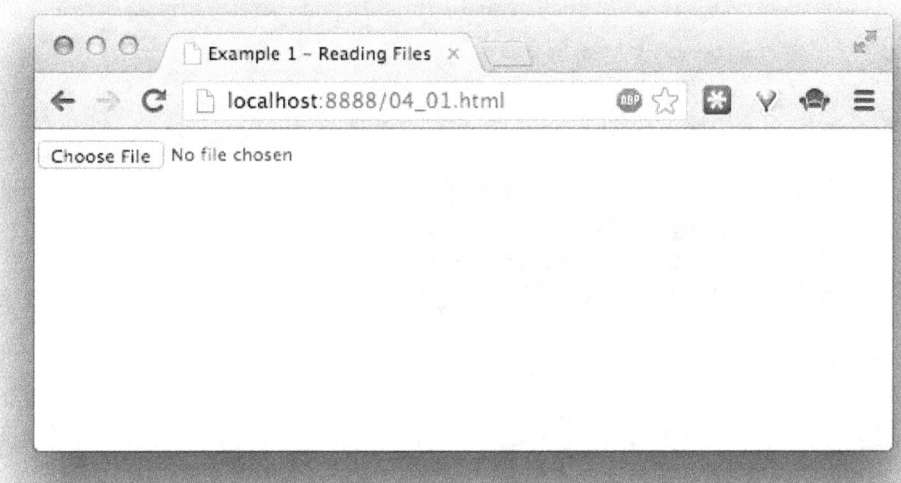

A single file is handled by this input.

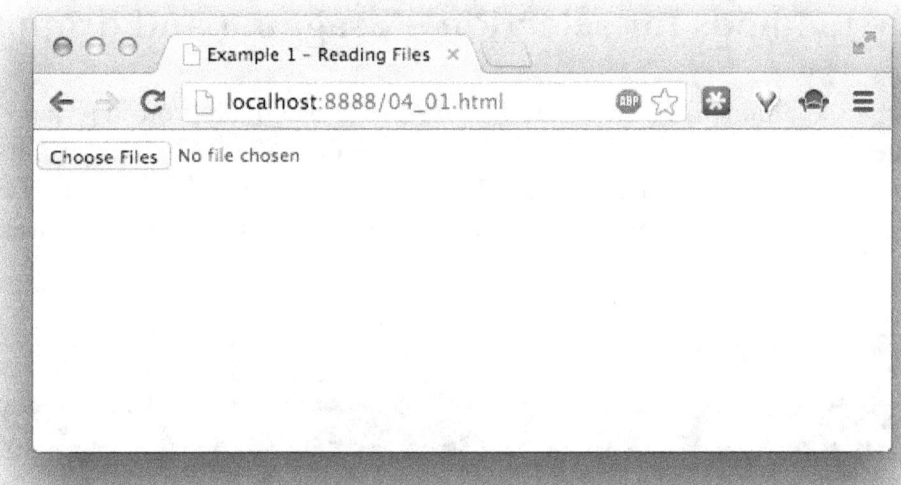

Multiple files can be handled by this input.

56   Reading Files with jQuery and HTML5 File API

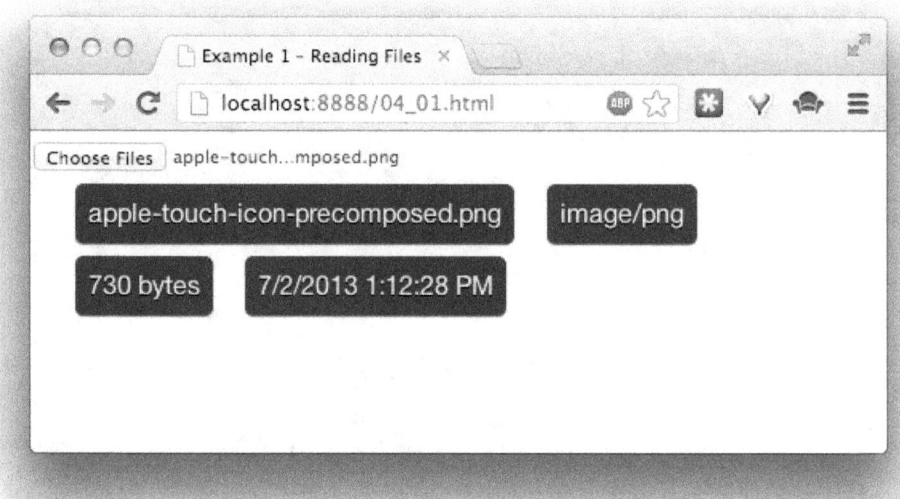

The `filesSelected()` function in action.

Alternative methods for selection – dragging and dropping

If you have ever used an email client in the browser, such as Gmail, you may have noticed that you can drag files from your desktop into the browser window, with the ability to attach files or a group of files to an email. This feature is called "Drag and Drop". Drag and Drop is also provided by HTML5, and is available in pretty much every modern browser past Internet Explorer 8.

Drag and Drop - Working Draft												
Method of easily dragging and dropping elements on a page, requiring minimal JavaScript.												
											*Usage stats:	Global
											Support:	64.86%
											Partial support:	13.25%
											Total:	78.11%
Show all versions	IE	Firefox	Chrome	Safari	Opera	iOS Safari	Opera Mini	Android Browser	Opera Mobile	Blackberry Browser	Chrome for Android	Firefox for Android
								2.1				
								2.2				
							3.2	2.3	10.0			
							4.0-4.1	3.0	11.5			
	8.0		26.0				4.2-4.3	4.0	12.0			
	9.0	21.0	27.0	5.1			5.0-5.1	4.1	12.1	7.0		
Current	10.0	22.0	28.0	6.0	15.0	6.0-6.1	5.0-7.0	4.2	14.0	10.0	27.0	22.0
Near future	11.0	23.0	29.0	7.0		7.0						
Farther future		24.0										

Drag and Drop is supported by quite a few desktop browsers.

Let's modify the previous page to handle the Drag and Drop events instead. But first, let's make a few visual modifications via CSS, so that the `<div class="output">` element will be a visibly identifiable box on the screen.

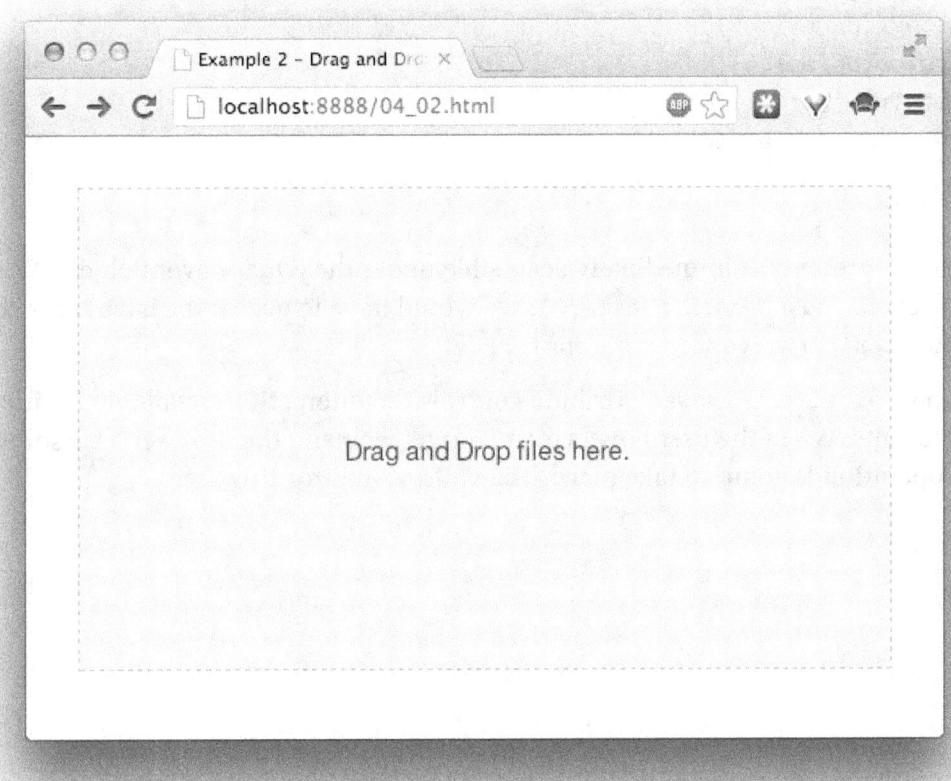

We will use Drag and Drop event handling on this box.

```
1  jQuery.event.props.push('dataTransfer');
2  $('.output')
3      .on('dragover', filesDragged)
4      .on('drop', filesDropped);
```

The `jQuery.event.props.push('dataTransfer')` line simply exposes the original event's `dataTransfer` property to the jQuery event object. I will show you this in the following code sample.

I didn't have to edit much to get this working. We are very spoiled as web developers these days! Let's write our functions for the separate Drag and Drop actions.

```
1  function filesDragged(e){
2      e.stopPropagation();
3      e.preventDefault();
4      e.dataTransfer.dropEffect = 'copy';
5      e.dataTransfer.effectAllowed = 'all';
6  }
```

The `dataTransfer` property is immediately accessible under the jQuery event object. Without using `jQuery.event.props.push('dataTransfer')`, we would have to access the `dataTransfer` attribute by digging into `e.originalEvent.dataTransfer`.

The `e.dataTransfer.effectAllowed` attribute controls the interactions available during `dragenter` and `dragover` events. When the user hovers over a target element, the browser's cursor will indicate what type of operation is going to take place. The valid values for this are:

- "none"
- "copy"
- "link"
- "move"

Instead of using the browser's default 'ghost image' feedback, you can optionally set a drag icon:

```
1  var dragIcon = document.createElement('img');
2  dragIcon.src = 'icon.png';
3  dragIcon.width = 150;
4  e.dataTransfer.setDragImage(dragIcon, -75, -75);
```

Forgot to get a screenshot of this while working on this sample code. Sorry!

Now let's handle the `drop` event.

```
1  function filesDropped(e){
2      e.stopPropagation(); // Stops some browsers from redirecting.
3      e.preventDefault();
4
5      var files = e.dataTransfer.files //FileList object
6          , output = [];
7
8      for(var i = 0, f; f = files[i]; i++){
9          output.push(
10             '<li>'
```

```
11                        , f.name.wrapSpans()
12                        , (f.type || 'no file type').wrapSpans()
13                        , (f.size + ' bytes').wrapSpans()
14                        , (f.lastModifiedDate ? f.lastModifiedDate.toLocaleString() : 'new fil
15  Spans()
16                        , '</li>'
17                );
18          }
19
20          $('.output').html('<ul>'+output.join('')+'</ul>');
21  }
```

The most important aspect of filesDropped() is the list of files accessible from e.dataTransfer.files. Notice that I can access the type, size, and lastModifiedDate attributes on each file.

To help present these differing attributes on each file, I created a function called wrapSpans(), which is added to the String class's prototype.

```
1  String.prototype.wrapSpans = function(){
2          return '<span>'+this.toString()+'</span>';
3  }
```

This simply takes any string, and returns the original content with <span> tags around it.

The end result, after dragging a number of files onto the page, looks like the following screenshot.

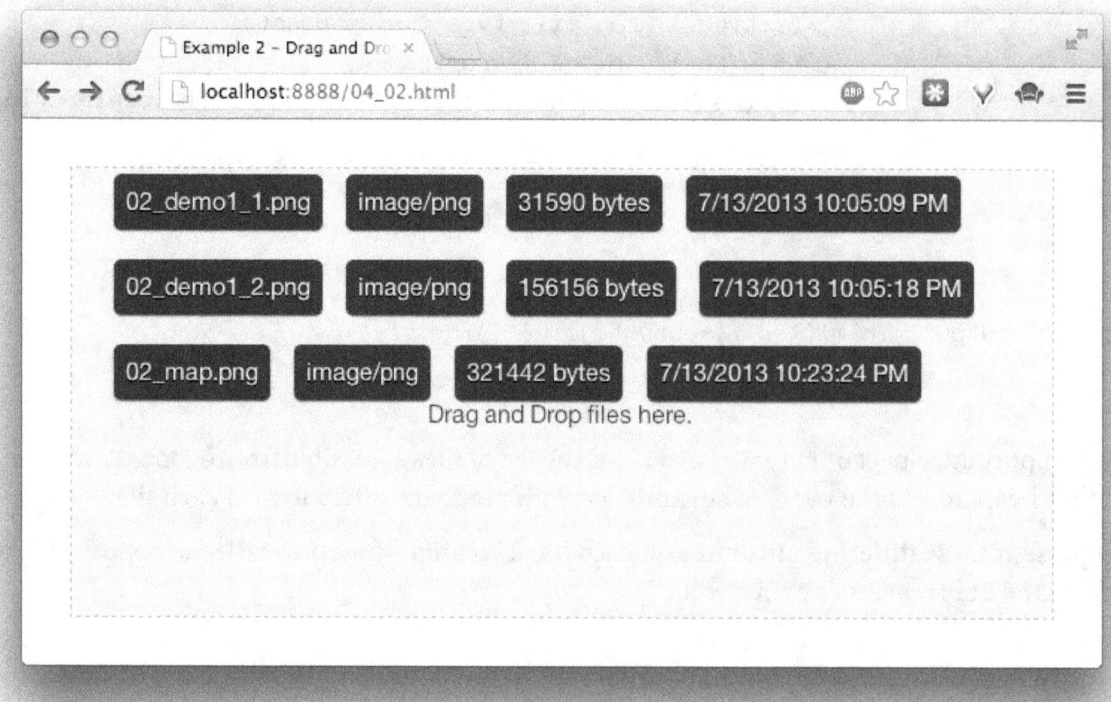

After dragging three files over the content.

Reading File Contents with the FileReader API

The typical application that will read a file from a browser will use a selection method as described above. Then, the developer (that's you!) can instantiate a `FileReader` to access the contents of those files.

There are four options to asynchronously read a file with `FileReader`:

- `FileReader.readAsText(file)`
- `FileReader.readAsDataURL(file)`
- `FileReader.readAsArrayBuffer(file)`
- `FileReader.readAsBinaryString(file)`

We will cover the paradigms that govern each of these in detail. But first, let's cover the main process of reading file contents.

In the previous example, when a file is dropped and handled by the `fileDropped()` function, there is a FileList reference (`e.dataTransfer.files`) passed with the jQuery event object. Each of the File objects within this FileList can be passed as an argument to `FileReader` functions. This simple API design is what will make developing applications very modular and extensible.

We will demonstrate how this is carried out by showing how to access the content of a file as plain text.

Reading Files as Plain Text

Let us go ahead and extend the `filesDropped()` function to append the file contents (as text) to `<div class="output">`.

```
function filesDropped(e){
        e.stopPropagation(); // Stops some browsers from redirecting.
        e.preventDefault();

        var files = e.dataTransfer.files //FileList object
            , output = []
            , promises = [];

        for(var i = 0, f; f = files[i]; i++){
            (function(file){
                    var dfd = $.Deferred();
                    promises.push(dfd.promise());
                    var reader = new FileReader();
                    reader.onload = function(e){
                            output.push(
                                    '<li>'
                                    , file.name.wrapSpans()
                                    , htmlEncode(e.target.result).wrapSpans()
                                    , '</li>'
                            );
                            dfd.resolve();
                    };
                    reader.readAsText(file);
            })(f);
        }

        $.when.apply($, promises).then(function(){
                $('.output').html('<ul>'+output.join('')+'</ul>');
        })
}
```

Let me walk you through this function:

1. `output = []` - This array will store the text to be concatenated, as in the previous example.
2. `promises = []` - This array will hold a list of jQuery Promises (to be discussed in more detail).
3. `for(var i = 0, f; f = files[i]; i++){ … }` - This loop will iterate over each file, and pass it as input to the IIFE (Immediately Invoked Function Expression) – pronounced "iffy".
4. `var dfd = $.Deferred()` - This creates a jQuery Deferred object, which can `resolve()` or `fail()`.

Why do we use an IIFE?

In JavaScript, We pass references to objects, not the objects themselves. In this case, `f` is a reference to the `i`-th file. If we did not pass `f` in through a *closure* (a function scope), then the code inside the `for` loop thinks `f` is `files[n-1]`. Thus, by passing in `f` as an argument to an IIFE, we have ensured that each file in `files` is called by `reader.readAsText(file);`

1. There is a jQuery Promise within this Deferred object which is used to deconstruct asynchronous calls:

    If you've used jQuery's `$.animate()` or `$.ajax()` functions (or some derivative such as `$.get()` or `$.post()`), then you have used jQuery Promises before. jQuery lets us wait to run something upon the conditional success of one or more Promises (in this case returned by `$.get()`).

```
function getSomething(){
    return $.get(…);
}

function getSomething2(){
    return $.get(…);
}

$.when(getSomething(), getSomething2()).then(function(){
    // our AJAX queries have completed!
});
```

The same can be done with `$.animate()`:

```
1  function animateSomething(){
2      return $('#div1').animate(...);
3  }
4
5  function animateSomething2(){
6      return $('#div2').animate(...);
7  }
8
9  $.when(animateSomething(), animateSomething2()).then(function(){
10     // our animations have completed!
11 });
```

In the IIFE, we return a Promise explicitly created in the code, instead of by `$.get()`.

2. `promises.push(dfd.promise())` - Save a Promise for this particular file.
3. `var reader = new FileReader()` - Create a `FileReader` to read the file.
4. `reader.onload = function(e){ ... }` - Tell the `FileReader` to run a function once the file has been read from the local file system.
5. `output.push( ... )` - Store the file's contents in the `output` list.
6. `dfd.resolve()` - Tell the Deferred object to signal to the Promise that it can return successfully once the `output` has been updated with the file's contents.
7. `reader.readAsText(file)` - Finally, tell the `FileReader` to attempt to read the file.

We perform a little bit more magic at the end of the `filesDropped()` function to update the HTML once **all** of the files have been successfully read:

```
1  $.when.apply($, promises).then(function(){
2      $('.output').html('<ul>'+output.join('')+'</ul>');
3  })
```

`$.when.apply($, promises)` is basically translating the list of promises into an argument list for `$.when()`. To the JavaScript engine, this would then read like:

```
1  $.when(promises[0], promises[1], ..., promises[n-1]).then(function(){
2      ...
3  });
```

This code produces the following screenshot.

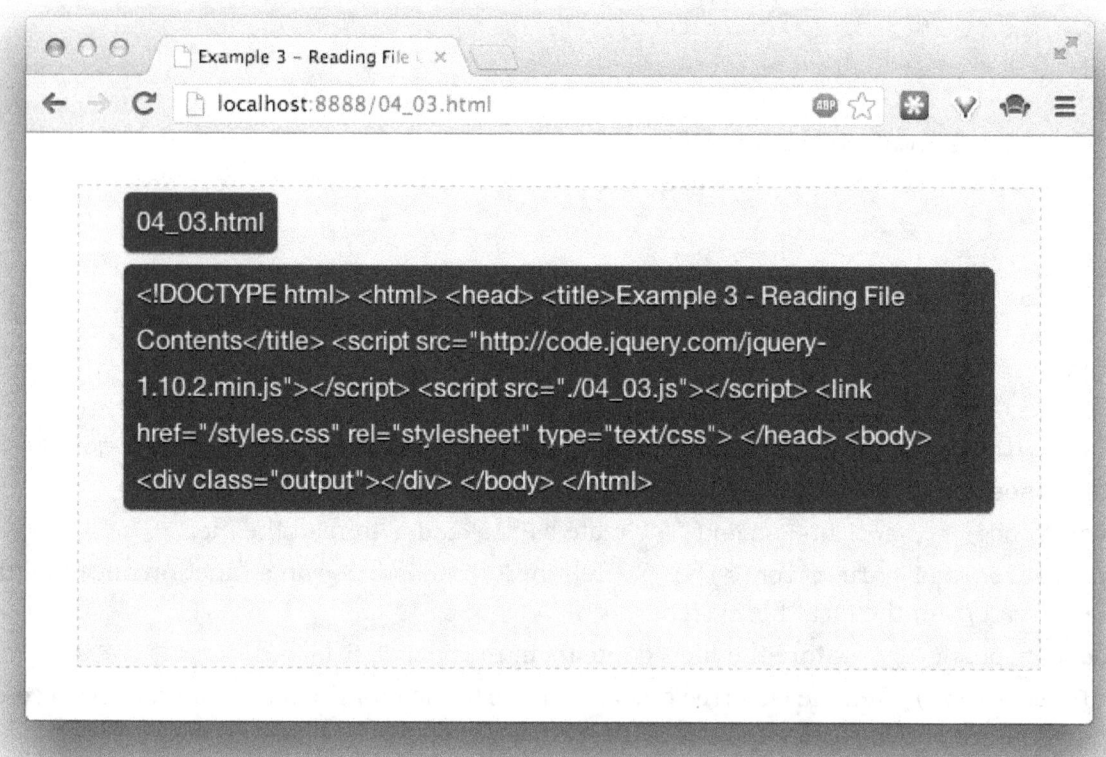

This web page just read its own contents from a file.

Reading Files as Images

Unfortunately, we do have to handle binary data - such as images - a little differently than when reading text files.

In order to read image data from files, we will use a technique called Base64 encoding, which attempts to represent the binary data of an image in hexadecimal alphanumeric digits (a through f, and 0 through 9).

This next snippet (yet again, rewriting `filesDropped()`) will demonstrate how to use `FileReader` to access and embed images from the local file system.

```
function filesDropped(e){
        e.stopPropagation(); // Stops some browsers from redirecting.
        e.preventDefault();

        var files = e.dataTransfer.files //FileList object
            , output = $('.output');

        for(var i = 0, f; f = files[i]; i++){
            (function(file){
                // only process image files
                if(!f.type.match('image.*')){
                    return;
                }
                var reader = new FileReader();
                reader.onload = function(e){
                    output.append('<img src="'+e.target.result+'">');
                };
                reader.readAsDataURL(file);
            })(f);
        }
}
```

Notice that we are testing the file type being accessed, in order to reject any non-image data. Then, we simply go on about our business as usual, accessing the result property underneath the event object that is propagated through our code. Finally, once the file is read we can set the src attribute on an image to be the contents from reader.readAsDataURL(file).

The following image, for example, will produce this drib-drab from reader.readAsDataURL(file):

```
data:image/png;base64,iVBORw0KGgoAAAANSUhEUgAABIQAAAK8CAYAAACeK2TMAAAYHW1DQqPjb2D\
wCAwCAwCg8AgMAgMAoPAIDAIDAKDwCAwCDwQgf8fkmNfHKAK0ecAAAAASUVORK5CYII=...
```

This page read an image from disk.

Browsers are able to interpret this data and render an image, instead of a large string of characters, onto the web page.

Reading Files as Blobs

In many scenarios, it may either be unnecessary or down-right impossible to read an entire file into memory.

Fortunately, we can specify slices of a file, or Blobs, to be read. This handy feature is supported by the `File` interface, where we can use the `File.slice()` method to feed segments of a file by a front and end byte, alongside an optional third argument to specify a content-type.

```
1  var blob = file.slice(frontByte, endByte);
2  reader.readAsBinaryString(blob);
```

Very simple, is it not? Let's go ahead and add another modification to our `filesDropped()` function, this time to work with blobs:

```javascript
function filesDropped(e){
    e.stopPropagation(); // Stops some browsers from redirecting.
    e.preventDefault();

    var list = $("<ul></ul>")
        , files = e.dataTransfer.files //FileList object
        , output = $('.output').append(list) && list;

    for(var i = 0, f; f = files[i]; i++){
        (function(file){
            var reader = new FileReader()
                , start = 0
                , end = Math.floor(Math.random()*(file.size-1))
                , blob = file.slice(start, end + 1);
            reader.onloadend = function(e){
                if(e.target.readyState == FileReader.DONE){
                    output.append(
                        [
                            '<li>'
                            , ('byte data: ' + htmlEncode(e.target
                            , ('byte range from: ' + start + ' to
 e file.').wrapSpans()
                            , '</li>'
                        ].join('')
                    );
                }
            };
            reader.readAsBinaryString(blob);
        })(f);
    }
}
```

Notice that the start is always 0, and end is a random value between 0 and the size of the file, in bytes. Also, I've taken changed the onload event callback to unloaded. This is because, when reading blobs, the onload event will fire multiple times, however the unloadend event will fire once the entire blob has been read.

Once the onloadend event is triggered, I am checking the readyState attribute for its equivalence to a variable on the FileReader API – FileReader.DONE.

If this check is successful, then I can access the blob's data, and write it as HTML to the webpage.

The following screenshot shows the result of the previous code.

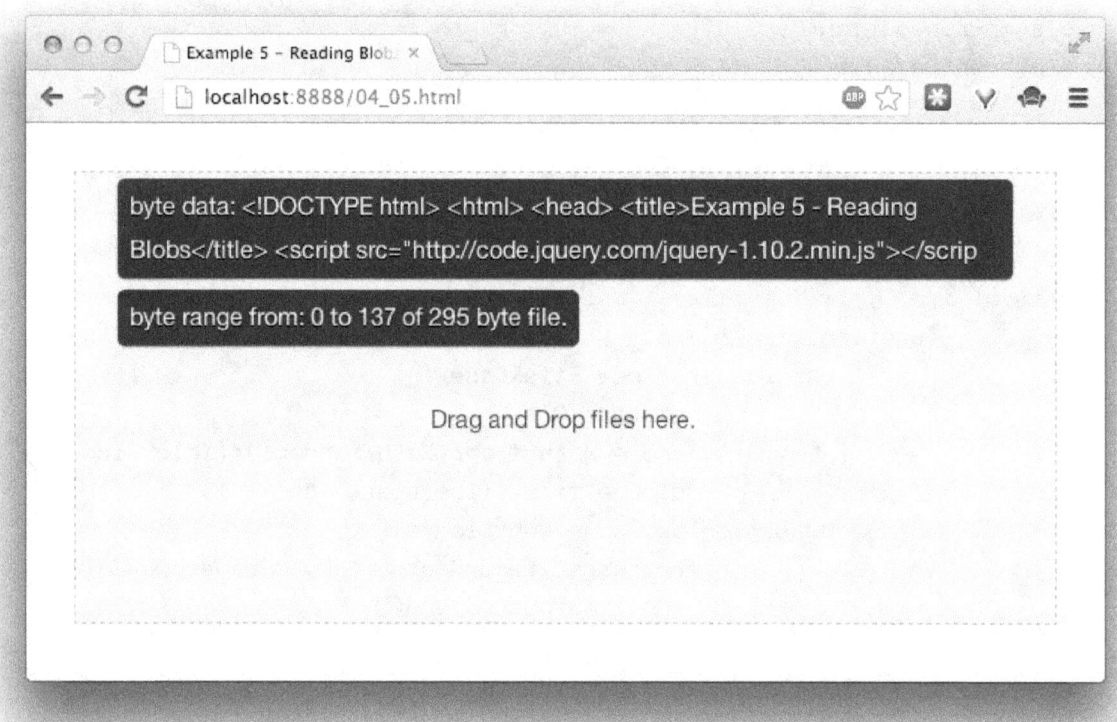

This webpage has read a partial blob representation of itself after I dragged the file into the page.

Monitoring Progress

There may be cases where we attempt to access files that are too large to be read, or the browser runs into conflicts. `FileReader` can trigger `onerror` callbacks to handle these issues.

```
reader.onerror = function (e) {
        switch(e.target.error.code) {
                case e.target.error.NOT_FOUND_ERR:
                        console.log('File Not Found:', file.name);
                        break;
                case e.target.error.NOT_READABLE_ERR:
                        console.log('File is not readable:', file.name);
                        break;
                case e.target.error.ABORT_ERR:
                        break; // noop
                default:
                        console.log('An error occurred reading file:', file.name);
```

```
13        }
14  };
```

This way, when an issue occurs, web app developers can gracefully handle issues without crashing or forcing the user to reload the webpage.

`FileReader` also provides us with progress events which tell us about the status of an attempt to read a file.

Here's the list of progress callbacks that can be used on `FileReader`:

- `reader.onloadstart`
- `reader.onprogress` - Provides an event with `loaded` and `total` attributes. To get the percent loaded, we can do: `Math.round((e.loaded / e.total) * 100)+'%'`.
- `reader.onabort`
- `reader.onloadstart`

Review from this Chapter

In this chapter we covered several aspects:

- The state of HTML5 File APIs and browser support
- The paradigms that govern the File APIs, and more specifically, FileReader
- Asynchronously loading a file as text
- How to handle one or more files at a time with the multiple attribute
- Drag and Drop
- Asynchronously loading images as DataURLs
- Asynchronously loading files as Blobs and reading only slices of a file
- Handling error and progress events

In the next chapter, we will dive into using webcam access natively from the browser.

5 Webcam Access with jQuery

Until recently, the video and webcam application realm was dominated by desktop applications such as Skype and iChat, and Adobe Flash applications such as Chatroulette. Users of the desktop applications typically had to download and install an application to the operating system of his or her choice. This included downloading a large file, in which the user would need special privileges to install the binary to the system. If the system or device supported this application download, then after Windows, Mac OS, Ubuntu, Android, iOS, and so on finished installing this application, the user would then typically initialize this application, login with a user account, and use the application to initiate a webcam chat. Furthermore, should the application need updates, it will have the user download a new binary and reinstall the application.

With Flash applications the experience is similarly cumbersome, as the support is not very widely harnessed, and updates must be distributed. In many cases, Flash has had its own problems in support on systems, especially with Mac OS and Linux. Moreover, Flash is now being phased out from iOS and Android – the two most ubiquitous mobile device platforms. So, users of Chatroulette, for instance, would login to the website, and Flash would startup. Commonly understood to have support problems with webcam and microphones, Flash also has a history of introducing many security flaws and exploits into widespread attacks on users.

These woes existed for users of the technology for years, meanwhile developers themselves had to implement multiple versions of code to support platforms where Flash's cross-platform support fell short.

Lo' and behold, there is a new champion in the online multimedia realm called `getUserMedia()` which prompts the latest browsers to use a media device (such as a camera or microphone) for multimedia streams to be read by open platform web applications. Using this, web developers can feed native, lightweight, speedy video and audio into website apps for a broad range of multimedia experiences – chat, video, streaming, surveillance, you name it!

In this chapter we shall learn:

1. Which browsers support `getUserMedia()` as of the time of this writing.
2. How to get video, audio, or both.
3. How to detect errors and what the error means.
4. How to listen for events from the webcam.
5. How to capture images and image data from the webcam.
6. Structuring jQuery for wrapping `getUserMedia()` into a reusable plugin.

Want to run the example code for this chapter? Grab and install the latest version of Node.js[1]. After installing, you can run a simple web server by opening the Chapter 5 code directory and using node to run the server:

`node my/directory/wrinklefree-jquery/ch5/server.js`

Afterwards, simply open a browser to `localhost:8888`.

Why WebRTC is Important

`getUserMedia()` comes packaged as part of the WebRTC specification for the Open Web Platform. The RTC in WebRTC is an acronym for Real-Time Communications, a collection of software technologies that enables browsers to natively handle both audio and video streams, as well as share data between two browsers in a peer-to-peer scheme - all without third party plugins!

Defining WebRTC Formally

WebRTC components can be utilized with JavaScript APIs made available to the JavaScript engine in the supported browsers. Here are a few of the APIs available under WebRTC:

1. The Network Stream API, which represents an audio or video data stream.
2. The PeerConnection API, which allows two or more users to communicate browser-to-browser.
3. The DataChannel API, which enables communication of other types of data for real-time gaming, text chat, file transfer, and so forth.

We can further break these APIs down into more granular service architectures: Stream APIs and PeerConnection APIs.

Beneath all of the layers of the Stream APIs, is the LocalMediaStreamInterface which grants us access to a locally available media stream, such as a webcam. The low-level functionality of this convention, however, is already provided for us by supported browsers, with a function named `getUserMedia()`.

The WebRTC project offers a complete solution of audio and video services. It includes, as of the time of this writing, three audio codecs and one video codec, as well as other components crucial for a great experience, such as software based acoustic echo cancellation (AEC), automatic gain control (AGC), noise reduction, noise suppression and hardware access and control across multiple platforms.

The WebRTC project builds on the VP8 codec, introduced in 2010 as part of the WebM Project http://webmproject.org/[2]. It includes components to conceal packet loss, clean up noisy images as well as capture and playback capabilities across multiple platforms.

---

[1] http://nodejs.org

[2] http://webmproject.org/

The following diagram gives a decent bird's eye view of the WebRTC project and where it stands in the application interface, which is between the browser and the web services.

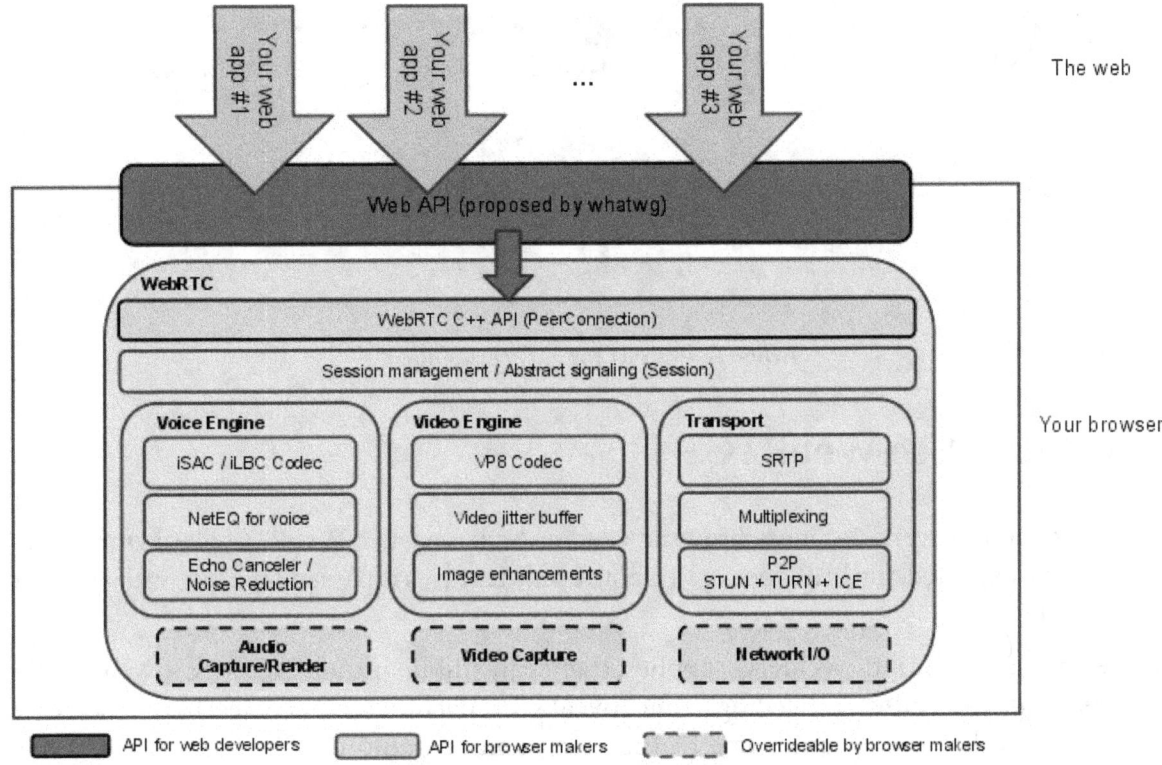

Overview of WebRTC

Browser Support for WebRTC

As of the time of this writing, the latest and most up-to-date version `getUserMedia()` and WebRTC spec is available and published to the W3C in June 2013. The draft is published here: http://www.w3.org/TR/webrtc/[3].

Here is a list of browsers and their versions that support `getUserMedia()`:

---

[3]http://www.w3.org/TR/webrtc/

Show all versions	IE	Firefox	Chrome	Safari	Opera	iOS Safari	Opera Mini	Android Browser	Opera Mobile	Blackberry Browser	Chrome for Android	Firefox for Android
								2.1				
								2.2				
						3.2		2.3	10.0			
						4.0-4.1		3.0	11.5			
	8.0		26.0 webkit			4.2-4.3		4.0	12.0			
	9.0	21.0 moz	27.0 webkit	5.1		5.0-5.1		4.1	12.1	7.0		
Current	10.0	22.0 moz	28.0 webkit	6.0	15.0	6.0-6.1	5.0-7.0	4.2	14.0	10.0 webkit	28.0	22.0
Near future	11.0	23.0 moz	29.0 webkit	7.0	16.0	7.0						
Farther future		24.0 moz										

Browser support for getUserMedia.

When Not to Use WebRTC

In the most common scenario, most browser vendors will find the WebRTC platform extremely helpful. As to be expected, the brilliance of this platform's features is passed on to the web application developers – us!

For whatever valuable utility WebRTC supplies, there can still be instances where a web developer may indeed find his software needing some tweaks or needing to meet certain requirements not provided. The license for using one of the video and/or audio codecs may not suffice for a particular businesses' use, or a codec's "lossiness" could spell trouble in certain applications where "losslessness" is extremely important. Moreover, the support of getUserMedia() may not be supplied for a range of devices or platforms that we need to support with our web applications. For instance, supporting audio and video streams in Internet Explorer 7 and 8 would be very difficult without a Java Applet or Adobe Flash.

Lossy Versus Lossless Codecs

The advantage of lossy methods over lossless methods is that in some cases a lossy method can produce a much smaller compressed file than any lossless method, while still meeting the requirements of the application. Lossy methods are most often used for compressing sound, images or videos. This is because these types of data are intended for human interpretation where the mind can easily "fill in the blanks" or see past very minor errors or inconsistencies.

Thus, lossy methods will help to improve performance of an application.

The Open Web Platform is the Perfect Blend of Technologies

getUserMedia() is only the tip of the WebRTC iceberg - whilst it indeed provides a very visible and somewhat tangible user experience, WebRTC's true power lies within the combinations of the

WebRTC and HTML5 APIs - where the union of visual, audio, storage, and other features can create an immersive experience right in your browser.

Streaming Screen Capture

Tab Capture is now available in the Chrome Dev channel. This makes it possible to capture the visible area of the tab as a stream, which can then be used locally, or with RTCPeerConnection's `addStream()` function.

This addition to WebRTC would be very useful for sceencasting, web page sharing, and taking screenshots.

> For more information see the WebRTC Tab Content Capture Proposal http://www.chromium.org/developers/design-documents/extensions/proposed-changes/apis-under-development/webrtc-tab-content-capture[4].

Examples of WebRTC in Action

Google / Mozilla / Opera WebRTC Demo

The Google / Mozilla / Opera WebRTC Demo https://apprtc.appspot.com/[5] is a WebRTC demo application hosted on App Engine. Developed by Google, Mozilla, and Opera, it enables both browsers to "talk" to each other using the WebRTC API.

The following screenshot depicts the author having a native WebRTC driven webcam chat.

---

[4]http://www.chromium.org/developers/design-documents/extensions/proposed-changes/apis-under-development/webrtc-tab-content-capture
[5]https://apprtc.appspot.com/

WebRTC Demo from Google

ASCII Camera

This real-time ASCII representation of your webcam video (http://idevelop.ro/ascii-camera/) demonstrates how combining `getUserMedia` with HTML5 Canvas can create some really powerful effects.

The following screenshot demonstrates what the ASCII Camera application looks like:

ASCII Camera Demo from Google

Tools of the Trade

Chrome Developer Tools

https://developers.google.com/chrome-developer-tools/[6]

The Chrome DevTools Suite is the de-facto standard for debugging in the browse. Learn to use this suite of tools first from Google's website if you want deep access to the internals of the browser with:

1. Logging and performance measurements
2. Rendering, cpu, and memory profiling
3. Debugging utilities and breakpoint tests
4. (and much, much more)

---

[6]https://developers.google.com/chrome-developer-tools/

It will make debugging everything from styles, to JavaScriptJavaScriptJavaScript, to page layout and CSS performance a much more trivial ordeal versus the "edit and refresh" approach!

The Details of `getUserMedia()`

Let's start off with an introduction to using the draft, and then we will dive into the details.

```
$.supportsGetUserMedia = function(){
        //--> including browser prefixes
        return navigator.getUserMedia
                || navigator.webkitGetUserMedia
                || navigator.mozGetUserMedia
                || false;
};

$.getUserMedia = function(constraints, success, error){
        var getMedia = $.supportsGetUserMedia();
        return getMedia && getMedia(constraints, success, error);
};

$.getUserMedia(
        { //--> options
                video: true,
                audio: true
        },
        function(stream){ //--> success function
                var myWebcam = $('#video');

                if(navigator.getUserMedia || navigator.webkitGetUserMedia){
                        var ObjectURL = (window.URL || window.webkitURL).createObjectURL(stream)
                        myWebcam.attr('src', ObjectURL);
                } else {
                        //--> for Mozilla browsers
                        myWebcam[0].mozSrcObject = stream;
                }

                video.on('loadedmetadata', function(){
                        var widthAndHeight = [this.videoWidth, this.videoHeight];
                        console.log(dimensions);
                        video[0].play();
                });
```

```
35                },
36                function(error){
37                        var error_string;
38                        switch(error.code){
39                                case 1:
40                                        error_string = "PERMISSION_DENIED - The user denied permission
41  evice required for operation.";
42                                        break;
43                                case 2:
44                                        error_string = "NOT_SUPPORTED_ERROR - A constraint specified i
45   by the browser.";
46                                        break;
47                                case 3:
48                                        error_string = "MANDATORY_UNSATISFIED_ERROR - No media tracks
49  cified in the constraints were found.";
50                                        break;
51                                default:
52                                        error_string = error;
53                        }
54                        console.log("Something went wrong:", error_string);
55                }
56  );
```

As in previous chapters, we have a simple test to detect support for getUserMedia(). Here we are using two vendor specific prefixes that come from webkit and mozilla browsers since those are the only known supporters of getUserMedia() at the time of this writing. Then, we simply wrap the process in a little jQuery function that checks for getUserMedia() support, taking a constraints input, and two callback functions – success and error.

The constraints object itself needs at least one of two flags set to a "truthy" value – video and audio. Setting video to true will trigger the call to look for a video source, and setting audio to true will trigger the call to look for an audio source. The success function itself is feed a LocalMediaStream object, which is a WebRTC MediaStream object returned by getUserMedia().

The stream object has some properties carried with it:

1. stream.audioTracks – A WebRTC MediaStreamTrackList object representing audio tracks being fed into stream.
2. stream.ended – A boolean that is true if the ended event has fired on the stream.
3. stream.label – A globally unique identifier (GUID) describing stream.
4. stream.onended – A writable property on stream that can handle what to do when the ended event has fired on stream.

5. `stream.videoTracks` – A WebRTC MediaStreamTrackList object representing video tracks being fed into stream.

The stream object also has an event that the developer can listen to instead of polling the `stream.onended` property for changes:

```
1  //--> Triggers when all of the tracks of this stream have ended, in which case st\
2  ream is said to be finished.
3
4  stream.ended = function(){ … };
```

The stream also has a stop method we can invoke to halt the stream.

```
1  stream.stop(); //--> returns nothing
```

Both `stream.audioTracks` and `stream.videoTracks`, as described before, are MediaStreamTrackList objects, the details of which we will not bother with.

WebRTC and HTML5 Canvas

We cover the HTML5 Canvas API in greater detail in another section of this book, but here we find that Canvas is quite useful when writing applications which provide interactions with WebRTC and `getUserMedia()`. One particularly useful application of `getUserMedia()` is the ability to pull in image data from the `<video>` element directly as a screenshot. Coincidentally, we choose to use Canvas here because the Canvas API is able to take image data and write it to the page, giving the developer access to an image buffer. Once this has happened, the image data can then be displayed by converting the Canvas element's image data to a base64 encoded image. This lets web developers take a screenshot function from any video element!

The HTML

Our HTML is going to be quite boilerplate. In fact, it will be so bare and minimal that you can count the elements with your hands:

1. The latest jQuery as of this writing
2. A stylesheet (same stylesheet from earlier examples)
3. Basic container and elements
4. A `<video>` element
5. A `<canvas>` element
6. An `<img>` element
7. A place to put our JavaScript

Here is the basic HTML:

```html
1  <!DOCTYPE html>
2  <html>
3  <head>
4      <title>Example 5a - getUserMedia() Screenshot</title>
5      <script src="//cdnjs.cloudflare.com/ajax/libs/jquery/2.0.3/jquery.min.js"></scri\
6  pt>
7      <link href="styles.css" rel="stylesheet">
8  </head>
9  <body>
10     <div class="container">
11         <div class="ten columns offset-by-three">
12             <form class="CatForm">
13                 <h3>My Video</h3>
14                 <h3 class="subheader">(click video to take screenshot)</h3>
15                 <hr>
16                 <video id="video" style="width:100%;display:none;"></video>
17                 <canvas style="display:none;"></canvas>
18
19                 <h3>Screenshot</h3>
20                 <hr>
21                 <img src="">
22             </form>
23         </div>
24     </div>
25     <script>
26         //--> The code will go here.
27     </script>
28 </body>
29 </html>
```

The following screenshot shows how this HTML will look on the browser, using the included stylesheet from previous chapters.

My Video
(click video to take screenshot)

Screenshot

Preview of the HTML

The jQuery / JavaScript

The initial jQuery code to a simple plugin project should begin to look quite familiar. In a similar design process as earlier chapters, we will:

1. Layout a jQuery plugin.
2. Wrap interoperability code and test for features into the plugin.
3. Take contextual functions from the chapter and refactor them for use with the plugin.

Determining Support

First and foremost, we would not need to write any more code if the browser that is attempting to run the code does not support getUserMedia(). Therefore, we can remedially test for support of getUserMedia() by identifying its vendor-specific attributes on the navigator object:

```
$.fn.getUserMedia = function(_options){
    var isSupported = function(){
        return (navigator.getUserMedia
                || navigator.webkitGetUserMedia
                || navigator.mozGetUserMedia
                || false);
    };
};
```

In the event that you really want to use a dedicated feature detection library, check out Modernizr http://modernizr.com/[7].

Defining the Options for `getUserMedia()`

Let's first consider options and defaults with this plugin, matching those defined earlier for our example code to `getUserMedia()`. We might want to author this plugin so that there is some understood default use, documented for our users. Then, adopters of our plugin will need to merely call a parameterless function to have basic features.

```
1   var defaults = {
2       constraints: { video: true, audio: true },
3       success: function(stream){
4           var getMedia = isSupported();
5           if(getMedia && getMedia.name.match(/^(getUserMedia|webkitGetUserMedia)$/g)){
6               var ObjectURL = (window.URL || window.webkitURL).createObjectURL(strea
7               video.attr('src', ObjectURL);
8           } else {
9               video[0].mozSrcObject = stream; //--> for Mozilla browsers
10          }
11          video
12              .css('display', 'block')
13              .on({
14                  loadedmetadata : function(){
15                      canvas.attr('width', this.videoWidth);
16                      canvas.attr('height', this.videoHeight);
17                      video[0].play();
18                  },
19                  click : function(){
20                      takeScreenshotOfVideo();
21                  }
22              });
23      },
24      error: function(error){
25          var error_string;
26
27          switch(error.code){
28              case 1:
29                  error_string = "PERMISSION_DENIED - The user denied permission
30  evice required for operation.";
```

---

[7] http://modernizr.com/

```
31                          break;
32                      case 2:
33                          error_string = "NOT_SUPPORTED_ERROR - A constraint specified is
34   by the browser.";
35                          break;
36                      case 3:
37                          error_string = "MANDATORY_UNSATISFIED_ERROR - No media tracks of
38   cified in the constraints were found.";
39                          break;
40                      default:
41                          error_string = error;
42              }
43
44              console.log("Something went wrong:", error_string);
45          }
46   };
```

Let's examine what this code is doing:

1. Here, we ask for both audio and video device access in the constraints object.
2. If the browser is granted access to the webcam/audio device streams, we attach the stream to our `<video>` element. Furthermore, we create two event listeners on the `<video>` element:
   - `loadedmetadata` is an event that fires when the browser knows the details about the stream's content, if any. If video is provided, we set the `<canvas>` element to the same width and height as our video stream's source so that we will be able to do a capture of all the pixel data in a given frame of the `<video>`.
   - `click` is of course listened for on our `<video>` element. This listener will drive the final feature of our plugin - taking a picture and saving it!

   Note that the default error callback is unchanged from the previous example.
3. The `loadedmetadata` event is provided by the browser to notify the developer that meta data for the specified video and audio has been loaded. This event occurs with several others that are triggered in the following order:
   - `loadstart` – Triggered when the loading process starts.
   - `durationchange` – Triggered when the duration of the specified video/audio changes. Changes from `NaN` to the actual duration of the video/audio once loaded.
   - `loadedmetadata` – Triggered when meta data for the video/audio is loaded
   - `loadeddata` – Triggered when data for the current frame is loaded, but not necessarily enough data for the next frame.
   - `progress` – Triggered when the browser is downloading the video/audio.
   - `canplay` – Triggered when the browser can begin playing the video/audio.
   - `canplaythrough` – Triggered when the browser estimates that it can play through the entire video/audio without having to stop for buffering.

So, what do we do now? Simply, we are building a jQuery plugin, so the desired interaction with our lovely plugin should be a simple user-facing API. Therefore, it is preferable to keep calls to our plugin as small and clean as possible. One possible call to the plugin could pass in a `<video>`, a `<canvas>`, and `<img>` elements within our jQuery object:

```
1  $('video, canvas, img').getUserMedia();
```

This usage would then initialize `getUserMedia()` and setup a feedback of the webcam/microphone stream in the `<video>` element. Once the `<video>` is clicked, then the `<canvas>` element's supplied JavaScript Canvas API will be utilized to capture a frame from the `<video>` source stream (if there is any pixel data) and render it into the `<img>` element.

To handle the required references to a `<video>`, `<canvas>`, and `<img>`, the plugin will filter the `this` reference inside the plugin's scope and test that all requirements are met. Then, we will store a reference to our `<video>`, `<canvas>`, and `<img>` items:

```
1   //--> storing elements
2
3   var video
4       , canvas
5       , img
6       , options = $.extend(defaults, _options);
7
8   //--> build up our video, canvas, and img list
9   this.each(function(i, el){
10      el = $(el);
11      if(el.is('canvas')){
12          canvas = el;
13      } else if(el.is('video')){
14          video = el;
15      } else if(el.is('img')){
16          img = el;
17      }
18  });
```

Notice that we have also taken the defaults object provided above, and extended it with the `_options` item (which will override any duplicate defaults).

Grabbing a screenshot

The next step is to actually write a function that can grab a screenshot from the video. To do this, we will make use of the HTML5 Canvas API. The W3C's Canvas Documentation http://www.w3.org/html/wg/drafts/canvas/[8] lists some details about this API:

---

[8] http://www.w3.org/html/wg/drafts/2dcontext/html5_canvas/

- `getContext()` returns a CanvasRenderingContext2D, which represents an interface implementation that can perform and manipulate two dimensional bitmap data.
- `drawImage()` takes an image buffer, or in this case, an HTML `<video>` element.
- `toDataURL()` returns a base64 encoded image of the data source, which in this case is a `<video>` element.

The HTML5 APIs handle much of the minute details, leaving them out of the developer's worry. However, it is still important to understand what is happening in the background.

```
var takeScreenshotOfVideo = function(){
        //--> Read in the video frame as image data to the canvas object
        canvas[0].getContext('2d').drawImage(video[0], 0, 0);

        //--> Write the canvas image data as a base64 encoded string to the image's src \
attribute
        //--> This will fallbackfallback to "image/png" if webm is not supported by the \
browser
        img.attr('src', canvas[0].toDataURL('image/webm'));
};
```

The first call to `canvas[0]` is accessing the actual HTML5 Canvas element, instead of the jQuery collection that we made earlier. We use the Canvas's 2D drawing context to draw the graphics data from our `<video>` element to the hidden `<canvas>` element, where the `<canvas>` is hidden because we set `display:none;` on the element's style attribute.

Once the `toDataURL()` function flattens and stores an image behind the scenes, it returns a base64 encoded string of data that represents the image.

Base64 encoded images can be interpreted by browsers as part of a feature set called DataURI's:

1. Base64-encoded images look like a long string of text. Basically, a super long string of gibberish characters. It's not gibberish to the browser, though!
2. This data is interpreted as the type of file you are saying it is.
3. DataURI's are supported by all major browsers except Internet Explorer 7 and older.

In our case, we are asking for a `webm` image, which is favored by our friendly Webkit browsers such as Google Chrome and Safari. In the event that `webm` is not supported, the Canvas API will automagically record the image as a `png`.

Finally, we set the `src` attribute of the image to the base64 encoded string. Most modern browsers today understand and interpret this data without any extra work by the developer. Thus, at this point we have saved and displayed a screenshot of our webcam, natively in the browser without a single plugin!

Did you know that you don't have to link to an external image file when using an `<img>` element in HTML, or declaring a background-image in CSS? You can embed the image data directly into the document with a Data URI.

Data URI is supported by the following browsers (from http://caniuse.com/#feat=datauri[9]):

Data URIs - Other												
Usage stats: Support: 73.08% Partial support: 21.05% Total: 94.13%												
Method of embedding images and other files in webpages as a string of text												
Show all versions	IE	Firefox	Chrome	Safari	Opera	IOS Safari	Opera Mini	Android Browser	Opera Mobile	Blackberry Browser	Chrome for Android	Firefox for Android
								2.1				
								2.2				
						3.2		2.3	10.0			
						4.0-4.1		3.0	11.5			
	8.0		26.0			4.2-4.3		4.0	12.0			
	9.0	21.0	27.0	5.1		5.0-5.1		4.1	12.1	7.0		
Current	10.0	22.0	28.0	6.0	15.0	6.0-6.1	5.0-7.0	4.2	14.0	10.0	28.0	22.0
Near future	11.0	23.0	29.0	7.0	16.0	7.0						
Farther future		24.0										

Browser support for DataURI

Putting It All Together

Finally, we can establish an init function which will run on construction of a new plugin instance:

```
1  var init = function(){
2      if(!video || !canvas || !img || !(getMedia = isSupported()) ){
3          return;
4      }
5
6      navigator[getMedia.name](options.constraints, options.success, options.error);
7  };
```

Here, you will notice that we invoke the `getUserMedia()` that exists with our browser by accessing the navigator object like a key-store. The final plugin now looks rather complete, and is extensible enough to add functionality to the success or error functions as needed:

---

[9]http://caniuse.com/#feat=datauri

```
 1  $.fn.getUserMedia = function(_options){ //--> _options -> { constraints: ..., suc\
 2  cess: ..., error: ... }
 3
 4       var isSupported = function(){
 5            return
 6                 navigator.getUserMedia
 7                 || navigator.webkitGetUserMedia
 8                 || navigator.mozGetUserMedia
 9                 || false;
10       };
11
12       var takeScreenshotOfVideo = function(){
13            //--> Read in the video frame as image data to the canvas object
14            canvas[0].getContext('2d').drawImage(video[0], 0, 0);
15
16            //--> Write the canvas image data as a base64 encoded string to the image's src\
17   attribute
18            //--> This will fallback to "image/png" if webm is not supported by the browser
19            img.attr('src', canvas[0].toDataURL('image/webm'));
20       };
21
22       var init = function(){
23            if(!video || !canvas || !img || !(getMedia = isSupported()) ){
24                 return;
25            }
26            navigator[getMedia.name](options.constraints, options.success, options.error);
27       };
28
29       var defaults = {
30            constraints: { video: true, audio: true },
31            success: function(stream){
32                 var getMedia = isSupported();
33
34                 if(getMedia && getMedia.name.match(/^(getUserMedia|webkitGetUserMedia)$/
35                      var ObjectURL = (window.URL || window.webkitURL).createObjectURL
36                      video.attr('src', ObjectURL);
37                 } else {
38                      video[0].mozSrcObject = stream; //--> for Mozilla browsers
39                 }
40
41                 video
42                      .css('display', 'block')
```

```
                            .on({
                                loadedmetadata : function(){
                                    canvas.attr('width', this.videoWidth);
                                    canvas.attr('height', this.videoHeight);
                                    video[0].play();
                                },
                                click : function(){
                                    takeScreenshotOfVideo();
                                }
                            });
                },
                error: function(error){
                    var error_string;
                    switch(error.code){
                        case 1:
                            error_string = "PERMISSION_DENIED - The user denied pe
device required for operation.";
                            break;
                        case 2:
                            error_string = "NOT_SUPPORTED_ERROR - A constraint spe
d by the browser.";
                            break;
                        case 3:
                            error_string = "MANDATORY_UNSATISFIED_ERROR - No media
ecified in the constraints were found.";
                            break;
                        default:
                            error_string = error;
                    }
                    console.log("Something went wrong:", error_string);
                }
            };

        //--> storing elements
        var video,
                canvas,
                img,
                options = $.extend(defaults, _options);

        //--> build up our video, canvas, and img list
        this.each(function(i, el){
                el = $(el);
```

```
85                    if(el.is('canvas')){
86                            canvas = el;
87                    } else if(el.is('video')){
88                            video = el;
89                    } else if(el.is('img')){
90                            img = el;
91                    }
92          });
93
94          init();
95     };
96
97     //--> call our plugin
98     $('video, canvas, img').getUserMedia();
```

Our finished product will look something like the following screenshot (funny faces not included):

Funny faces, courtesy of yours truly.

Summary

Whew! That was quite a thorough snapshot (wink, wink) of getUserMedia(), don't you think? In this chapter, we discussed a lot of the shortcomings of plugin-based webcam apps that are driven by Adobe Flash, Silverlight, or Java Applets, and brought to light the scenarios and design requirements that would create the "perfect storm" for native media experience. Moreover, we discussed the design architecture of the WebRTC platform, how it affects the demands on the evolving browser experience, and the future possibilities for the young yet mature project.

We also discussed tools that can be used to help debug and profile WebRTC platform code, and the status of major browsers and which versions support getUserMedia() (and for some, WebRTC).

Finally, after addressing drawbacks of plugin based designs, we put together a tiny, modular front-end app by formulating a jQuery plugin around the use of getUserMedia() and HTML5 Canvas.

In the next chapter, we take a deep look intensive data processing and multi-threaded high-performance JavaScript with HTML5 Web Workers.

6 Web Workers

In the history of web applications, no one could attest to a JavaScript solution as the centerpiece for high-performance computing and data-crunching. Data-intensive use cases have historically been the domain of highly specialized software built for native desktop applications. These native applications required the multi-core and multi-threaded resources available to desktop applications, in order to solve complex problems in many different domains, such as:

1. Engineering programs
2. 3D rendering
3. Physics simulations
4. Data-crunching mathematical and probabilistic applications
5. Visual computing such as Movement tracking from a webcam with WebRTC
6. Cryptographic functions

Overall, computing resources on desktop class applications are able to make use of extensive multi-core, multi-threaded memory, processor, and even General Purpose GPU computing-power allocation.

> Want to run the example code for this chapter? Grab and install the latest version of Node.js[1]. After installing, you can run a simple web server by opening the Chapter 6 code directory and using node to run the server:
>
> `node my/directory/wrinklefree-jquery/ch6/server.js`
>
> Afterwards, simply open a browser to `localhost:8888`.

In contrast to desktop applications, JavaScript-heavy web applications that written just a few years ago were forced to be as efficient as possible, where memory, image, and file resources must be approached with extreme caution. As of ten years ago, the idea that one could quickly process and ray-trace a 3-dimensional scene in the browser would have been approached with a smirk and a snort.

Just as in compiled platform applications, such as server side code or Mac and Windows desktop software, simply running an infinitely-repeating while loop in a single-threaded app will crash it:

---

[1] http://nodejs.org

```
1  while(true){
2          //--> do something
3  }
```

Not unlike desktop and native applications, there is a need for multi-threading in web apps, too. If instead we could run the infinite loop, but still keep the operating system happy - *and therefore the user happy* - then heavy processing tasks can be conquered in web apps.

Fortunately, we can already do this today. Consider a scenario where we want to calculate prime numbers. Here is what a single-threaded JavaScript application would look like:

```
1  //--> Master.js
2
3  var n = 1;
4  while (true) {
5          n += 2;
6
7      for (var i = 3; i <= Math.sqrt(n); i += 2){
8              if (n % i == 0){
9                      continue;
10             }
11     }
12
13     //--> found a prime number!
14         console.log("A new prime number has been found! --> ", n);
15 }
```

Now, while this will work, this will also hang the browser. The user will have no opportunity to make use of the interface at all while these calculations are taking place.

Consider instead how simple it is to create a rudimentary multi-threaded version of this:

```
1  //--> Master.js
2
3  var worker = new Worker('Worker.js');
4  worker.onmessage = function (event) {
5          console.log("A new prime number has been found! --> ", event.data);
6  };
7
8  //--> Worker.js
9
10 var n = 1;
11 while (true) {
```

```
12              n += 2;
13
14              for (var i = 3; i <= Math.sqrt(n); i += 2){
15                  if (n % i == 0){
16                      continue;
17                  }
18              }
19
20              //--> found a prime number!
21              postMessage(n);
22          }
```

If this is the reader's first time seeing Web Worker code, then it's his lucky day! With merely three more lines of code overall, we have added the ability for this web app's main thread to receive updates asynchronously without needing any extra intervention. This is the common protocol for **all** Web Workers, where a Worker will simply have a conversation with our code (or not, if it is to do nothing) by merely implementing use of two main pieces:

1. Worker.onmessage

    An event handlerwhich allows the main thread to receive message from our Worker.

2. Worker.postMessage()

    Sends a message back to the main thread, alongside some event data that represents some result of our calculations.

Most of the JavaScript applications being written even **today** are applied to work within the resources of a single **thread**. In contrast, 3-dimensional rendering and others classes of multi-threaded applications listed above are not going to play well without some parallelism in processing.

The introduction of resources such as the HTML5 File API, WebStorage, and others has made it possible for modern web applications to undertake some serious client-side computations. Despite the improvements in browser JavaScript engines, it is not yet common to find buttery user interfaces as the browser churns through intensive calculations. The dawn of Web Workers is intended to give us web developers a means to process large tasks in the background, thus preventing the UI from freezing up!

Examples of Web Workers

Before we move any further into details, let's have a gander at some example applications which employ Web Workers to help with the heavy-lifting.

Oliver's JS RayTracer

Check out this demo[2] for an example of the performance impact that using workers can have. First set the number of workers to `disabled` and notice that time it takes for the image to be drawn. Then, try `1 worker`.

If we're using a browser that supports Web Workers and we don't witness a considerable performance benefit in the time taken to draw an image, I'll be a monkey's uncle!

Web Worker Ray Tracing

John Robinson's Web Worker Clock

Web Workers can be used to not only speed up distributable calculations, but they can serve to lighten load on the UI thread so that user interactions and rendering can be updated whilst some calculations are done.

Take this example[3]. Test the code out by running a long string of operations in the `main thread` first. One will notice that the user interface and the time on the screen does not update while the processing continues.

---

[2][http://nerget.com/rayjs-mt/rayjs.html]

[3][http://www.storminthecastle.com/projects/webworkers/workers.html]

Then compare that scenario to running the job in a `Web Worker`. Whilst the processing time of the job with a single Web Worker should be near to the same processing time on the main thread, the Web Worker approach allowed the main UI thread to update the clock on the screen without a hitch.

HTML5 Web Workers

Article and Sample App by John Robinson.

This sample app allows you to run a long running job either within the main thread or within a webworker thread. Running this on the main thread will result in the UI becoming non-responsive until the function completes. Running this same job within a webworker allows the main thread to remain available for interaction even as the longJob function is executed in parallel.

[Run long job in web worker] *Notice that the clock continues to run while this is progress.*

[Run long job in main thread] *Notice that the clock stops running while this is in progress*

11:26:40 PM

Web Worker Processing with Clock

HTML5Rocks

HTML5Rocks[4] wrote a sample application that makes use of the bleeding edge in Web Workers. Normally when sending large amounts of data to a Web Worker (an `Image`, or `Blob`, or `File`), the browser copies the data to ensure that all threads stay safe. However, bleeding edge browsers allow large amounts of data to be directly transferred over, resulting in significant performance gains.

---

[4]http://html5-demos.appspot.com/static/workers/transferables/index.html

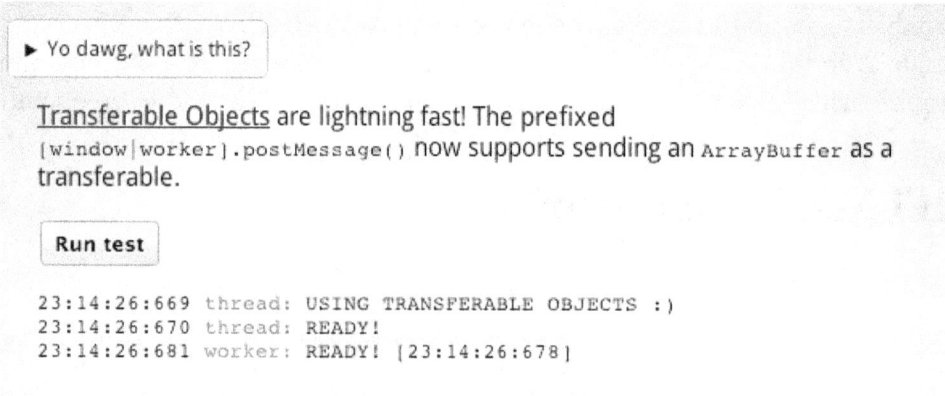

Transferable Objects are Fast

Browser Support

Web Workers have just arrived, and they are already supported across the board quite well:

1. Internet Explorer 10
2. Firefox 19+
3. Safari 5.1+
4. Chrome 25+
5. Opera 12.1+
6. iOS Safari 5.0+
7. Blackberry 7+

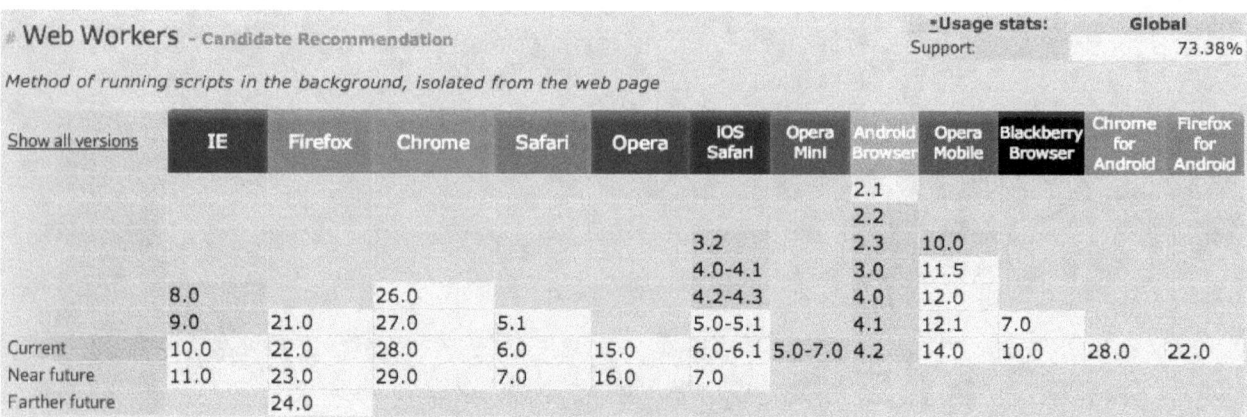

Browser support for Web Workers

We will also cover the Shared Web Workers Draft, which are supported by these browsers:

1. Chrome 25+
2. Safari 5.1+
3. Opera 12.1+
4. iOS Safari 5.0+
5. Blackberry 7.0+

Browser support for Shared Web Workers

Detecting Support

The best and most supported method of testing for Web Worker and Shard Web Worker support is to make use of the brilliant Modernizr library[5].

```
1  if(Modernizr.webworkers){
2      //--> Woohoo! We have Web Workers!
3  }
```

If you don't want to use Modernizr[6], you could also roll your own:

---

[5]http://modernizr.com/
[6]http://modernizr.com/

```
1   function ICanHasWebWorkers(){
2
3       //--> returns true or false
4       return !!window.Worker;
5
6   }
7
8   if( ICanHasWebWorkers() ){
9
10      //--> Use some Web Workers
11
12  } else {
13
14      //--> Don't use some Web Workers
15
16  }
```

However, Modernizr[7] still provides the ability to specify complex load and test operations with ease. The `Modernizr.load()` function lets the developer test for different features, and load different scripts based on support. For instance, if a user's browser doesn't support Web Workers, we can specify a different file to be loaded, or load a polyfill:

```
1   Modernizr.load([
2     {
3       test : Modernizr.webworkers,
4
5       nope : 'singlethreading.js',
6
7       yep  : ['master.js', 'webworkers.js'],
8
9       both : [ 'extra.js' ],
10
11      complete : function () {
12        // Run this after everything in this group has downloaded
13        // and executed, as well everything in all previous groups
14        myApp.init();
15      }
16    },
17
18    // Run your analytics after you've already kicked off all the rest
19    // of your app.
```

---

[7]http://modernizr.com/

```
20      'analytics.js'
21   ]);
```

With a plethora of choices for testing support, there should be a flavor of support that fits every developer's preferences.

Running Examples

If we load a local HTML file into our browser of choice, the URL will look something like http://localhost/.... In this page, we can load a Worker by pointing to the relative location on our filesystem. Thus, if our HTML file is at http://localhost/index.html, and a script worker.js that we want to load into the page is under a scripts folder in the same directory, then we would load that file by simply referencing scripts/worker.js.

At the time of this writing, this works fine in all browsers, except the latest versions of Chrome. There are two workarounds if you want to use Chrome:

1. Host your own server at the location of the code. A simple Node.js[8] script is available in the online source code that allows the developer to setup a simple webserver at http://localhost.
2. Run Chrome with the --allow-file-access-from-files flag set. Please note: It is not recommended to run your primary browser with this flag set. It should only be used for testing purposes and not permanent, every-day browsing.

Without --allow-file-access-from-files

```
1  Modernizr.load([
2    {
3      test : Modernizr.webworkers,
4      yep  : ['scripts/worker.js']          //--> fails silently
5    }
6  ]);
```

With --allow-file-access-from-files

---

[8]http://nodejs.org

```
Modernizr.load([
  {
    test : Modernizr.webworkers,
    yep  : ['scripts/worker.js']         //--> works as expected
  }
]);
```

Threads

Consider a thread to be a big laundry list of todo tasks. When we write JavaScript, each of the tasks written is applied to this thread, where the browser loading the website will work its way through the each consecutive item. However it does not matter if these tasks can be done in parallel, because historically there was no defined standard to address and create *new* execution contexts to process data. In fact, if some JavaScript tasks take too long to execute, even common interface interactions such as mouse hovering, clicking, and scrolling will suffer as a result - leaving your application to be slow and quite unresponsive.

> In computer science, a thread of execution is the smallest sequence of programmed instructions that can be managed independently by an operating system scheduler.

In single-process applications, the idea of multithreading occurs by dividing processor time between different time-slots, effectively allowing for different tasks to execute in chunks. This is called multiplexing.

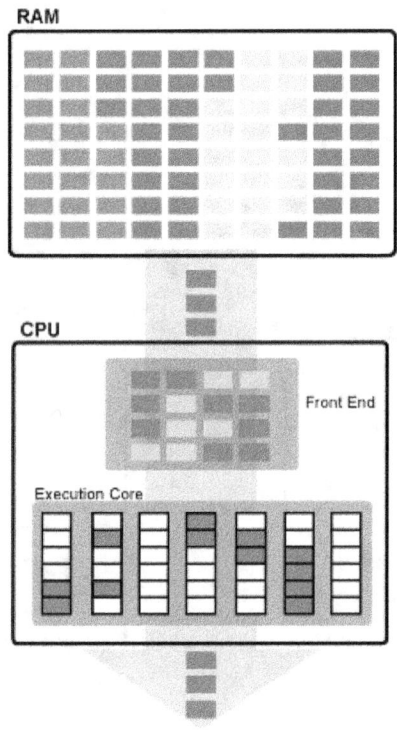

Single CPU

Now, consider a true multi-threading solution, where two or more executing contexts occur at a given slice in time. These simultaneous threading models can process disjoint tasks far more efficiently than the single-core multi-plexing solution. These parallel threads can spawn from the new Web Worker API.

Web Workers facilitate creating new execution threads that support data-processing, therefore allowing the user-interaction and rendering duties of the main thread to stay unhindered. (We like to call this *jank*.)

What does our system look like when we run a multi-threaded application?

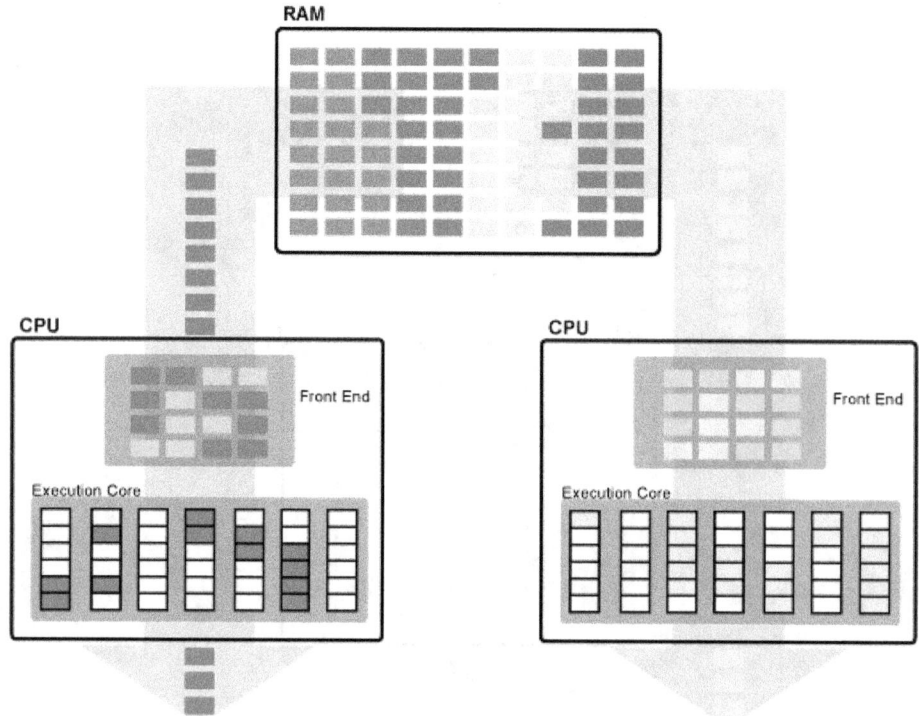

Dual CPU

As you can see, if we specify two or more Web Workers in the application, and we are letting the first threading engine run the UI, and the second one run the background processing, the browser has more time available in the main UI thread to handle interactions and rendering.

Now that you have an understanding of the role that web workers play in JavaScript applications lets take a look at how you can use them in your own projects.

When Not To Use Web Workers

Web Worker contexts can be heavy and should not be attributed too many resources. Spawning more Web Workers than threading engines (or CPU cores for non-HyperThreading processors) available will provide a loss of responsiveness and would over-allocate available processing power.

Defining Web Workers Formally

The `Worker` interface actually spawns a legitimate OS-level thread on your system. It is very important to write modular and simple code to employ concurrency without causing harmful effects. Fortunately, the browsers which implement the `Worker` interface control inter-thread communication very carefully, so there is no access to some non-thread safe components (including the DOM itself), and the developer will be forced to pass data to and from the main thread with serialized objects.

This leads us to the limitations of Web Workers.

Limitations of Web Workers

Web Workers are fantastic but there are several resources restricted by the browser to keep Web Workers as safe and happy as possible.

1. Same Origin Policy

   All of your worker scripts must be served from the same domain as the script that is attempting to create the worker. This also applies to the protocol. For example a `https://` page cannot call on a worker served using `http://`.

2. Limited Access

   Due to the fact that your Web Workers run outside of the main application thread they do not have the same access to JavaScript features as your main application does. Your workers do not not have access to: 1. The `DOM` 2. The `document` object 3. The `window` object 4. The `parent` object

   If you are using a worker to handle a task that ultimately needs to update the main user interface, you will need to use `postMessage()` to pass the data between the worker and the main application. The main application is then responsible for updating the UI. Similarly, if your worker needs access to data from the `document`, `window` or `parent` objects you will need to send it in the `postMessage()` call that is used to start the worker.

3. Restricted Local Access

   Web Workers will not work if the web page is being served directly from the filesystem on Google Chrome (using `file://`). Instead you will need to use a local development server such as XAMPP[9], host your own `Node.js`[10] server (the author's preferred solution), or just use another browser.

4. No Shared Memory

   Also, keep in mind that the standard `Worker` does not share any memory with any other threads, which is why variables within a `Worker` and the main JavaScript of an application cannot access each other's variables.

The Properties of Web Workers

- `void close();` Terminates the worker thread.

---

[9] http://sourceforge.net/projects/xampp/
[10] http://nodejs.org

- `void importScripts(urls);` A comma-separated list of additional JavaScript files.
- `void postMessage(data);` Sends a message to or from the worker thread.
- `location` Represents an absolute URL, including protocol, host, port, hostname, pathname, search, and hash components.
- `navigator` Represents the identity and online state of the user agent client.
- `self` The worker scope, which includes the `WorkerLocation` and `WorkerNavigator` objects.
- `onerror` Event handler for when runtime errors occur.
- `onmessage` Event handler for when message data is received.
- `void clearInterval(handle);` Cancels an interval identified by handle.
- `void clearTimeout(handle);` Cancels a timeout identified by handle.
- `long setInterval(handler, timeout value, arguments);` Schedules a timeout to be run repeatedly after the specified number of milliseconds. Note that you can now pass additional arguments directly to the handler. If handler is a DOMString, it is compiled as JavaScript. Returns a handle to the timeout. Clear with `clearInterval`.
- `long setTimeout(handler, timeout value, arguments);` Schedules a timeout to run after the specified number of milliseconds. Note that you can now pass additional arguments directly to the handler. If handler is a DOMString, it is compiled as JavaScript. Returns a handle to the timeout. Clear with `clearTimeout`.

Spawning a new Web Worker

As demonstrated earlier, to create a Web Worker we just call the `Worker` constructor, specifying the URI of a script to execute in that `Worker`'s thread.

```
//--> Master.js

var worker = new Worker('Worker.js');

worker.onmessage = function(event){
        console.log('The worker sent us some data: ', event.data);
};
```

Alternatively, we can use `addEventListener()` to handle when to signal to `worker` to begin processing.

```javascript
//--> Master2.js

var worker2 = new Worker('Worker.js');

worker2.addEventListener('message', function(event){
        console.log('The worker sent us some data: ', event.data);
}, false);

//--> tell the worker to start
worker2.postMessage('');
```

Remember that the URI passed to the Worker constructor must also obey the Same Origin Policy. There is currently some disagreement among browsers on what URIs are of the same origin, however. When using data URIs, browsers such as Firefox 10+ allow Worker to be invoked with a data URI, whereas Internet Explorer 10 does not.

The following is an example data URI Web Worker:

```javascript
var dataURIWorker = new Worker("data:text/JavaScript;charset=US-ASCII,onmessage%3\
Dfunction(event)%7B+postMessage(event.data)%3B+%7D");
```

The code inside the invocation to Worker is simply an escaped version of the following:

```javascript
onmessage=function(event){
        postMessage(event.data);
}
```

Embedded Workers

While there is not some standard for writing the code for a Worker directly into the main application's page (in a <script> tag processed as type="text/JavaScript"), it is possible in some browsers to still to create a Worker with code embedded into the <html>. If we, instead, create a <script> tag with no mime-type that is processed by the browser (e.g. <script type="text/js-worker">), then the code inside that tag will not be executed, and instead be considered a "data block" - which is a general HTML5 feature that carries any textual data.

Let's write the previous Worker as a "data block" in a webpage:

```html
 1  <!-- Index.html -->
 2
 3  <!DOCTYPE html>
 4  <html>
 5      <head>
 6          <meta charset="UTF-8" />
 7      </head>
 8      <body>
 9          <script type="text/js-worker">
10              //--> NOT executed
11          </script>
12          <script type="text/JavaScript">
13              //--> executed
14              //--> Remember the HTML5 File APIs?
15              var blob = new Blob(document.querySelector("script[type=\"text\/js-worker
16  .textContent, {type: "text/JavaScript"});
17              //--> Creating a new worker, and pass a URL created which points to our
18  n the page createObjectURL()
19              var objectURL = window.URL.createObjectURL(blob);
20              var worker = new Worker(objectURL);
21              worker.onmessage = function (event) {
22                  postMessage(event.data);
23              };
24              //--> And finally, start the worker!
25              window.onload = function() { worker.postMessage(""); };
26          </script>
27      </body>
28  </html>
```

The key takeaways of the previous example are:

1. Embed the `Worker` in a non-standard mime-type `<script>` tag.
2. Create a `Blob()` with our `<script>`'s content.
3. Then, finally create a `Worker` by invoking the constructor and passing it the URL of the `Blob()`. On my local server, that URL looks like:

```
1  blob:http%3A//localhost%3A8888/36c72a2e-6f1b-43c4-b749-d3ec697cb2d2
```

Want to remove that URL before the user has refreshed the page? Simply call the `revokeObjectURL()` function.

```
1  window.URL.revokeObjectURL(objectURL);
```

Creating Embedded Workers is supported under these browsers:

1. Chrome 8+
2. Firefox 4+
3. Internet Explorer 10
4. Safari (Nightly)
5. Chrome for Android 18+
6. Android 4.0+
7. Firefox Mobile 14+
8. Safari Mobile 6+

Communicating with a Web Worker

Communication between a worker and the main JavaScript of a web application is quite simple, and more recent browser releases make that simple communication amazingly easier still. We have already seen the two Web Worker functions that we will use for the foundations of our applications:

1. `Worker.onmessage`
2. `Worker.postMessage`

Let's write a quick example on sharing a JSON object with a `Worker`. This JSON object, passed to and from a `Worker`, is serialized into a compressed and safe version of itself, where it is received by the other thread and then deserialized.

```
1  //--> Master.js
2
3  var worker = new Worker('Worker.js');
4
5  worker.onmessage = function(event){
6      console.log('The worker said: ', event.data);
7  };
8
9  var myUser = {
10     name: "Matt",
11     dogOwner: true,
12     date: new Date()
13 };
14
```

```
15  worker.postMessage(myUser);
16
17  //--> Worker.js
18
19  //--> not received by the Master, because the onmessage
20  //--> handler is processed after this worker started
21  postMessage("Worker, reporting for duty!");
22
23  onmessage = function(event){
24      setTimeout(function(){
25          postMessage("Hello "+event.name".");
26      }, 4000);
27  };
```

As we create our Worker called worker, the Master passes myUser to worker using the structured cloning algorithm[11]. Structured cloning is a new JSON serialization specification that offers more than typical string to JSON serialization.

Some browser versions do not support structure cloning, and thus must resort to using JSON.parse(largeStringTo and JSON.stringify(largeJSONToString) to send and receive strings to the Web Workers, instead of JavaScript objects.

Structured Cloning is supported by:

1. Chrome 13+
2. Firefox 8+
3. Internet Explorer 10
4. Opera 11.5+
5. Safari 5.1+
6. Chrome for Android 0.16+
7. Firefox Mobile 8+

Structure Cloning

Structured cloning provides:

1. Standard JSON serialization (We can post JSON and objects to Web Workers instead of strings!)
2. Serialization of cyclic JSON

---

[11]http://www.w3.org/html/wg/drafts/html/master/infrastructure.html#safe-passing-of-structured-data

```
1   //--> example cyclic JSON
2   var json = {};
3   json.item = json;
4
5   //--> error
6   JSON.parse(json);
```

3. Can duplicate `RegExp` objects
4. Can duplicate `Blob`, `File`, and `FileList` objects
5. Can duplicate `ImageData` objects

Structured cloning cannot:

1. Duplicate `Error` and `Function` objects
2. Duplicate `DOM` elements
3. Preserve the `lastIndex` field of `RegExp` objects
4. Preserve descriptors, setters, getters, and `prototypes` of JavaScript objects

> If an object is marked read-only using a property descriptor, it will be read-write in the duplicate.

It is important to understand that data passed by an application to a `Worker` is **copied**, not shared. Thus, in the previous example, after sending `myUser` to worker, modifying `myUser`'s name to be `"Mark"` instead of `"Matt"` after the `postMessage()` call will not propagate to worker.

```
1   //--> Master.js
2
3   var worker = new Worker('Worker.js');
4
5   worker.onmessage = function(event){
6       console.log('The worker said: ', event.data);
7   };
8
9   var myUser = {
10      name: "Matt",
11      dogOwner: true,
12      date: new Date()
13  };
14
15  worker.postMessage(myUser);
16
17  myUser.name = "Mark"; <-- This change is not visible to worker
```

Using prototypes with `postMessage()`

Remember that the structured cloning algorithm does not copy over properties from the `prototype` chain? Consider adding a class with a `prototype` to a new `myUser2` object:

```
1   //--> Master.js
2
3   function ProtoObj(){
4   }
5   ProtoObj.prototype.callme = "maybe";
6
7   var worker = new Worker('Worker.js');
8   worker.onmessage = function(event){
9           console.log('The worker said: ', event.data);
10  };
11
12  var myUser = {
13          name: "Matt",
14          dogOwner: true,
15          date: new Date(),
16          protoobj: new ProtoObj()
17  };
18
19  var myUser2 = {
20          name: "Bob",
21          dogOwner: false,
22          date: new Date(),
23          protoobj: $.extend(true, {}, new ProtoObj())
24  };
25
26  worker.postMessage(myUser);
27  worker.postMessage(myUser2);
28
29  //--> Worker.js
30
31  onmessage = function(event){
32          event.data.protoobj;
33  };
34
35  //--> myUser produces: {}
36  //--> myUser2 produces: { callme: "maybe" }
```

As we can see from the last line in the previous code, the `myUser2` object passed with an actual `callme` property on `protoobj`. In order to take a property off of the `prototype` and set it directly on the object itself, we made use of jQuery's `$.extend()` method instead of writing our own (although rolling your own is entirely fine).

In order to make a proper `deep copy` of an object with `prototype` attributes by way of `jQuery.extend()`, use the following method:

```
//--> Shallow copy
var newObject = jQuery.extend({}, oldObject);

//--> Deep copy
var newObject = jQuery.extend(true, {}, oldObject);
```

jQuery provides the helpful `deep copy` functionality for us.

Transferrable Objects

There is a new high-performance standard on the block, supported only by:

1. Firefox 18+
2. Chrome 17+

Whereas using a `worker.postMessage(argObject)` would send a **copy** of `argObject` to `worker` as either a string or structured clone, using Transferrable Objects instead simply **transfers** an object via reference to the `worker`'s thread. The main thread will no longer be able to use or access the transferred object.

Recently introduced alongside Web Workers is a speed-focused feature called `ArrayBuffer()`. `ArrayBuffer()`'s are datatypes that represent arrays of generic, fixed-length binary data. For example, we can create a buffer for 32-bit integers[12] with `Int32Array()`:

---

[12] https://developer.mozilla.org/en-US/docs/JavaScript/Typed_arrays

```
1   var arr = new Int32Array(1024*1024*32); //--> 32MB
2   for (var i = 0; i < arr.length; ++i) {
3         uInt8View[i] = i;
4   }
5   worker.postMessage(arr.buffer, [arr.buffer]);
6   if (!arr.byteLength) {
7     //--> Transferables are not supported in your browser
8   } else {
9     //--> Transferables are supported in your browser
10  }
```

This is especially helpful in transferring ownership of unsharable or expensive resources across worker boundaries. Consider the previous task of making a copy of a 32MB object in memory when sending that object to a Worker. This will prove to be orders of magnitude faster when using Transferable Objects[13].

Terminating a Web Worker

If you need to terminate a Worker without letting any other operations or clean-up occur:

```
1   //--> Master.js
2
3   var worker = new Worker('Worker.js');
4   worker.onmessage = function(event){};
5   worker.terminate();
```

Workers can also close themselves with their close() method:

```
1   //--> Worker.js
2
3   self.close();
```

Shared Web Workers

All of our examples thus far have been Dedicated Workers. Dedicated Workers have a one-to-one relationship with the script/page that created them. This, in effect, can be limiting to certain use cases. SharedWorkers, on the other hand, can be distributed across multiple pages that originate from the same origin (note: Same Origin Policy). This would allow us to in effect create multiple references to a single SharedWorker from two different browser tabs.

SharedWorkers make use of a slightly different API, given that each SharedWorker must manage multiple connections.

---

[13]http://html5-demos.appspot.com/static/workers/transferables/index.html

Creating a Shared Worker

SharedWorkers are constructed just we create a Dedicated Worker, only we can also provide a name for the SharedWorker so that any other connections can identify with that SharedWorker on this origin.

```
var worker = new SharedWorker('Worker.js'); //--> no name provided
//--> will attach to a SharedWorker in
//--> this origin named 'someName', or create a new one
var namedWorker = new SharedWorker('Worker.js', 'someName');
```

Communicating with a Shared Worker

SharedWorkers communicate via port objects defined on them. As more connections are made to namedWorker, more ports are added to namedWorker's internal list. Messages for SharedWorkers are handled with events on the port property.

```
worker.port.onmessage = function (event) { ... };
worker.port.postMessage('some lovely text');
worker.port.postMessage({
        structured: [
                'data',
                'is',
                'also',
                {
                        possible: 1
                }
        ]
});
```

We also now have the ability to check not only when the SharedWorker receives a message (with onmessage), but can listen for new connections with the onconnect handler, since there can be more than one connection to it.

```
//--> new SharedWorker created!
onconnect = function (event) {
        var newGuy = event.ports[0];
        // set up a listener
        newGuy.onmessage = function (event) { ... };
        // send a message back to the port
        newGuy.postMessage('ready!'); // can also send structured data, of course
};
```

Capturing Errors from Web Workers

As with many JavaScript application patterns, it is recommended to capture and handle any errors a user may encounter. To do this, we can simply listen for the error event on a worker:

```
function handleError(e) {
        console.log('ERROR at line: ', e.lineno, ' in ', e.filename, ' --> ', e.message);
}

function handleMessage(e) {
        console.log(e.data);
}

var worker = new Worker('Worker.js');

//--> standard message event
worker.addEventListener('message', handleMessage, false);

//--> standard error event
worker.addEventListener('error', handleError, false);

//--> start our Worker
worker.postMessage(); // Start worker without a message.
```

Using Web Workers in our Own Web Applications

Since you don't have access to the window object from a Worker, you won't be able to access the Local Storage (which doesn't seem to be thread-safe anyway). Those limitations may look too constraint for developers used to multi-threaded operations in other environments. However, the big advantage is that we won't fall into the same problems we usually encounter: locks and race conditions. We won't have to think about that with Web Workers. This makes the Web Workers something very accessible, while allowing some interesting performance boosts in specific scenarios.

Here are some interesting scenarios that could use Web Workers to enhance a realtime experience:

1. Image processing by using the data extracted from the `<canvas>` or `<video>` elements. You can divide the image into several zones and push them to the different `Workers()` that will work in parallel. You'll then benefit from the new generation of multi-cores CPUs. The more you have, the faster you'll go.
2. Retrieving large amounts of data with an `XMLHTTPRequest` call and parsing it. If the time needed to process this data is important, you'd better do it in the background inside a Web Worker to avoid freezing the UI Thread.
3. Background auto-correct or assisted typing: parsing out and calculating spelling corrections and retrieving popular keywords based on input being typed be a user right now, without impacting the UI experience. Think about an application like Word (of our Office Web Apps suite) leveraging such possibility: background search in dictionaries to help the user while typing, automatic correction, etc.
4. Making concurrent requests against a local database. `IndexedDB` will allow what the `Local Storage` can't offer us: a thread-safe storage environment for our Web Workers.
5. AI or Physics Engines on Web Workers: Artificial Intelligence engines and Physics calculations can be done in the background while the user is still interacting with the application (and the application is still drawing).

But in a general manner, as long as you don't need the DOM, any time-consuming JavaScript that may impact the user experience is a good candidate for using Web Workers. However, you need to pay attention to 3 points while using the Workers:

1. The initialization time and the communication time with the worker shouldn't be superior to the processing itself.
2. The memory cost of using several Workers is large.
3. Writing parallelized Web Workers is not a simple task, so try to organize the code blocks so that dependency of one `Worker` on another is few and far between.

Using Web Workers with Libraries

Web Workers have taken a rather infamous turn for being used with libraries, as major app developers are beginning to see the benefits of them. Since we have already explored the depths of Web Workers and their API, we may grasp an understanding of how these libraries work. Let's take a look at a few libraries that are now wrapping around `Workers`.

jQuery Hive

jQuery Hive is a simplistic abstraction (and jQuery plugin!) that wraps a bunch of features into a nice friendly package. The jQuery Hive API provides the developer with the ability to:

1. Simplify the client/main page worker setup API
2. Wrap Worker constructor and functions in syntax that jQuery developers are familiar with
3. Normalize cross-implementation inconsistencies; message serialization/deserialization, Structured Cloning, and Transferrable Objects
4. Worker-to-Worker Direct Messaging (Shared Workers)
5. Worker memoization

jQuery Hive exists in duality with another piece of code called Pollen.js, included as part of jQuery Hive. Pollen is the code that runs inside a `Worker`, providing:

1. AJAX, Worker-to-Worker Direct Messaging, Worker memoization
2. Object, Array and String Manipulation
3. Query JSON objects with JSONPath
4. Variable evaluation and logic control flow utilities
5. Syntax that jQuery developers will recognize and understand

Let's take a look at a small example of how jQuery Hive works in a page:

```html
 1  <!-- index.html -->
 2
 3  <!DOCTYPE html>
 4  <html>
 5  <head>
 6      <script src="//cdnjs.cloudflare.com/ajax/libs/jquery/2.0.0/jquery.js"></script>
 7      <script src="scripts/jquery.hive.min.js"></script>
 8  </head>
 9  <body>
10      <script>
11      $(function() {
12          $.Hive.create({
13              count: 2,
14              worker: 'worker.js',
15              receive: function(data) {
16                  console.group('RECEIVED MESSAGE - WORKER: #' + data._from_);
17                  console.log(data);
18                  console.groupEnd();
```

```
                        },
                        created: function(hive) {
                                // fired when all of the Web Workers have been created
                        }
                });

                //--> send all Workers a message
                $.Hive.send({
                        "message": {
                                "a": "a-value",
                                "b": "b-value",
                                "c": "c-value"
                        }
                });

                //--> send only the first Worker a message
                $.Hive.get(1).send({
                        "message": {
                                "d": "d-value"
                        }
                });
        });
        </script>
</body>
</html>

//--> worker.js

importScripts('jquery.hive.pollen.js');
$(function(data) {
        // this equals WorkerGlobalScope
        $.ajax.get({
                url: 'get-data-from-the-server.php',
                dataType: 'json',
                data: $.param(data.message),
                success: function(json) {
                        //--> get unique items underneath the json
                        //--> object returned by the ajax request
                        $.send($.unique(json));
                }
        });
});
```

The previous example gives us a simple method to create two Workers, where we can then send messages to all or a single Worker. We are able to listen for message events in the creation of our Hive, and one may notice that the jQuery Hive code provides a data._from_ property on the message event which tells us the Worker that posted the message.

In the Worker created, we can see that the first order of business is to import the jquery.hive.pollen.js file. While this is not necessary, and we could simply use the onmessage handler and the postMessage() function to send and receive data, the Pollen.js file provides many niceties for us to use. In this example, we make an ajax request to a URL, turn the event.data object into a query parameter, and then process a returned value json, which we then send the $.unique() items back to our Hive with $.send().

Communist.js

There is another library, Communist, that takes a different approach to providing an API for creating Workers. First of all, Communist does not use jQuery as a prerequisite. Even more so, Communist doesn't create new Workers by taking a file as input, instead it receives functions, and creates a number of specified Workers on the fly.

Let's have a look at the API:

```
var worker = communist({
    sum: function (a, b, cb){
        cb(a+b);
    },
    square: function(a){
        return a*a;
    }
});

//--> get the sum of 2 and 5
worker.sum(2,5).then(function(a){ console.log(a); }); //--> prints 7

//--> get the square of 5
worker.square(5).then(function(a){ console.log(a); }) //--> prints 25

worker.close() //--> closes the worker
```

Providing an object as input, we can pass a list of functions, such as the sum() and square() functions above. However, we can send functions to Communist with two different signatures, one that uses a callback function and one which returns a result. In each case, we can see that sum() and square() functions can be used by following up with a then(function(a){ ... }) function, where a is either the value returned by square() or the value given as input to the cb() function in sum().

Summary

In this chapter, we covered the foundations of Web Workers, including multiple scenarios in creating Web Workers, the fundamentals of Message Passing with Web Workers, and the limitations of the Web Worker API. On top of this, we also discussed typical issues such as error capturing, resource management, and other quirks such as the `file://` issue under Google Chrome.

Additionally, we took a look at some examples uses of Web Workers, example libraries that are built on top of them, and built a jQuery plugin ourselves to use.

Next, we will examine the world of WebSockets and the expanding possibilities of Real-Time Communication on web applications.

7 jQuery and WebSockets – Low Latency Networking in JavaScript

Real-time connections in HTML and JavaScript web applications are historically a difficult process. The old limitations of HTTP requests were restricted to the request-response model, where the browser itself must send a message to a server to get information needed for an application. This typical dialog follows an accepted and commonplace story:

1. A client loads a web page from a server.
2. Nothing occurs until the client processes a click on the page to navigate to a new page.
3. The client loads a page where some AJAX code loads 'live' updates on a news feed.
4. The client runs the JavaScript to load some new data from the server every 10 seconds.

The standard means of requesting data from a web server is via HTTP request. This involves a request from the browser to the server hosting the data, which acknowledges the request, processes some data, and sends that data back to the browser in a response.

Consider the typical scenario for a stock ticker on a webpage. In the stone-age of the web, these requests would occur at some recurring interval – let's say ten seconds is the interval. This method is called polling. When browsers poll servers frequently, there is a large amount of data sent to and from the server, without guarantee of 'fresh' stock prices. In other words, those stock prices may not have changed at all.

This leaves polling seemingly disadvantaged at handling "real time communications":

1. Typical HTTP request and response headers would contain 871 bytes and this number doesn't include any data! HTTP header data can even surpass 2000 bytes, so this could get worse. What happens when you need to deploy this data to a large number of users, in quick succession, every few seconds?
2. There is no guarantee of stock price "freshness".
3. There is no method for the server to initiate communication with a browser when there are updated stock prices.
4. Browsers must make frequent requests to update their data.
5. Depending on the scenario, "real-time" could require "fresh" data within 0.5 seconds, making it nearly impossible to support this model via polling.

Let us address the HTTP request size issue. A typical polling client may make a single request every second. Given the average size of HTTP requests to be 871 bytes, we could map out the scenario of network throughput needed for a server to handle those users.

Consider that this stock price ticker has 1,000 browsers polling the server every second. Network throughput would be (871 x 1,000) = 871,000 bytes every second. This comes out to 6,968,000 bits per second or 6.6 Mbps, which is already approaching total bandwidth capacity and speed limits for many price levels on web-hosting packages.

Now imagine this stock ticker gained some larger adoption and is now utilized by 10,000 clients, each polling the server still every second. This makes the required network throughput (871 X 10,000) = 8,710,000 bytes = 69,680,000 bits per second = 66 Mbps!

If that number wasn't daunting enough, imagine designing a polling solution for a popular stock ticker today, which typically reach well over 100,000 clients. If 100,000 clients were to poll the stock ticker server every second, the server would be bombarded with (871 X 100,000) = 87,100,000 bytes = 696,800,000 buts per second, or 665 Mbps. This would cripple many server infrastructures.

Fortunately, after polling was invented, some new methods of server-side signaling were introduced, bundled under the blanket term "Comet" [http://en.wikipedia.org/wiki/Special:Search/Comet_programming][1]. These "hacks" created the illusion of a server initiated connection by keeping the request or response connection open.

Here is a list of the most popular designs:

1. Long-polling
2. Streaming
3. FlashSocket

Comet delays the completion of an HTTP response to deliver subsequent messages to the client, making use of JavaScript techniques like long-polling. Long-polling lets the app send a request and the server keeps that request open for a set period of time and writes into it, updating the app with some new HTTP packets. If the request times out, the server sends a response to terminate the connection and the process is repeated. Streaming, on the other hand, sends a complete request just like polling. However, the server sends and maintains a response (kept open indefinitely or for a set amount of time) that is continuously updated with more information. There is, however some predictably large overhead with this method, since these streaming methods still encapsulate HTTP.

---

[1] http://en.wikipedia.org/wiki/Special:Search/Comet_programming

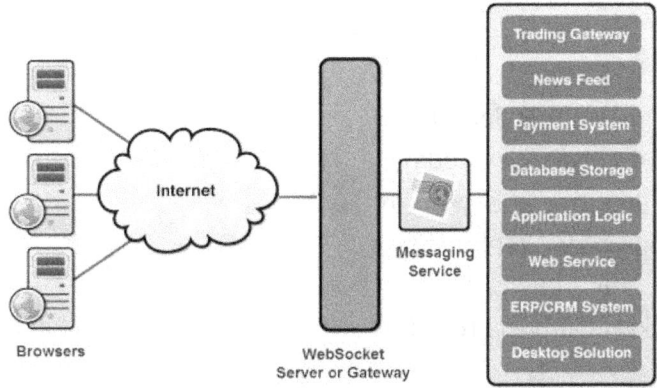

From http://www.websocket.org/aboutwebsocket.html

Because this still piggybacks on HTTP, firewalls and proxy servers may also buffer this activity, adding latency to the response. One such way around this buffering is to use TLS and SSL connections, however those connections themselves are much more expensive to setup.

Each of these Comet methods requires a significant amount of extra headers and packet data. This is especially important if you are using cloud-hosting services which charge you or your company money based traffic volume. They also rely on a half-duplex mechanism, meaning that extra and unnecessary effects must be added to simulate Server-to-Client signals. It gets worse when attempting to scale Comet solutions to the masses, as:

1. Simulating bi-directional communication is error-prone and complex.
2. Roundtrip cost of fresh data incurs a high price tag of latency.
3. The server suffers an unnecessary increase in traffic.
4. HTTP packets still incur a higher CPU and memory cost to create and send large amounts of encapsulated data.
5. The server still lacks the ability to initiate communication.

The only workaround that many developers saw as a scalable solution was to implement server-to-client connections with browser plugins such as Adobe Flash, which supplied the independent background TCP connections needed with FlashSockets, in order reduce the extra `871 bytes to 2000 bytes` of HTTP request header information, which could mean as much as a 50% reduction in packet size.

However, this still left app developers with no native, in-browser method to scaling server-to-client connections.

The HTML5 spec addresses this native need of server-push enabled connections, with the introduction of WebSockets. These APIs adopt the WebSocket protocol for full-duplex communication between client and server. This communication can be initiated from the client JavaScript, provided the server supports upgrade requests to WebSocket protocol.

Let's take a look at the list of features we address in this chapter:

1. The Benefits of WebSockets
2. When to Use or Not Use WebSockets
3. Examples of WebSockets In Use Today
4. Which Browsers Support WebSockets Today
5. Libraries that Encapsulate WebSockets
6. WebSocket API Details
7. A jQuery/WebSockets Coding Project

Want to run the example code for this chapter? Grab and install the latest version of Node.js[2]. After installing, you can run a simple web server by opening the Chapter 7 code directory and using node to run the server:

```
node my/directory/wrinklefree-jquery/ch7/server.js
```

Afterwards, simply open a browser to `localhost:8888`.

The Benefits of WebSockets

WebSockets are full duplex channels that operate over a single TCP socket. This means both the client and server can write to the channel (full duplex), and the server can initiate communication for live updates on our stock ticker (TCP)!

By allowing the server to send updates to connected browsers, the bandwidth utilization is lower. This means less processing is needed over the network, and servers may even be able to scale more linearly due to the reduction of excess networking operations.

The server can also "push" live updates to browsers, meaning updates to software applications – such as stock tickers – can listen for new data. This data is "fresh" because the server initiated the "push" itself to distribute updates.

WebSockets also makes use of TCP packets, instead of HTTP packets, leading to a reduction of packet data from 2kb HTTP requests to 2 bytes of TCP packet data.

Furthermore, WebSockets help reduce latency of typical HTTP packet scenarios from 150ms to 50ms, by bypassing typical proxies and routing schemas of HTTP requests.

Let us consider the advent of WebSockets over polling in the scenario of the stock ticker. With the common size of WebSocket headers being around 2 bytes, 1,000 clients could receive server-initiated communication every second, where the server's throughput would need to meet (2 x 1,000) = 2,000 bytes = 16,000 bits per second = 0.015 Mbps. This is already an easily attainable metric.

Consider the other two numbers as well for further comparison:

---

[2] http://nodejs.org

1. 10,000 clients would receive 1 message per second, meaning the server would need to be able to support (2 x 10,000) = 20,000 bytes = 160,000 bits per second = 0.153 Mbps.
2. 100,000 clients would receive 1 message per second, meaning the server would need to be able to support (2 x 100,000) = 200,000 bytes = 1,600,000 bits per second = 1.526 Mbps.

In order to withstand 100,000 clients using the stock ticker, the bandwidth and processing power of the stock ticker's server infrastructure on HTTP polling would need to support nearly 436 times more bandwidth than it would with WebSockets!

This is a dramatic difference and an amazing evolution in communication protocols for the web. Don't forget that WebSockets are also faster to process, requiring less CPU, and incur less latency cost in sending packets.

When to Use or Not Use WebSockets

WebSockets provide a very fast, very reliable transport of data from client to server, **and** server to client. However, there are some cases where WebSockets shouldn't be used, even if WebSockets are supported.

> When is using WebSockets not a good idea?

1. Serving basic content such as a blog or publishing focus, would best to be served over HTTP. Why? Well, SEO and indexing, for starters. Web technologies, browsers, and search engines (hey, Google!) haven't quite evolved to track WebSockets and dynamic content (without extra code to handle in-app analytics). Serving documents over HTTP is the best approach to allow indexing of a site.
2. Mobile devices may not support WebSockets, so be sure not to serve essential content over WebSockets and fail to ignore a large portion of an audience.
3. Finally, on low-bandwidth connections (not just mobile devices) WebSocket sessions (and the handshakes that establish the connections) can be difficult to setup. With that being said, most smartphones and tablets today support 4G and HSPA+ connections, which meet the bandwidth and latency requirements for WebSockets to be effectively used. Attempting to establish WebSocket connections over EDGE or 2G connections is risky, and the connection may be lost.

This leads us to the next question:

> When is using WebSockets a good idea?

Let's take a look at a few developer scenarios where WebSockets would be a good fit:

1. "My project management app needs to receive notifications from the server when I have updates to the projects I work on. My users are mostly using desktop browsers, instead of mobile."
2. "My chat application needs to be able to handle sending messages to multiple users of a chatroom."
3. "My collaboration app sends and receives a lot of JSON data to the server when modifying different tasks and projects, and I need to be able to send and receives updates in real-time."

While these aren't the only applicable uses for WebSockets, if the reader is considering WebSockets on a project – and the project fits one of the previous descriptions – then the technology might be a viable option.

Examples of WebSockets in Use

Trello

Trello [http://trello.com][3] uses WebSockets to push and pull data to the browser. With Websockets, the Trello developers have implemented some great usability features into the application, such as live update notifications, fast multi-file uploads, and very fast data transfer for app data.

---

[3] http://trello.com

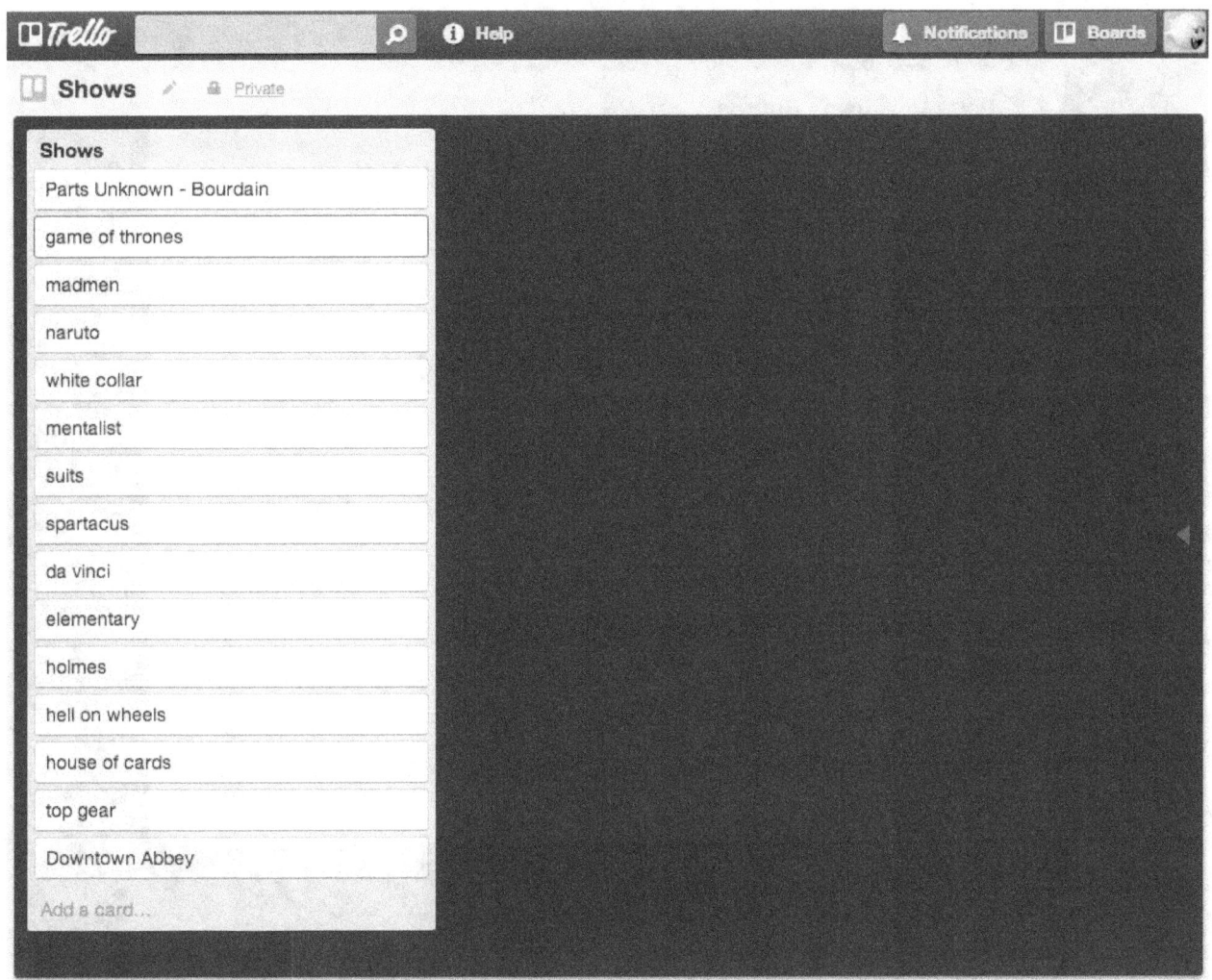

Trello Screenshot

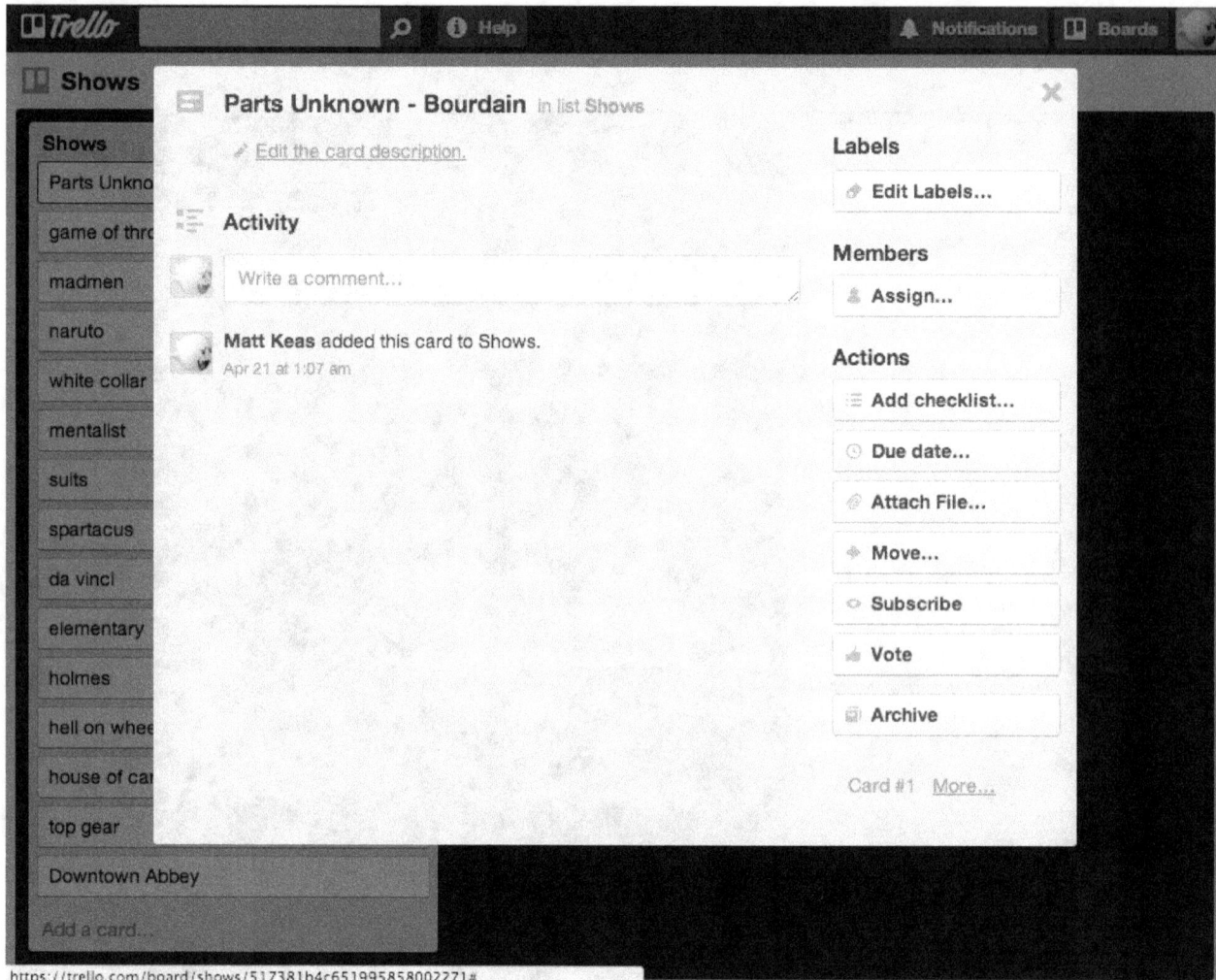

Trello Screenshot

WebSocket.org

WebSocket.org has a plethora of information available to developers, describing the inner-workings of WebSockets as well as providing some examples. One such example shows how to implement a simple messaging system with WebSockets.

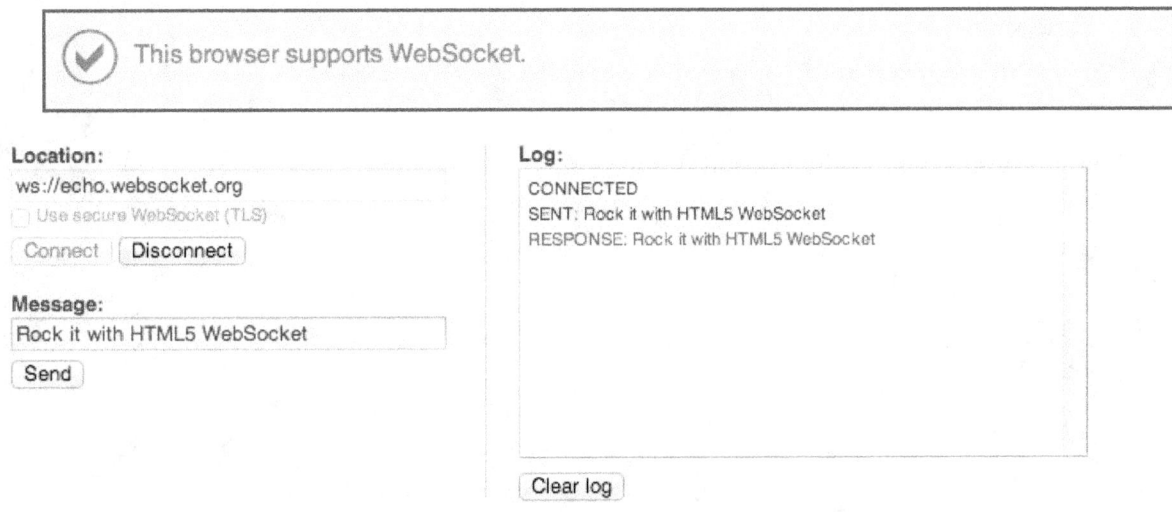

WebSocket.org - Support Test

Google's WebGL Aquarium

With no reservations for WebSocket's power to amaze, we saved the best example for last.

A developer team representing Google has put together an application that draws a 3-dimensional aquarium scene in WebGL (covered later in this book in Chapter 10). To further modernize the application, they decided to implement a scene control with WebSockets.

Essentially, the Aquarium can be connected with multiple browsers, which can collaborate on rendering different camera views from the same scene.

View the single rendered scene at Google Aquarium [http://webglsamples.googlecode.com/hg/aquarium/aquari

To enable multiple machine / multiple window rendering, read the directions at Google Aquarium README [http://webglsamples.googlecode.com/hg/aquarium/README.html][5].

If the reader's machine doesn't support WebGL, see an example video on Youtube [http://www.youtube.com/wat

---

[4]http://webglsamples.googlecode.com/hg/aquarium/aquarium.html
[5]http://webglsamples.googlecode.com/hg/aquarium/README.html
[6]http://www.youtube.com/watch?v=64TcBiqmVko

Google's WebGL and WebSockets Aquarium

Browsers Currently Supporting WebSockets

As of the time of this writing, WebSockets is fully supported by these browsers:

1. Internet Explorer 10
2. Firefox 19+
3. Chrome 25+
4. Safari 6.0+ (An older implementation is supported under 5.1)
5. Opera 12.1+
6. iOS Safari 6.0+ (An older implementation is supported under 4.2, 4.3, 5.0, and 5.1)
7. Blackberry 7+
8. Opera Mobile 12.1+ (An older implementation is supported under 11.5 and 12.0)
9. Chrome for Android 25+
10. Firefox for Android 19+

Show all versions	IE	Firefox	Chrome	Safari	Opera	iOS Safari	Opera Mini	Android Browser	Opera Mobile	Blackberry Browser	Chrome for Android	Firefox for Android
								2.1				
								2.2				
						3.2		2.3	10.0			
						4.0-4.1		3.0	11.5			
	8.0		26.0			4.2-4.3		4.0	12.0			
	9.0	21.0	27.0	5.1		5.0-5.1		4.1	12.1	7.0		
Current	10.0	22.0	28.0	6.0	15.0	6.0-6.1	5.0-7.0	4.2	14.0	10.0	28.0	22.0
Near future	11.0	23.0	29.0	7.0	16.0	7.0						
Farther future		24.0										

Browser support for WebSockets

For a detailed view of browser and platform support of WebSockets, check out http://caniuse.com/#feat=websocke

But never fear, as there are fallbacks and libraries that can help us in our endeavors to support older browsers, or situations where WebSocket handshakes may fail such as on low-bandwidth connections and users behind firewalls.

Server Side WebSocket Frameworks

Implementing WebSockets adds a new level of complexity to standard HTTP web servers. Traditional stacks such as LAMP[8] work with the HTTP request/response cycle. For each subsequent request, a browser must also send a cookie or some other data that ties the new request to **session**. This helps HTTP become scalable and fault-tolerant.

WebSockets, on the other hand, have to maintain an established handshake with the server. This is because the server must be able to initialize communication and send messages back to the client.

Hence the design focus of HTTP is to not use large amounts of memory to maintain connections, and the design focus of WebSockets is to maintain an open connection – even if the client migrates between locations or IP addresses.

More simply stated, HTTP is **stateless** and WebSockets are **stateful**.

New server architectures and add-on modules are designed to handle non-blocking I/O and implement threading, helping to maintain the high rate of I/O operations needed to take advantage of WebSockets. Here is a list of popular frameworks on a variety of platforms today which support WebSockets:

---

[7] http://caniuse.com/#feat=websockets
[8] http://lamp.org

.NET Frameworks

- SignalR[9]
- Internet Information Services (IIS) 8, ASP.NET 4.5[10]
- SuperWebSocket[11]

Nginx

- Proxy[12]

PHP

- php-websocket[13]
- Ratchet[14]

Python

- pywebsocket[15]
- Tornado[16]

Ruby

- EventMachine[17]

Node.js

- Socket.io[18]
- WebSocket-Node[19]
- ws[20]

Since we are using JavaScript for this book, and Node.js runs on JavaScript, we will use the ws[21] library to implement our examples.

---

[9] http://en.wikipedia.org/wiki/SignalR
[10] http://en.wikipedia.org/wiki/ASP.NET
[11] http://superwebsocket.codeplex.com/
[12] http://nginx.com/news/nginx-websockets.html
[13] https://github.com/nicokaiser/php-websocket
[14] http://socketo.me/
[15] http://code.google.com/p/pywebsocket/
[16] https://github.com/facebook/tornado
[17] https://github.com/igrigorik/em-websocket
[18] http://Socket.io
[19] https://github.com/Worlize/WebSocket-Node
[20] https://github.com/einaros/ws
[21] https://github.com/einaros/ws

The WebSocket API - Getting Started

Polling with jQuery

Using jQuery's `$.ajax()` method, we can create a simple polling method to get "live" updates from the server every five seconds.

Let's have a look at the code:

```
(function GetUpdates() {
    setTimeout(function () {
        $.ajax({
            type: 'POST',
            dataType: 'json',
            url: 'http://localhost/api/notifications',
            success: function (data) {
                //--> do something with our code
            },
            complete: GetUpdates
        });
    }, 5000);
})();
```

This code simply uses `setTimout()` to make a request to `http://localhost/api/notifications` after `5000ms` or five seconds. Once the request fails or succeeds, `GetUpdates()` is called to start the process over again. This results in a common way of achieving HTTP polling.

Breaking Out the Sockets

Let's open a WebSocket connection simply by calling the WebSocket constructor:

```
var connection = new WebSocket('ws://localhost', ['soap']);
```

Breaking down the protocol.

Notice the `ws:` URL schema. To implement secure connections (just like `https:`) we can use `wss:`. Also, the IANA Registry[22] defines the WebSocket subprotocols that can be used in the optional parameter to the `WebSocket()` constructor, which in this case is `soap`.

We can setup our WebSocket to handle messages from the server with a few event handlers:

```
1  //--> When the connection opens, 'Ping' the server
2  connection.onopen = function () {
3    connection.send('Ping');
4  };
5  //--> When an error occurs, log it
6  connection.onerror = function (error) {
7    console.log('WebSocket Error ' + error);
8  };
9  //--> Log messages from the server
10 connection.onmessage = function (e) {
11   console.log('Server: ' + e.data);
12 };
```

That's all there is to listening on different events from our `WebSocket()` and sending messages.

Sending Messages Over WebSockets – A Deeper Look

The latest spec of WebSockets [http://dev.w3.org/html5/websockets/][23] allows developers to send not only strings, but `Blobs` and `ArrayBuffers` as well. Thus, just as we worked with `ArrayBuffers` while putting together `WebWorker` powered applications in the previous chapter, `connection.send()` can take those items as input as well to share basic data.

Sending a string over WebSockets is pretty basic:

```
1  //--> sending a string
2  connection.send("Some string");
```

Sending a file over WebSockets (think file uploads, fast!) is also super simple:

```
1  //--> send a file via WebSockets === fast asynchronous upload!
2  var file = document.querySelector('input[type="file"]').files[0];
3  connection.send(file);
```

Finally, sending simple image data can be done with the help of Canvas:

---

[22] http://www.iana.org/assignments/websocket/websocket.xml
[23] http://dev.w3.org/html5/websockets/

```
1  //--> send images from canvas
2  var img = canvas.getImageData(0, 0, 800, 600),
3          binary = new Uint8Array(img.data);
4  connection.send(binary.buffer);
```

Just as we can send binary data over WebSockets to a server from the browser, a server can send the browser binary data. The onmessage = function(e){} event object carries a data property which would represent the Blob or ArrayBuffer sent from our server.

```
1   //--> specify that we are receiving an ArrayBuffer
2   connection.binaryType = 'arraybuffer';
3   connection.onmessage = function(e) {
4     console.log(e.data.byteLength);
5     //--> do something with the image data, such as print it out with canvas
6   };
7   //--> specify that we are receiving a Blob
8   connection.binaryType = 'blob';
9   connection.onmessage = function(e) {
10    console.log(e.data);
11    //--> do something with the file, such as use the FileAPI to save it
12  };
```

Same Origin Policy and WebSockets

Historically, XMLHTTPRequests are subject to the Same Origin Policy, where the requests made must adhere to these restrictions:

1. The same scheme must be used - requests to http:// must come from http:// pages.
2. The same hostname - requests to test.my.example.com must come from test.my.example.com.
3. The same port - requests to test.my.example.com:9090 must come from test.my.example.com:9090.

However, given that WebSockets is a very forward-looking protocol, cross-domain communication is baked right in. The only restriction is based on the accepted domains that connect to our WebSocket-enabled server, defined as loosely and strictly as needed by the application developer.

Encapsulating WebSockets with ws

The WebSocket protocol is still a young technology. However, some **awesome** libraries (like ws), are already fully handling the wonderful world of WebSockets for the Node.js platform.

In this case, we use ws as an example due to the speed, reliability, and up-to-date support for the latest WebSocket protocols.

The benefit of ws is not just ease of handling WebSocket connections, but the tools provided for the developer:

1. Very easy to install with npm[24]

```
1    $ npm install ws
```

2. Support for the latest WebSocket drafts, with the ability to send and receive binary messages (ArrayBuffers, Blobs, etc)

3. Ships with a simple command-line utility called wscat, which can either act as a server (–listen), or client (–connect). use it to debug simple websocket services.

```
1    $ npm install -g ws
2    $ wscat -c ws://echo.websocket.org -p 8
3    connected (press CTRL+C to quit)
4    > hi there
5    < hi there
6    > are you a happy parrot?
7    < are you a happy parrot?
```

ws works in Node.js to provide WebSocket client functions. The following code goes into a Node.js script file which is run by Node.js with the command node file.js:

1. sending text and open / message events

```
1    var WebSocket = require('ws');
2    var ws = new WebSocket('ws://www.me.site.example.com/path');
3    ws.on('open', function() {
4        ws.send('something');
5    });
6    ws.on('message', function(data, flags) {
7        //--> flags.binary will be set if a binary data is received
8        //--> flags.masked will be set if the data was masked
9    });
```

2. sending binary objects over ws

---

[24]http://npmjs.org

```
1   var WebSocket = require('ws');
2   var ws = new WebSocket('ws://www.me.site.example.com/path');
3   ws.on('open', function() {
4       var array = new Float32Array(5);
5       ws.send(array, {binary: true, mask: true});
6   });
```

Masking of WebSocket traffic from client to server is required because of the unlikely chance that malicious code could cause some broken proxies to do the wrong thing and use this as an attack of some kind. Nobody has proved that this could actually happen. However browser vendors made sure to protect from this attack vector, and masking was added to remove the possibility of it being used.

ws also provides the ability to run a WebSocket server. The following code goes into a Node.js script file which is run by Node.js with the command node file.js:

```
1   var WSS = require('ws').Server
2     , server = new WSS({port: 8080});
3   server.on('connection', function(ws) {
4       ws.on('message', function(message) {
5           console.log('received: %s', message);
6       });
7       ws.send('some message to the client');
8   });
```

We can pass callback functions that handle errors if something goes wrong. This is also the best way to ensure that a message did not fail:

```
1   ws.send('something', function(error) {
2       //--> if error is null, the send has been completed,
3       //--> otherwise the error object will indicate what failed.
4   });
```

Coding our example application - Boots' Return!

In Chapter 2 - Geolocation, we built an application to handle a popularity-building application for our friend Jeremy which allowed dog-lovers to "like" the "Boots' Supporters Club". For our next example, we will extend this further so that visitors can join a live chat room, powered by the Node.js ws library and WebSockets.

Let us begin with the basic HTML, where we will define a simple <div> that will act as the container for our tiny micro-application, and create a form with an input field and button.

```
 1  <!DOCTYPE html>
 2  <html>
 3  <head>
 4          <script src="//cdnjs.cloudflare.com/ajax/libs/modernizr/2.6.2/modernizr.min.js">\
 5  </script>
 6      <script src="//cdnjs.cloudflare.com/ajax/libs/jquery/2.0.3/jquery.min.js"></s\
 7  cript>
 8          <link href="bootstrap.min.css" rel="stylesheet">
 9  </head>
10  <body>
11      <div class="container">
12          <h2>Leave a message</h2>
13          <input type="text" class="input-block-level" placeholder="What's would yo\
14  u like to say?">
15          <button class="btn btn-med" type="submit">Send</button>
16      </div>
17      <div class="container">
18         <h4>Messages</h4>
19         <ul class="unstyled messages">
20         </ul>
21      </div>
22  </body>
23  </html>
```

This will give us a page that looks like the following image.

Leave a message

[What's would you like to say?]

[Send]

Messages

Our initial markup.

We can add in a few styles to make our messages look more presentable:

```css
.messages {
        position: relative;
}
.messages > li {
    -webkit-transition: all .3s ease-out;
    -moz-transition: all .3s ease-out;
    transition: all .3s ease-out;
    -webkit-transform: translateX(-50%);
    -moz-transform: translateX(-50%);
    transform: translateX(-50%);
    opacity: 0;
    border: 1px lightblue solid;
    background: lightcyan;
    padding: 1em 1em;
    margin-bottom: 1em;
}
.messages > li.incoming {
        -webkit-transform: translateX(50%);
    -moz-transform: translateX(50%);
    transform: translateX(50%);
}
.messages > li.show {
    -webkit-transform: translateX(0);
    -moz-transform: translateX(0);
    transform: translateX(0);
    opacity: 1;
}
```

This gives us a little color for our messages, such as in the following image.

CSS3 makes everything better.

Next, we'll begin by testing for WebSocket support with `Modernizr` when `jQuery` is ready to start working on the page. Then, we'll call a jQuery plugin that we are about to create:

```
$(function(){
        if(Modernizr.websockets){
                $('.container').BootsChat();
        } else {
                alert("Your browser doesn't support websockets!")
        }
});
```

Next, let's go ahead and define our `BootsChat` plugin. In this process, we initially the following interactions:

1. When the button is clicked, we send a message to the server.
2. When the user types into the input field and presses enter, we send a message to the server.
3. When a message is sent, clear the input field and refocus on it.
4. When a message is sent, print out incoming and outgoing messages as list items into the list.

```
$.fn.BootsChat = function(){
   if(this.length > 1){
      return;
   }

   var container = this.first(), //--> our container
       input = container.find('input').first(), //--> our input text
       button = container.find('button'), //--> our button
       list = container.find('ul'); //--> our list

   var addMessage = function(text){
       //--> Not Yet Implemented
   }

   container.on('keyup', 'input', function(e){
         //--> Not Yet Implemented
   }).on('click', 'button', function(e){
         //--> Not Yet Implemented
   });
};
```

If you haven't gotten used to this pattern, what we have done here is extended jQuery with a function that will work on a jQuery `selection` as the context. Thus, in a call to `$('.container').BootsChat();`, `this` refers to `$('.container')`.

We have also setup some references to the different fields needed in the application for creating the interactions.

The next step is to add in the interaction events `keyup` and `click` delegated to the `container`.

```
container.on('keyup', 'input', function(e){
        if(e.which === 13){ //--> return was pressed
                addMessageFromInput();
        }
}).on('click', 'button', function(e){
        addMessageFromInput();
});
```

The `addMessageFromInput()` function will be the function to get the `input`'s text, call `addMessage()`, and refocus the `input` after resetting the `input`'s text:

```
var addMessageFromInput = function(){
        var text = input.val();
        input.val('').focus();
        addMessage(text);
}
```

This leaves the `addMessage()` function, which will simply create a new list item and add it to the list:

```
var addMessage = function(text){
        if($.trim(text)){
                var newListItem = $('<li/>').text(text);
                list.prepend(newListItem);
                setTimeout(function(){
                        newListItem.addClass('show');
                }, 100)
        }
}
```

As a small-touch, we can also have the `input` take focus right when the webpage loads:

```
1  $.fn.BootsChat = function(){
2      //--> other implementation code here
3      ..
4      //--> focus on the input
5      input.focus();
6  });
```

At this point, we have defined the interactions and user experience needed, but what about our WebSockets data? In this case, it might be beneficial to write a jQuery wrapper for WebSockets on the client side.

Let's start with a basic skeleton for this wrapper, which we can call Banjo (because it is light, small, and fast!):

```
1  $.Banjo = function(){
2      return new function(){
3          var ws;
4          var connect = function(url){
5              //--> connect to server and establish events
6          }
7          var close = function(){
8              //--> close the connection
9          }
10         var send = function(message){
11             //--> send a message
12         }
13         //--> return only the functions we want to be publicly accessible
14         return {
15             connect: connect,
16             send: send,
17             close: close
18         }
19     }
20 };
```

The above code establishes a few things:

1. ws will be a local reference to a WebSocket object.
2. connect will connect to a server and establish onopen, onmessage, and onclose callbacks.
3. close will close the connection.
4. send will send a message to the server.

Before we move further, let us discuss a helpful development pattern that will simplify the process of using the `Banjo` plugin with the `BootsChat` plugin. This pattern, called `PubSub`, falls under a category of architectures called `mediator patters`. PubSub is short for `publish/subscribe`.

```
(function(){
        var o = $({});
        $.subscribe = function() {
                o.on.apply(o, arguments);
        };
        $.unsubscribe = function() {
                o.off.apply(o, arguments);
        };
        $.publish = function() {
                o.trigger.apply(o, arguments);
        };
})();
```

The goal of this is to let any number of distinct code modules interact with one another by defining events. This process works almost exactly the same as handling `click` events with `jQuery`. The following code will provide an example on using PubSub versus `$.click()`.

```
//--> click method <--
        $('a').click(function(){
                //--> do something when an anchor tag is clicked
        });

        $('input').change(function(){
                //--> when an input changes, tell the anchor to handle a click event above, to
                $('a').trigger('click');
        });

//--> PubSub method <--
        $.subscribe('anchorClicked', function(e, arg1, arg2, …){
                //--> do something when an anchor tag is clicked
        });

        //--> make the above function run with the provided inputs
        $.publish('anchorClicked', ['a', 'b', 'c', 1, 2, 3]);
```

Now in some cases the `click` method definitely works better. However, the `PubSub` pattern has a less rigid application, allowing different pieces of code to asynchronously hook together to build very scalable front-end architectures.

Banjo publishes to an event whenever it receives an incoming message. BootsChat will then consume this event with $.subscribe and print an incoming message to the screen. The following code will implement the PubSub event and simple WebSocket wrapper code for Banjo.

```javascript
$.Banjo = function(){
    return new function(){
        var ws;
        var connect = function(url){
            ws = new WebSocket(url);
            ws.onopen = function(event){
                send('Greetings.');
            }
            ws.onclose = function(event){
                //--> do something when the WebSocket closes
                alert('Connection ended.');
            }
            ws.onmessage = function(event) {
                $.publish('Banjo-incoming-message', [event.data]);
            };
        }

        var close = function(){
            ws.close();
        }

        var send = function(message){
            ws.send(message);
        }

        return {
            connect: connect,
            send: send,
            close: close
        }
    }
};
```

Then, we can add the code to BootsChat to handle the incoming messages.

```
1  $.fn.BootsChat = function(){
2          //--> Other code not shown
3          ...
4          //--> modified to use banjo
5          var addMessageFromInput = function(){
6                  var text = input.val();
7                  input.val('').focus();
8                  addMessage(text);
9                  banjo.send(text);
10         }
11         //--> subscribe to the event for incoming messages
12         $.subscribe('Banjo-incoming-message', function(e, message){
13                 addIncomingMessage(message);
14         });
15         //--> create our local banjo
16         var banjo = $.Banjo();
17         banjo.connect("ws://localhost:8080");
18 };
```

Next to do is to code our Node.js server with the ws library.

Remember that all code is available for download on this book's website.

First, install ws with npm:

```
1  $ npm install ws
```

Then, modeling after previous tactics, we can simply have our ws module create a local websocket server and listen on a defined port in server.js:

```
1  //--> server.js
2
3  var ...,
4      ws = require("ws"),
5      server = new ws.Server({port: 8080});
6
7  server.on('connection', function(ws) {
8      ws.on('message', function(message) {
9          ws.send('You said: "'+message+'"');
10     });
11     ws.send('Welcome!');
```

```
12  });
13
14  //--> other webserver code provided online
```

This code sets up a WebSocket server which listens for new connections, and whenever a connection or data is received, this server will echo a message back.

To run the server, simply open the command line and run:

```
1   $ node server.js
```

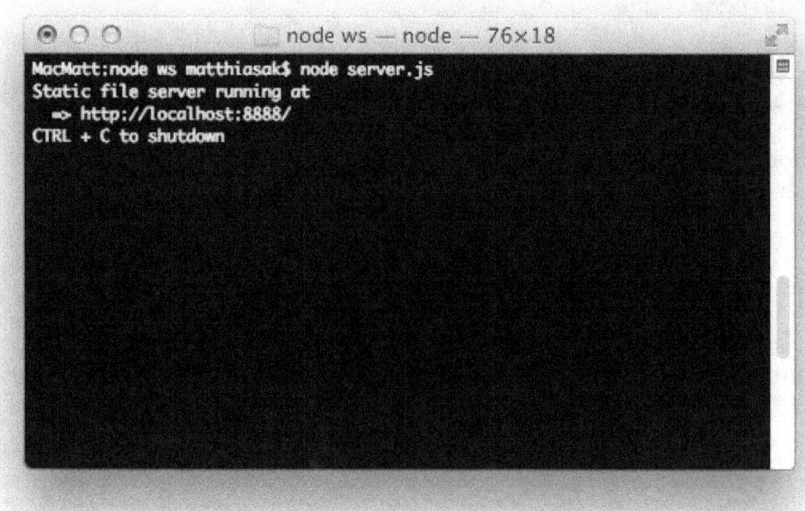

Node.js running in the terminal.

Now with the a plugin and a library completed and loosely coupled with `PubSub`, we can send and receive messages to the *Boots' Supporters* chat room in real-time!

The live chat example, live!

Summary

In this chapter, we covered the foundations of the WebSocket protocol, including creating WebSockets, the fundamentals of Message Passing with WebSockets, sending files and binary data to and from the server, and the limitations of the WebSockets Spec. On top of this, we also discussed typical issues such as error capturing, wrapping and handling WebSocket events, and features provided by some libraries today (with specific focus on the Node ws module).

Additionally, we took a look at some example uses of WebSockets, how to use the PubSub pattern to loosely couple two independent pieces of code, and built a jQuery plugin and one small JavaScript library in a live chat example.

In the next chapter, we will examine the multimedia powerhouse APIs - HTML5 Web Audio and HTML5 Video.

8 HTML5 Audio, Video and jQuery

Before the arrival of the `<audio>` and `<video>` HTML5 tags, Adobe Flash or other plugins were required to cut through the silent and colorless web. Audio and video, the foundations of a multimedia experience, can now be set free from the bounds of black-box binaries running behind a browser.

Recently, both `<audio>` and `<video>` became real members of the HTML clan – they received their own tag, graduating from the archaic `<object>`. Accompanying these shiny tags are HTML5 JavaScript APIs that provide access to and control of the Audio and Video objects. Insurmountable to this is the ability to then turn back time (edit the timeline data) and perform tricky visual and aural effects on media streams.

In this chapter we shall learn:

- The ins-and-outs of the HTML5 Audio and Video elements
- How to programmatically use these elements
- The basics of SVG filters
- How to make fullscreen web applications

Examples of HTML5 Audio and Video

As always, we will begin this section with some inspiration, and then move along to the details and implementation of our own jQuery plugins to use the HTML5 media features!

Youtube

Not a single person could browse the web and not have visited Youtube [http://www.youtube.com][1]. We're in luck, as Youtube has an optional HTML5 version of the site, letting users who opt-in to skip the use of Adobe Flash!

Join the HTML5 Trial by going to http://www.youtube.com/html5[2].

---

[1] http://www.youtube.com
[2] http://www.youtube.com/html5

152   HTML5 Audio, Video and jQuery

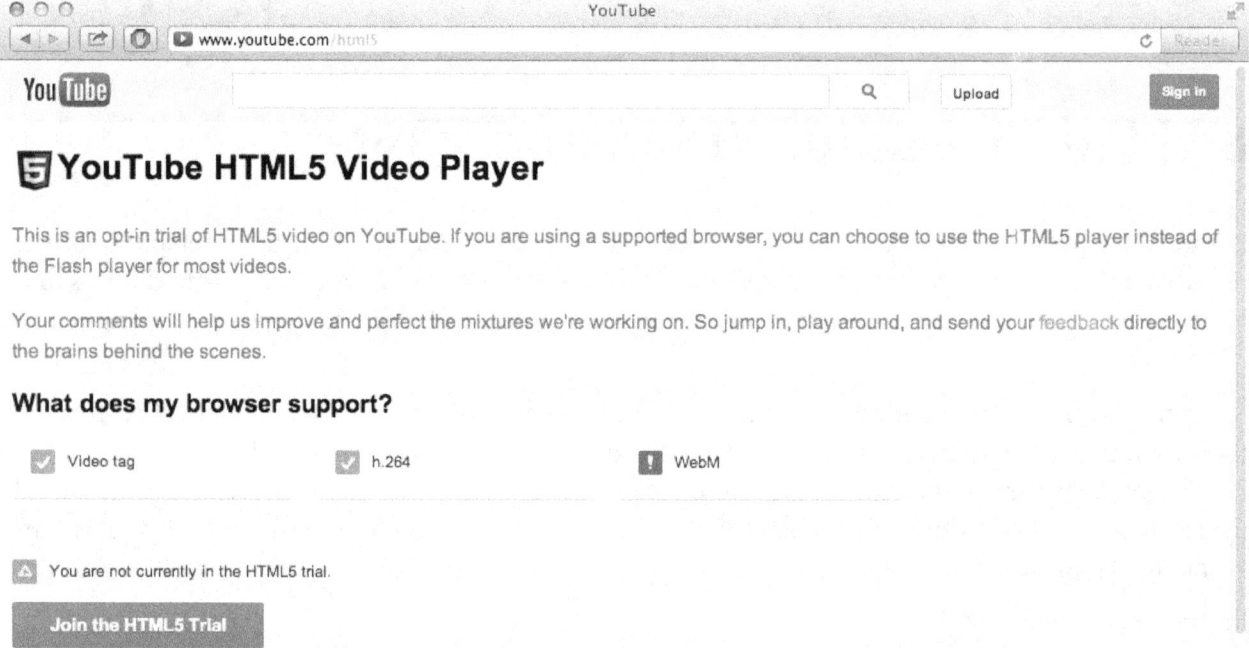

YouTube Screenshot

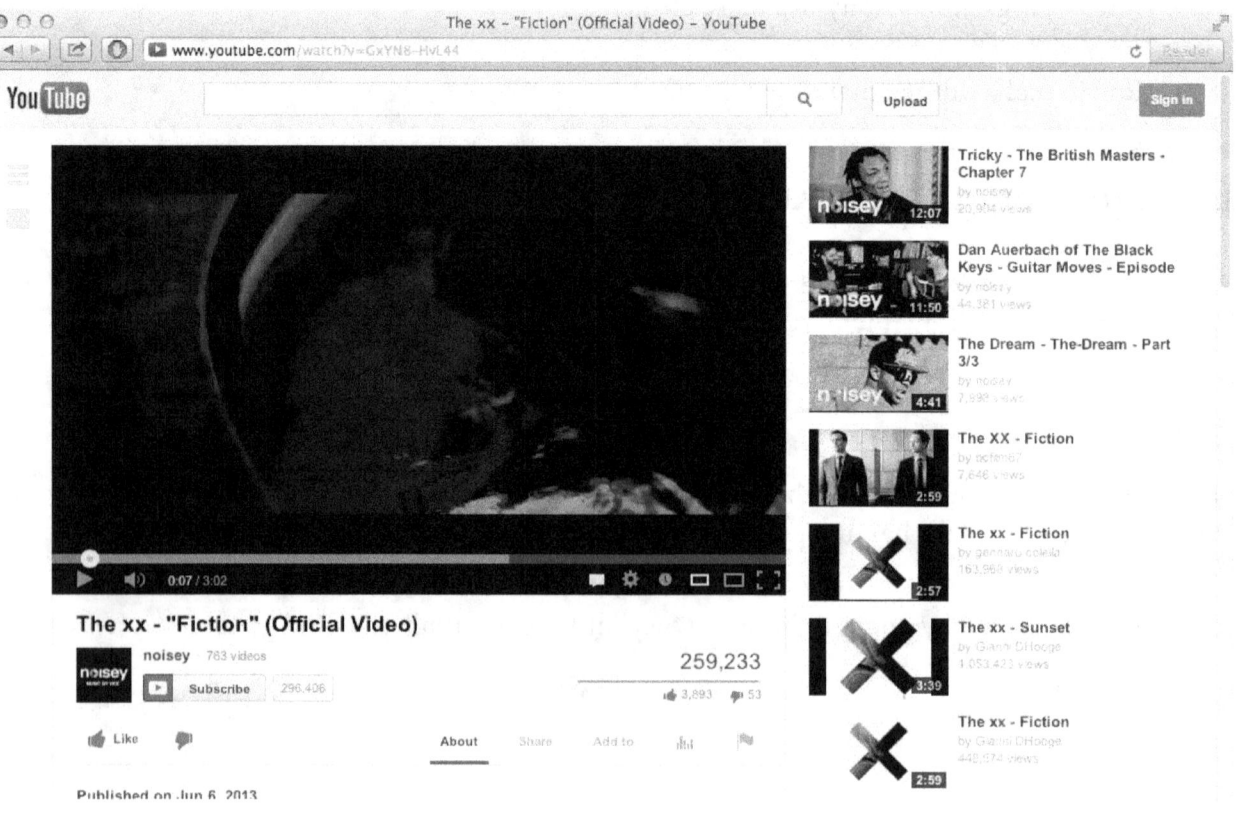

YouTube Screenshot

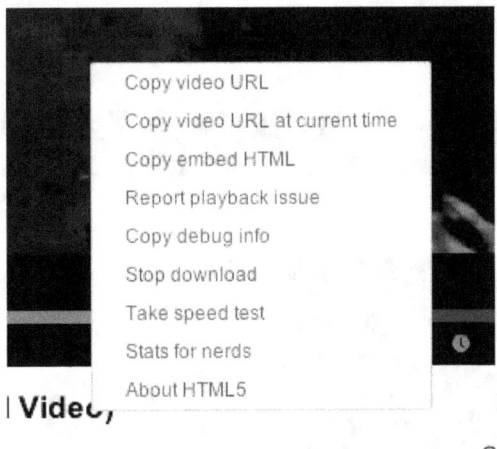

YouTube Screenshot

SoundCloud

Another popular service that is now using HTML5 Audio is SoundCloud [https://soundcloud.com/][3]. SoundCloud touts itself as "The largest community of artists, bands, podcasters and creators of music & audio". Only, they have all the materials to back up that claim.

The SoundCloud application is a sublime and delightful experience, creating an immersive user experience which rivals even the most polished desktop applications.

---

[3]https://soundcloud.com/

SoundCloud Screenshot

Grooveshark

Grooveshark is, while younger than Youtube, an older competitor in the browser-based media player market. The service initially depended on Adobe Flash to stream and play music, however after some time back in the think-tank, Grooveshark released an HTML5 version [http://html5.grooveshark.com/][4] that lets anyone share and stream music via the native browser.

---

[4]http://html5.grooveshark.com/

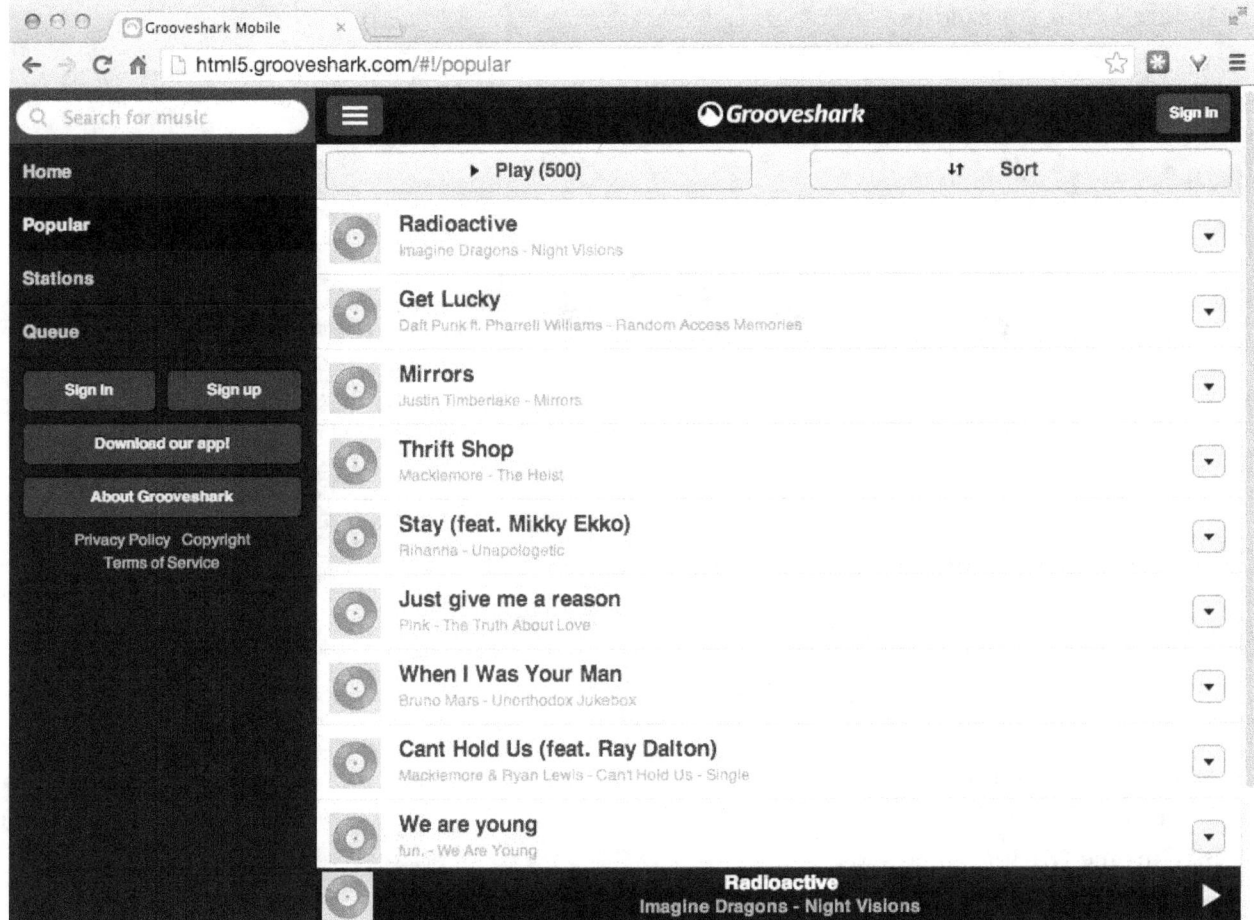

SoundCloud Screenshot

Browsers Currently Supporting HTML Video and Audio

The HTML5 Audio element is supported by:

1. Internet Explorer 9+
2. Firefox 20+
3. Chrome 26+
4. Safari 5.1+
5. Opera 12.1+
6. iOS Safari 4.0+
7. Android Browser 2.3+
8. Blackberry Browser 7+
9. Opera Mobile 11.5+
10. Chrome for Android 25+

11. Firefox for Android 19+

For more info, visit http://caniuse.com/#feat=audio[5].

Audio element - Working Draft												
Method of playing sound on webpages (without requiring a plug-in)												
Show all versions	IE	Firefox	Chrome	Safari	Opera	iOS Safari	Opera Mini	Android Browser	Opera Mobile	Blackberry Browser	Chrome for Android	Firefox for Android
								2.1				
								2.2				
						3.2		2.3	10.0			
						4.0-4.1		3.0	11.5			
	8.0		26.0			4.2-4.3		4.0	12.0			
	9.0	21.0	27.0	5.1		5.0-5.1		4.1	12.1	7.0		
Current	10.0	22.0	28.0	6.0	15.0	6.0-6.1	5.0-7.0	4.2	14.0	10.0	28.0	22.0
Near future	11.0	23.0	29.0	7.0	16.0	7.0						
Farther future		24.0										

Browser Support for HTML5 Audio

The HTML5 Video element is supported by:

1. Internet Explorer 9+
2. Firefox 20+
3. Chrome 26+
4. Safari 5.1+
5. Opera 12.1+
6. iOS Safari 3.2+
7. Android Browser 2.1+
8. Blackberry Browser 7+
9. Opera Mobile 11.5+
10. Chrome for Android 25+
11. Firefox for Android 19+

For more info, visit http://caniuse.com/#feat=video[6].

---

[5]http://caniuse.com/#feat=audio
[6]http://caniuse.com/#feat=video

Video element - Working Draft													*Usage stats:	Global
Method of playing videos on webpages (without requiring a plug-in)													Support:	84.33%
													Partial support:	0.29%
													Total:	84.62%
Show all versions	IE	Firefox	Chrome	Safari	Opera	iOS Safari	Opera Mini	Android Browser	Opera Mobile	Blackberry Browser	Chrome for Android	Firefox for Android		
								2.1						
								2.2						
						3.2		2.3	10.0					
						4.0-4.1		3.0	11.5					
	8.0		26.0			4.2-4.3		4.0	12.0					
	9.0	21.0	27.0	5.1		5.0-5.1		4.1	12.1	7.0				
Current	10.0	22.0	28.0	6.0	15.0	6.0-6.1	5.0-7.0	4.2	14.0	10.0	28.0	22.0		
Near future	11.0	23.0	29.0	7.0	16.0	7.0								
Farther future		24.0												

Browser Support for HTML5 Video

The Full Screen API is supported by:

1. Internet Explorer 11
2. Firefox 20+
3. Chrome 26+
4. Safari 5.1+
5. Opera 12.1+
6. Opera Mobile 14
7. Blackberry Browser 10
8. Firefox for Android 19

For more info, visit http://caniuse.com/#feat=fullscreen[7].

Full Screen API - Working Draft													*Usage stats:	Global
API for allowing content (like a video or canvas element) to take up the entire screen.													Support:	36.28%
													Partial support:	17.78%
													Total:	54.06%
Show all versions	IE	Firefox	Chrome	Safari	Opera	iOS Safari	Opera Mini	Android Browser	Opera Mobile	Blackberry Browser	Chrome for Android	Firefox for Android		
								2.1						
								2.2						
						3.2		2.3	10.0					
						4.0-4.1		3.0	11.5					
	8.0		26.0 webkit			4.2-4.3		4.0	12.0					
	9.0	moz 21.0	moz 27.0	webkit 5.1	webkit	5.0-5.1		4.1	12.1	7.0				
Current	10.0	22.0	moz 28.0	webkit 6.0	webkit 15.0	webkit 6.0-6.1	5.0-7.0	4.2	14.0 webkit	10.0	28.0	22.0 moz		
Near future	11.0	ms 23.0	moz 29.0	webkit 7.0	webkit 16.0	webkit 7.0								
Farther future		24.0	moz											

Browser Support for Fullscreen API

---

[7]http://caniuse.com/#feat=fullscreen

Audio File Support

Ogg Vorbis (.ogg)

1. Firefox 20+
2. Chrome 26+
3. Opera 12.1+
4. Firefox for Android 19+

MP3 (.mp3)

1. Safari 5.0+
2. Chrome 26+
3. Internet Explorer 9+

WAV (.wav)

1. Firefox 20+
2. Safari 5.0+
3. Opera 12.1+
4. Internet Explorer 9+

Video File Support

MPEG-4/H.264 (.mp4)

1. Internet Explorer 9+
2. Firefox 21+
3. Chrome 26+
4. Safari 5.1+
5. iOS Safari 3.2+
6. Android 2.1+
7. Opera Mobile 11.5+
8. Blackberry Browser 7+
9. Chrome for Android 25+
10. Firefox for Android 19+

WebM/VP8 (.webm)

1. Firefox 20+
2. Chrome 26+
3. Opera 12.1+
4. Android 2.3+
5. Opera Mobile 14+
6. Chrome for Android 25+
7. Firefox for Android 19+

Ogg/Theora (.ogg/.ogv)

1. Firefox 20+
2. Chrome 26+
3. Opera 12.1+
4. Firefox for Android 19+

HTML5 Audio and Video Attributes

The specification for the `<audio>` and `<video>` elements defines some similar attributes on both:

1. A `src` attribute, consisting of a valid URL for the content source.
2. An `autoplay` boolean attribute, specifying whether the file should play as soon as it is loaded and buffered.
3. A `loop` boolean attribute, specifying whether the content should be repeatedly played.
4. A `controls` boolean attribute, specifying whether the browser should display its default media player controls.
5. A `preload` attribute, consisting of either `none`, `metadata`, or `auto` – where `metadata` means preload only the content's metadata, and `auto` means the browser will decide when and how to preload the content.

HTML5 Audio and jQuery

An exciting, long-awaited feature has arrived. Now as developers we are able to insert a single HTML element and we are able to get audio playback that can provide a feature to play soundtracks from movies, music from a local band, or even podcasts from our favorite talk-show hosts.

How simple is it to add native audio to a webpage?

Don't blink:

```
1  <audio src="http://somewebsite.com/audiofile.mp3" preload="auto" autoplay="true" \
2  loop="false" controls>
```

Whoa! What happened there? Well, we inserted some audio into a webpage.

Programmatic Control of HTML5 Audio

We can control the `<audio>` element with jQuery as well, as shown in the following code:

```
1  <!DOCTYPE html>
2  <html>
3      <head>
4          <title>HTML5 Audio example 1</title>
5          <script src="http://code.jquery.com/jquery-2.0.3.min.js"></script>
6      </head>
7      <body>
8          <audio preload="auto" controls></audio>
9      </body>
10     <script>
11         var audio;
12         $(function(){
13             var $audio = $('audio');
14             audio = $audio.get(0);
15             audio.src = "https://api.soundcloud.com/tracks/69018397/download?clie\
16 nt_id=b45b1aa10f1ac2941910a7f0d10f8e28"
17             audio.play();
18
19             setTimeout(function(){
20                 audio.pause();
21             }, 10*1000); //--> 10 seconds = 10,000 milliseconds
22
23                      //--> tells us the start and end time of the buffered part of the file
24             audio.buffered;
25
26             //--> asks the browser whether the given mime type can be played
27             audio.canPlayType("audio/wav"); //--> "maybe"
28         })
29     </script>
30 </html>
```

The following image shows what this code produces in Chrome on Mac OS X.

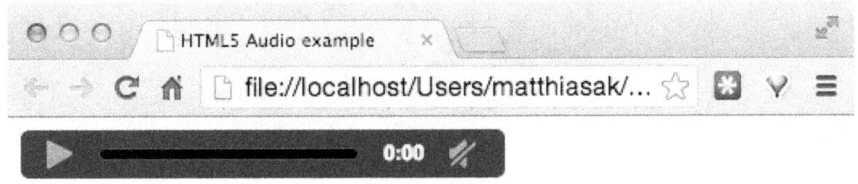

A built-in audio player!

Here's what the same code looks like without the controls flag set on the <audio> element.

A blank page.

Now, unfortunately some users will still visit your site with browsers that (*cough*) were released ten years ago or which doesn't support the particular audio format given in the src.

HTML5 Audio and the <source> Element

To coerce browsers into playing the sweet, sweet sounds for us, we can make use of the <source> element, which provides methods for us to try multiple sources, and even embed a Flash player if all else fails.

```
1   <!DOCTYPE html>
2   <html>
3       <head>
4           <title>HTML5 Audio example 2</title>
5           <script src="http://code.jquery.com/jquery-2.0.3.min.js"></script>
6       </head>
7       <body>
8           <audio preload="auto" controls>
9               <source src="freefalling.mp3" />
10              <source src="freefalling.ogg" />
11              <source src="freefalling.wav" />
12              <!-- now include flash fall back -->
```

```
13            </audio>
14        </body>
15        <script>
16            var audio;
17            $(function(){
18                var $audio = $('audio');
19                audio = $audio.get(0);
20                audio.play();
21
22                setTimeout(function(){
23                    audio.pause();
24                }, 10*1000); //--> 10 seconds = 10,000 milliseconds
25            })
26        </script>
27 </html>
```

Checking Compatibility

If we intend to gracefully degrade features based on each browser's capabilities, we need feature detection code to tell us if HTML5 Audio is supported. We can do this in two ways. Our favorite and preferred method is to use Modernizr, and there is of course an alternative method – roll our own!

1. Feature detection with Modernizr

```
1    <!DOCTYPE html>
2    <html>
3        <head>
4            <title>HTML5 Audio example 3</title>
5            <script src="http://code.jquery.com/jquery-2.0.3.min.js"></script>
6            <script src="http://cdnjs.cloudflare.com/ajax/libs/modernizr/2.6.2/moder\
7  nizr.min.js"></script>
8        </head>
9        <body>
10       </body>
11       <script>
12           var audio;
13           $(function(){
14               //--> we can create <audio> elements programatically, too!
15               audio = new Audio();
16               var supportsAudio = Modernizr.audio;
17               var name = "freefalling";
18               if(supportsAudio){
```

```
19                    if(supportsAudio.ogg){
20                        //--> set src to ogg file
21                        audio.src = name+".ogg";
22                    } else if(supportsAudio.mp3){
23                        //--> set src to mp3 file
24                        audio.src = name+".mp3";
25                    } else if(supportsAudio.wav){
26                        //--> set src to wav file
27                        audio.src = name+".wav";
28                    } else if(supportsAudio.m4a){
29                        //--> set src to m4a file
30                        audio.src = name+".m4a";
31                    }
32
33                    audio.play();
34                    setTimeout(function(){
35                        audio.pause();
36                    }, 10*1000); //--> 10 seconds = 10,000 milliseconds
37                }
38            })
39        </script>
40    </html>
```

2. Roll our own

```
1     <!DOCTYPE html>
2     <html>
3         <head>
4             <title>HTML5 Audio example 4</title>
5             <script src="http://code.jquery.com/jquery-2.0.3.min.js"></script>
6         </head>
7         <body>
8         </body>
9         <script>
10            function supportsAudio(audioType){
11                var element = document.createElement('audio');
12                var result = element.canPlayType;
13                //--> if we pass in a type, return whether or not that audio type is\
14     supported,
15                //--> else just return whether or not any audio type is supported
16                return audioType ? !!(result) : !!(result(audioType));
17            }
18            var audio = new Audio();
```

```
19              var name = "freefalling";
20              if(supportsAudio('audio/ogg; codecs="vorbis"')){
21                  //--> set src to ogg file
22                  audio.src = name+".ogg";
23              } else if(supportsAudio('audio/mpeg')){
24                  //--> set src to mp3 file
25                  audio.src = name+".mp3";
26              } else if(supportsAudio('audio/wav')){
27                  //--> set src to wav file
28                  audio.src = name+".wav";
29              } else if(supportsAudio('audio/m4a')){
30                  //--> set src to m4a file
31                  audio.src = name+".m4a";
32              } else {
33                  //--> use a Flash player
34              }
35
36              if (audio.src){
37                  audio.play();
38                  setTimeout(function(){
39                      audio.pause();
40                  }, 10*1000); //--> 10 seconds = 10,000 milliseconds
41              }
42          </script>
43  </html>
```

Creating a jQuery HTML5 Audio Plugin - jAudio

So far, we have covered:

1. How to insert an <audio> element into a page both programatically and as a direct HTML tag
2. How to configure an <audio> element
3. How to detect supported audio file types

Bundling this code up into a single jQuery plugin won't be very difficult. The following code will allow for inserting an <audio> element into the page, and automatically detect the best supported filetype for use as the src.

```
1   <!DOCTYPE html>
2   <html>
3       <head>
4           <title>HTML5 Audio example 5</title>
5           <script src="http://code.jquery.com/jquery-2.0.3.min.js"></script>
6       </head>
7       <body>
8           <div id="audio-div"></div>
9       </body>
10      <script>
11          //--> (1)
12          $.supportsAudio = function(audioType){
13              var element = document.createElement('audio');
14              var result = element.canPlayType;
15              //--> if we pass in a type, return whether or not that audio type is \
16  supported,
17              //--> else just return whether or not any audio type is supported
18              return audioType ? !!(result) : !!(result(audioType));
19          };
20
21          $.fn.jAudio = function(options){
22              //--> (2)
23              var defaults = {
24                  src: "",
25                  autoplay: false,
26                  preload: "auto",
27                  controls: true,
28                  loop: false,
29                  sources: [] //{url: ..., type: ...}
30              };
31
32              options = $.extend(defaults, options || {});
33
34              //--> (3)
35              //--> check that we have some files to load
36              if(!options.sources || !options.sources.length){
37                  return;
38              }
39
40              //--> determine the file to use, if any
41              var fileTypesPossible = [{name: "audio/mpeg", type:".mp3"}, {name:"au\
42  dio/wav", type:".wav"}, {name:'audio/ogg; codecs="vorbis"', type:".ogg"}, {name:"\
```

```
43      audio/m4a", type:".m4a"}];
44
45                  //--> (4)
46                  //--> determine which types are supported
47                  var fileTypesSupported = {};
48                  for(var i = 0; i < fileTypesPossible.length; i++){
49                      var possibleType = fileTypesPossible[i];
50                      if($.supportsAudio(possibleType.name)){
51                          fileTypesSupported[possibleType.type] = true;
52                      }
53                  }
54
55                  //--> (5)
56                  //--> determine which supported types are given in the sources list
57                  var fileTypesAvailable = [];
58                  for(var i = 0; i < options.sources.length; i++){
59                      var source = options.sources[i];
60                      if(fileTypesSupported[source.type]) {
61                          fileTypesAvailable.push(source);
62                      }
63                  }
64
65                  //--> (6)
66                  //--> check that a supported file type was provided
67                  if(!fileTypesAvailable.length){
68                      return;
69                  }
70
71                  //--> (7)
72                  //--> create and inject a supported Audio object with the properties \
73      provided
74                  var $this = this.first();
75                  var audio = new Audio(fileTypesAvailable[0].url);
76                  audio.autoplay = options.autoplay;
77                  audio.preload = options.preload;
78                  audio.controls = options.controls;
79                  audio.loop = options.loop;
80                  $this.append(audio);
81              }
82
83          $('#audio-div').jAudio({
84              sources: [{url: "https://api.soundcloud.com/tracks/69018397/download?\
```

```
85      client_id=b45b1aa10f1ac2941910a7f0d10f8e28", type:".ogg"}]
86          });
87      </script>
88  </html>
```

Let's break this down into steps:

1. Use the function created previously which checks for support, and add it to jQuery ($.supportsAudio).
2. Setup some default options for our code.
3. Check that we provided at least one source.
4. Determine a list of audio types supported in this browser.
5. Determine which file types were provided to the plugin.
6. Check that the browser supports any of those file types provided.
7. Create an <audio> element from the first item in the list of supported sources.

Finally, using this plugin works like the last few lines of the previous code:

```
1  $('#audio-div').jAudio({
2         sources: [{url: "https://api.soundcloud.com/tracks/69018397/download?client_id=b\
3  45b1aa10f1ac2941910a7f0d10f8e28", type:".ogg"}]
4  });
```

HTML5 Video and jQuery

While covering the topic of HTML5 Audio, we picked up a few points about the design of the new media interfaces of HTML5:

1. Common attributes like src, autoplay, controls, preload, and loop
2. An accompanying HTML tag (<audio>)
3. Programmatic APIs for accessing the elements (new Audio(…))

Fortunately for us, these common pieces also apply to HTML5 <video> tags!

Let's see how easy it is to add a <video> to a page:

```
 1  <!DOCTYPE html>
 2  <html>
 3      <head>
 4          <title>HTML5 Video example 1</title>
 5          <script src="http://code.jquery.com/jquery-2.0.3.min.js"></script>
 6      </head>
 7      <body>
 8          <video width="640" height="360" src="../movie.mp4" controls preload="auto\
 9  " poster="http://www.google.com/logos/2013/childrens_day_2013-1516005-hp.jpg">
10              <p>
11                  Try this page in a compatible browser, or you can
12                  <a href="../movie.mp4"> download the video </a>
13                  instead.
14              </p>
15          </video>
16      </body>
17  </html>
```

Notice the long string that is the `src` attribute of the `<video>`. This is a direct URL to a video file, instead of just a YouTube link.

Programmatic Control of HTML5 Video

Just as we controlled the `<audio>` element with jQuery and JavaScript, we can control the the `<video>` element:

```
 1  <!DOCTYPE html>
 2  <html>
 3      <head>
 4          <title>HTML5 Video example 2</title>
 5          <script src="http://code.jquery.com/jquery-2.0.3.min.js"></script>
 6      </head>
 7      <body>
 8          <video width="640" height="360" preload="auto" poster="http://www.google.\
 9  com/logos/2013/childrens_day_2013-1516005-hp.jpg">
10              <p>
11                  Try this page in a compatible browser, or you can
12                  <a href="#"> download the video </a>
13                  instead.
14              </p>
15          </video>
16          <script>
```

```
17          var src="../movie.mp4";
18          var video;
19          $(function(){
20              var $video = $('video');
21              video = $video.get(0);
22              video.src = src;
23              video.play();
24
25              setTimeout(function(){
26                  video.pause();
27              }, 10*1000); //--> 10 seconds = 10,000 milliseconds
28          })
29      </script>
30   </body>
31 </html>
```

The following image shows what this code produces in Chrome on Mac OS X.

Video with controls flag set to true.

Here's the same code, with the controls flag removed from the `<video>` element.

Video without controls flag.

HTML5 Video and the `<source>` Element

Surprise! We can use the `<source>` tag with HTML5 Video as well! This is very necessary, as there is a multitude of encodings supported by different browsers, and, being web developers, we must also account for no support at all (and thus may wish to include an Adobe Flash fallback).

```
1  <!DOCTYPE html>
2  <html>
3      <head>
4          <title>HTML5 Video example 3</title>
5          <script src="http://code.jquery.com/jquery-2.0.3.min.js"></script>
6      </head>
7      <body>
8          <video width="640" height="360" preload="auto" poster="http://www.google.\
9  com/logos/2013/childrens_day_2013-1516005-hp.jpg">
10             <source src="../movie.webm" type='video/webm; codecs="vp8, vorbis"' />
11             <source src="../movie.mp4" type='video/mp4; codecs="avc1.42E01E, mp4a\
12  .40.2"' />
13             <source src="../movie.ogv" type='video/ogg; codecs="theora, vorbis"' \
14  />
15             <p>
16                 Try this page in a compatible browser, or you can
17                 <a href="../movie.mp4"> download the video </a>
18                 instead.
19             </p>
20         </video>
21     </body>
22 </html>
```

Checking Compatibility

Yet again, we have the support by the user's browser for compatibility with Modernizr or our own detection code:

1. Feature detection with Modernizr

```
 1  <!DOCTYPE html>
 2  <html>
 3      <head>
 4          <title>HTML5 Video example 4</title>
 5          <script src="http://code.jquery.com/jquery-2.0.3.min.js"></script>
 6          <script src="http://cdnjs.cloudflare.com/ajax/libs/modernizr/2.6.2/moder\
 7  nizr.min.js"></script>
 8      </head>
 9      <body>
10          <video></video>
11      </body>
12   <script>
13       var video;
14       $(function(){
15           video = $('video').get(0);
16           var supportsVideo = Modernizr.video;
17           var name = "../movie";
18           if(supportsVideo){
19               if(supportsVideo.ogg){
20                   //--> set src to ogv file
21                   video.src = name+".ogv";
22               } else if(supportsVideo.webm){
23                   //--> set src to webm file
24                   video.src = name+".webm";
25               } else if(supportsVideo.h264){
26                   //--> set src to mp4 file
27                   video.src = name+".mp4";
28               }
29
30               video.play();
31               setTimeout(function(){
32                   video.pause();
33               }, 10*1000); //--> 10 seconds = 10,000 milliseconds
34           }
35       })
36   </script>
37  </html>
```

2. Roll our own

```html
1   <!DOCTYPE html>
2   <html>
3       <head>
4           <title>HTML5 Video example 5</title>
5           <script src="http://code.jquery.com/jquery-2.0.3.min.js"></script>
6       </head>
7       <body>
8           <video></video>
9       </body>
10      <script>
11          $(function(){
12              var $video = $('video');
13              video = $video.get(0);
14
15              function supportsVideo(videoType){
16                  var element = document.createElement('video');
17                  var result = element.canPlayType;
18                  //--> if we pass in a type, return whether or not that video typ\
19  e is supported,
20                  //--> else just return whether or not any video type is supported
21                  return videoType == result ? !!(result) : !!(result(videoType));
22              }
23
24              var name = "../movie";
25              if(supportsVideo('video/ogg; codecs="theora, vorbis"')){
26                  //--> set src to ogv file
27                  video.src = name+".ogv";
28              } else if(supportsVideo('video/webm; codecs="vp8, vorbis"')){
29                  //--> set src to mp3 file
30                  video.src = name+".webm";
31              } else {
32                  //--> use a Flash player
33              }
34
35              if(video.src){
36                  video.play();
37              }
38          })
39      </script>
40  </html>
```

Creating a jQuery HTML5 Video Plugin - jVideo

So far, we have covered the equivalent functionalities of `<video>` which translate to the `<audio>` element:

1. How to insert a `<video>` element into a page as a direct HTML tag
2. How to configure the `<video>` element
3. How to detect supported video file codecs

So, let us follow suit and build another jQuery plugin, only this time we will wrap the funcionality for the video up into a ncie and neat little package!

```
1   <!DOCTYPE html>
2   <html>
3       <head>
4           <title>HTML5 Video example 6</title>
5           <script src="http://code.jquery.com/jquery-2.0.3.min.js"></script>
6       </head>
7       <body>
8           <div id="video-div"></div>
9       </body>
10      <script>
11          //--> (1)
12          $.supportsVideo = function(videoType){
13              var element = document.createElement('video');
14              var result = element.canPlayType;
15              //--> if we pass in a type, return whether or not that video type is \
16  supported,
17              //--> else just return whether or not any video type is supported
18              return videoType ? !!(result) : !!(result(videoType));
19          };
20
21          $.fn.jVideo = function(options){
22              //--> (2)
23              var defaults = {
24                  src: "",
25                  autoplay: false,
26                  preload: "auto",
27                  controls: true,
28                  loop: false,
29                  sources: [] //{url: ..., type: ...}
30              };
```

```
            options = $.extend(defaults, options || {});

        //--> (3)
        //--> check that we have some files to load
        if(!options.sources || !options.sources.length){
            return;
        }

        //--> determine the file to use, if any
        var fileTypesPossible = [{name: 'video/ogg; codecs="theora, vorbis"',\
 type:".ogv"}, {name:'video/webm; codecs="vp8, vorbis"', type:".webm"}];

        //--> (4)
        //--> determine which types are supported
        var fileTypesSupported = {};
        for(var i = 0; i < fileTypesPossible.length; i++){
            var possibleType = fileTypesPossible[i];
            if($.supportsVideo(possibleType.name)){
                fileTypesSupported[possibleType.type] = true;
            }
        }

        //--> (5)
        //--> determine which supported types are given in the sources list
        var fileTypesAvailable = [];
        for(var i = 0; i < options.sources.length; i++){
            var source = options.sources[i];
            if(fileTypesSupported[source.type]) {
                fileTypesAvailable.push(source);
            }
        }

        //--> (6)
        //--> check that a supported file type was provided
        if(!fileTypesAvailable.length){
            return;
        }

        //--> (7)
        //--> create and inject a supported Audio object with the properties \
provided
```

```
73              var $this = this.first();
74              var video = document.createElement("video");
75              video.src = fileTypesAvailable[0].url;
76              video.autoplay = options.autoplay;
77              video.preload = options.preload;
78              video.controls = options.controls;
79              video.loop = options.loop;
80              $this.append(video);
81          }
82
83          $('#video-div').jVideo({
84              sources: [{url: "../movie.mp4", type:".mpeg"}]
85          });
86      </script>
87  </html>
```

Let's break this down into steps, some of which repeat what was done for the `<audio>` element:

1. Use the function created previously which checks for support, and add it to jQuery ($.supportsVideo).
2. Setup some default options for our code.
3. Check that we provided at least one source.
4. Determine a list of video types supported in this browser.
5. Determine which file types were provided to the plugin.
6. Check that the browser supports any of those file types provided.
7. Create a `<video>` element from the first item in the list of supported sources.

Reader Challenge

The previous two plugins use much of the same code, where there is mostly a logical split when handling `<audio>` or `<video>`. Since much of the code could be refactored to write a single jQuery plugin, it may be good exercise to try it on your own.

Grab a copy of the source code from this chapter on this book's website, and have a go!

The `canplay` Event

One event triggered by `<video>` and `<audio>` elements is the `canplay` event, which fires once preloaded content has enough data buffered to begin playing.

```
1  $('video').on('canplay', function(e) {
2    this.volume = 0.4;
3    this.currentTime = 10;
4    this.play();
5  });
```

HTML5 Video and SVG

SVG code provides a solution to rendering some filters on HTML5 Video elements. Some filters are supplied by the browser, thus not requiring us to write our own: Blur, Composite, Tiles, and others.

```
1  <svg style="filter:url(#blur);" version="1.1" xmlns="http://www.w3.org/2000/svg">
2    <defs>
3      <filter id="blur">
4        <feGaussianBlur stdDeviation="1" />
5      </filter>
6    </defs>
7  </svg>
```

One may notice that we defined a `<filter>` element inside the `<svg>`. Each type of filter has its own tag, e.g. blur has a tag called `<feGaussianBlur>`.

Here is an example of an SVG filter at work with a `<video>` element from a previous example:

```
1  <!DOCTYPE html>
2  <html>
3    <head>
4        <title>Fullscreen example 1</title>
5        <script src="http://code.jquery.com/jquery-2.0.3.min.js"></script>
6        <style>
7        video{
8            -webkit-filter:url(#blur);
9            -moz-filter:url(#blur);
10           -ms-filter:url(#blur);
11           -o-filter:url(#blur);
12           filter:url(#blur);
13       }
14       </style>
15   </head>
16   <body>
17       <video poster="http://www.google.com/logos/2013/childrens_day_2013-151600\
18  5-hp.jpg">
```

```
19              <p>
20                  Try this page in a compatible browser, or you can
21                  <a href="#"> download the video </a>
22                  instead.
23              </p>
24          </video>
25          <svg version="1.1" xmlns="http://www.w3.org/2000/svg">
26              <defs>
27                  <filter id="blur">
28                      <feGaussianBlur stdDeviation="4" />
29                  </filter>
30              </defs>
31          </svg>
32          <script>
33              var src="../movie.mp4";
34              var video;
35              $(function(){
36                  var $video = $('video');
37                  video = $video.get(0);
38                  video.src = src;
39                  video.load();
40                  video.play();
41              })
42          </script>
43      </body>
44  </html>
```

This example will create a filter on the `<video>` element, as depicted in the following image.

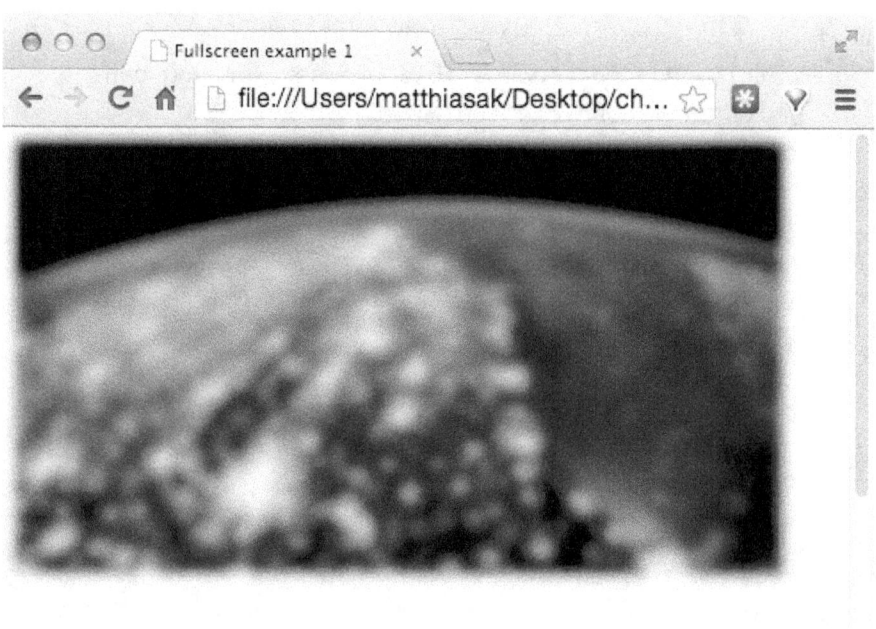

Effects with SVG Filters

The Fullscreen API

The Fullscreen API let's us take advantage of the screen real-estate available to desktop and tablet devices. This allows web apps to programatically tell any content on the page to enter the browser's fullscreen viewing mode. Now WebGL games, digital magazines, animated SVGs, audio histograms, and of course videos, can be a part of the experience offered through web content.

How does this API work? Well, simply tell the API which HTMLElement to zoom into for fullscreen exposure:

```
1  video = $('video').get(0);
2  video.webkitRequestFullscreen();
3  video.mozRequestFullScreen();
4  video.requestFullscreen();
```

To exit the fullscreen, we can programatically handle this event as well:

```
1  document.webkitExitFullscreen();
2  document.mozCancelFullscreen();
3  document.exitFullscreen();
```

Content in the fullscreen context will still need to be styled with CSS. Fortunately, the Fullscreen API let's use use some CSS3 pseudo-selectors for this!

```
1  video:-webkit-full-screen {
2    width: 100% !important;
3  }
4  video:-moz-full-screen {
5    width: 100% !important;
6  }
```

This is very easily rolled into existing applications. In fact, we will adopt the Fullscreen API into a previous HTML5 Video example that we wrote to use the new Fullscreen API.

```
1   <!DOCTYPE html>
2   <html>
3       <head>
4           <title>Fullscreen example 1</title>
5           <script src="http://code.jquery.com/jquery-2.0.3.min.js"></script>
6       </head>
7       <body>
8           <video poster="http://www.google.com/logos/2013/childrens_day_2013-151600\
9   5-hp.jpg">
10              <p>
11                  Try this page in a compatible browser, or you can
12                  <a href="#"> download the video </a>
13                  instead.
14              </p>
15          </video>
16          <script>
17              var src="../movie.mp4";
18              var video;
19              $(function(){
20                  var $video = $('video');
21                  video = $video.get(0);
22                  video.src = src;
23                  video.load();
24                  video.play();
25
```

```
26                $('html').on('keyup', function(e){
27                    if(e.which === 32){ //--> space bar
28                        video.requestFullScreen && video.requestFullScreen() || v\
29 ideo.webkitRequestFullScreen && video.webkitRequestFullScreen() || video.mozReque\
30 stFullScreen && video.mozRequestFullScreen();
31                    } else if(e.which === 27){ //--> escape key
32                        document.webkitExitFullscreen && document.webkitExitFulls\
33 creen();
34                        document.mozCancelFullscreen && document.mozCancelFullscr\
35 een();
36                        document.exitFullscreen && document.exitFullscreen();
37                    }
38                })
39            })
40        </script>
41    </body>
42 </html>
```

This last example detects which Fullscreen API function is supported (prefixed "webkit", "moz", or none at all). By listening on keystrokes, we can then set the video loaded as either fullscreen when the user taps the space bar, or exit fullscreen when the user taps the escape key.

The following screenshots depict how this will look in Google Chrome.

Before fullscreen is initialized.

Fullscreen video.

Summary

In this chapter, we conquered the multimedia landscape, embedded <audio> and <video> elements, programatically controlled those media objects, and detected and embedded file types based on browser support.

We also built jQuery plugins for the <audio> and <video> objects.

Furthermore, we covered some outlandish HTML recipes which use SVG filters to add effects to a <video> object, and immersed ourselves in video with the Fullscreen API.

In the next chapter, we will step into the wide world of pixel-based graphics by introducing ourselves to the HTML5 Canvas API – so stay sharp!

9 HTML5 Canvas

In Chapter 5 - Webcam Access with jQuery - we wrote a sample photobooth application which captures a video stream from a webcam, and then displays screenshots as images on the page. The utility that allows us to get the image data from the webcam and save it as an image in our HTML is HTML5 Canvas!

Canvas is a multifaceted 2D graphics powerhouse which lets us draw shapes, manipulate photos, create interactive games, and animate virtually anything. Better yet, neither Adobe Flash nor any other plugins are required to carry out these tasks in their entirety.

Examples

http://cssdeck.com/labs/xeheqrb1

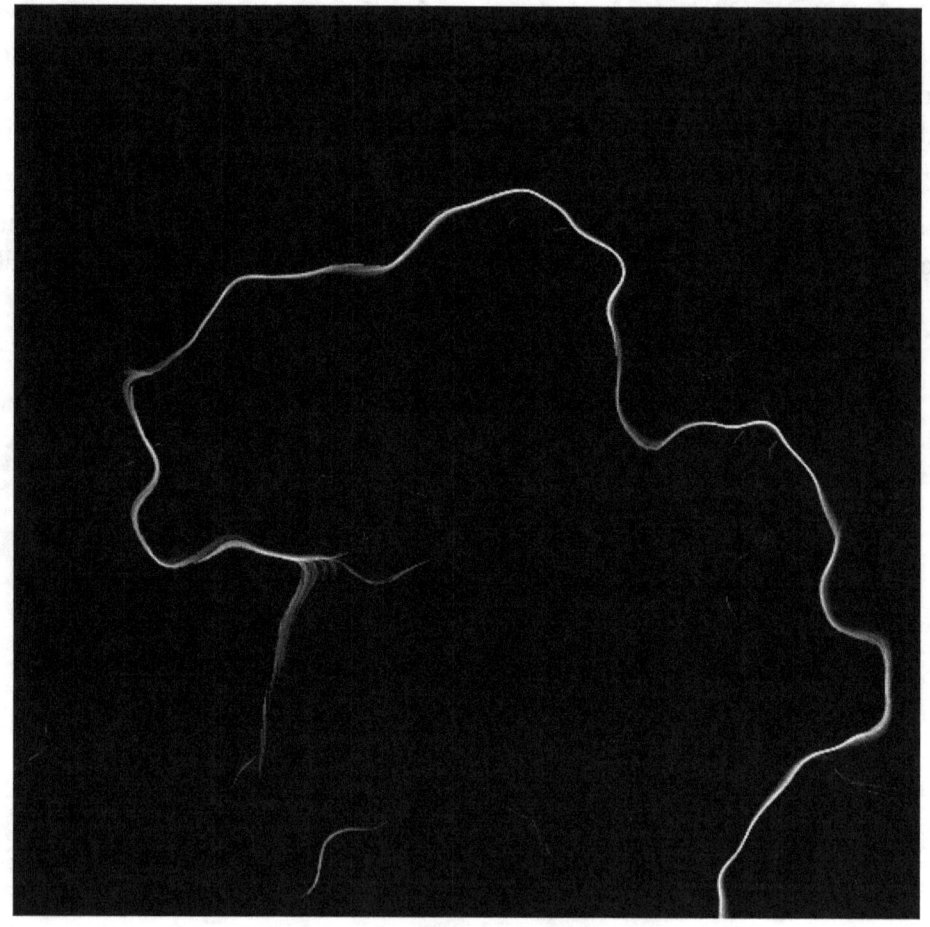

Canvas Example

http://jonobr1.github.io/two.js/

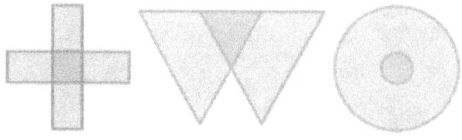

Canvas Example 2 - Two.js Library

Browser Support for HTML5 Canvas

HTML5 Canvas is supported by these browsers:

1. Internet Explorer 9+
2. Firefox 20+
3. Chrome 26+
4. Safari 5.1+
5. Opera 12.1+
6. iOS Safari 3.2+
7. Android 2.1+
8. Opera Mobile 10.0+
9. Blackberry 7.0+
10. Chrome for Android 25+
11. Firefox for Android 19+

Get more details at http://caniuse.com/#search=canvas[1].

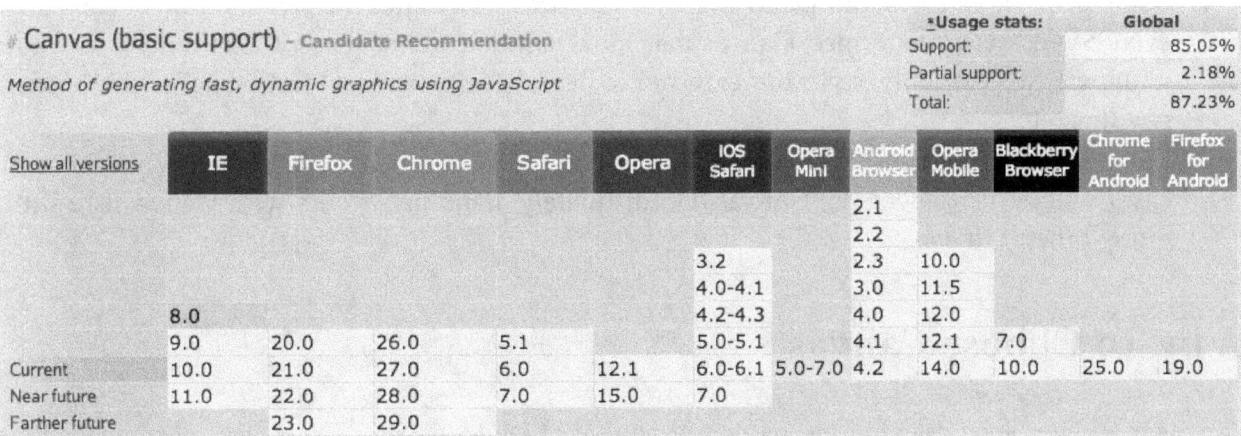

Browser support for HTML5 Canvas

Canvas - The Basics

Canvas is a 2D drawing API. This means that we recognize and respond to coordinates as (x,y) coordinate pairs ((x,y,z) is reserved for WebGL - next chapter). If you can imagine it, we can draw it with Canvas:

1. lines

---

[1] http://caniuse.com/#search=canvas

2. shapes
3. images
4. text
5. etc.

Moreover, it is so powerfully mobile that it can be used to create cross-device applications. In fact, Apple itself developed Canvas to be used with the Dashboard widgets and Safari on Mac OS X.[2]

Most importantly, it is important to understand that Canvas was built to paint pixels to the screen. There is no built-in concept of vectors, no modification of DOM-like objects, and no built-in event handlers.

Right now, there are four methods of drawing items natively in the browser:

1. Using SVGs, which are vector representations which act like DOM objects. SVG elements can be manipulated quite the same as regular HTML elements. They can even receive and trigger events, such as `click` or `hover`. The important thing to note about SVGs, is that they can be resized to fit any screen or device. Since they are vector-based, the rendering is slower than that of Canvas, however there is no risk of pixellating images.
2. Using CSS, we can style our DOM elements and drastically alter the presentation of elements, even SVGs. However, since Canvas has no DOM elements (except the outer `<canvas>` wrapper), we can only style the external styles of the Canvas object, such as the border, padding, etc.
3. Using DOM animation, such as with JavaScript or CSS, can be very hit or miss, and in most cases will be far slower the Canvas. Unfortunately, handling events with Canvas is a little more difficult to do.

Why To Choose Canvas

Canvas is a lower level drawing mechanism than that of DOM, CSS, or SVGs. This also means that we have more control over what is drawn, and can do it with better performance and less memory usage.

The drawback is this: we have to write more code.

This makes charts, graphs, dynamic diagrams, video games, and other interactive drawing scenarios ripe for Canvas's picking.

---

[2] See Ian Hickson's response to Apple's new tag at http://ln.hixie.ch/?start=1089635050

Simple Drawing

We are ready to see some Canvas code! Let's first take a look at a basic "Hello World" example for Canvas – drawing a box on the screen.

Let's start off with some basic HTML which will be used generically throughout the rest of the chapter:

```html
<!DOCTYPE html>
<html>
    <head>
        <meta charset="utf-8">
        <meta http-equiv="X-UA-Compatible" content="IE=edge,chrome=1">
        <meta name="description" content="">
        <meta name="viewport" content="width=device-width">
        <link rel="stylesheet" href="css/normalize.css">
        <link rel="stylesheet" href="css/main.css">
        <script src="js/vendor/modernizr-2.6.2.min.js"></script>
    </head>
    <body>
        <canvas id="jqueryCanvas" width="800" height="600"></canvas>
        <script src="js/vendor/jquery-2.0.3.min.js"></script>
        <script src="js/main.js"></script>
    </body>
</html>
```

That is all the HTML we will need! Now let's get to the good stuff – creating a rectangle on the `<canvas>` element:

```javascript
function demo1(){
    var canvas = document.getElementById('jqueryCanvas');
    var context = canvas.getContext('2d');
    context.fillStyle="salmon";
    context.fillRect(50,50,100,100);
}
demo1();
```

The previous code produces the following screenshot:

The Salmon Box

The first and foremost step is to get the two-dimensional context for our <canvas> with getContext(). After that, we can manipulate any number of drawing tasks for our Canvas object, which will procedurally run each item. Thus, if we set the fillStyle such as in the previous example, this will persist until we change the fillStyle attribute again.

```
function demo1(){
        var canvas = document.getElementById('jqueryCanvas');
        var context = canvas.getContext('2d');
        context.fillStyle="salmon";
        context.fillRect(50,50,100,100);
        context.fillStyle="hotpink"; //--> The rectangle will still have a 'salmon' fill\
 color
}
demo1();
```

It is important to distinguish and engrain in ourselves what Canvas is and what Canvas isn't.

Canvas is:

- for drawing pixels to the screen
- fast pixel-painting code that has to repaint screens as frames

Canvas is not:

- an abstraction for layers or shapes (SVG)
- an event handler for different painted sections (pixels are simply pixels, nothing more)

Furthermore, there are multiple drawing functions provided by Canvas which provide us the opportunity to draw more than just recangles! For instance, let's draw a triangle by defining a path for our pen to follow:

```
1  function demo2(){
2      var canvas = document.getElementById('jqueryCanvas');
3      var context = canvas.getContext('2d');
4      context.fillStyle = "salmon";
5      context.beginPath();
6      context.moveTo(50,20);
7      context.lineTo(400,150);
8      context.lineTo(150,380);
9      context.closePath();
10     context.fill();
11     context.strokeStyle = 'red';
12     context.lineWidth = 10;
13     context.stroke();
14 }
15 demo2();
```

The previous code produces the following screenshot:

The Salmon Triangle

Note that the context keeps track of the fill and stroke colors as separate variables. Moreover, these fillStyle and strokeStyle variables can take typical styles that would work in CSS, such as #aabbcc, blue, or rgb(100, 50, 200).

Another thing to take note of is how the path is stored intrinsically within the context object. However context.closePath() must occur before context.fill() or else no fill will be drawn.

Furthermore, calling `context.fill()` and `context.stroke()` merely depends on the current attributes stored on the current path, so calling `context.stroke()` and `context.fill()` can be in any order, so much as the state of the path produces the desired output (a triangle).

Working With Paths

To draw non-rectangular shapes, we must employ the use of paths with greater detail. Paths are merely series of straight or curved lines segments. As seen in the previous example, we begin creating every path with `context.beginPath()`. Afterwards, we can use three functions at our disposal:

1. `context.moveTo()`
2. `context.lineTo()`
3. `context.bezierCurveTo()`

We have already seen (1) and (2), and (3) is reserved for creating (surprise!) curved lines.

Let's first use a bezier curve, and then dig into how it works.

```
function demo3(){
        var canvas = document.getElementById('jqueryCanvas');
        var context = canvas.getContext('2d');
        context.fillStyle = 'salmon';
        context.beginPath();
        context.moveTo(50,20);
        context.bezierCurveTo(100, 100, 300, 200, 400, 100);
        context.lineTo(150,380);
        context.closePath();
        context.fill();
        context.lineWidth = 10;
        context.strokeStyle = 'red';
        context.stroke();
}
demo3();
```

The previous code produces this screenshot:

The Salmon Bezier

This is exactly the same triangle as created in the previous path example, however the top edge is bent inwards. This is due to the bezier curve created with context.bezierCurveTo(100, 100, 300, 200, 400, 100). This function simply calculates a curved path based on three points provided to bezierCurveTo().

```
context.bezierCurveTo(
    inflectionPoint1_X, inflectionPoint1_Y,
    inflectionPoint2_X, inflectionPoint1_Y,
    to_X, to_Y
);
```

As one might notice, there are six arguments provided to bezierCurveTo(). Each pair of points represents an (X,Y) pair to be used. The inflection points represent to points that will "pull" the path in the direction towards it.

Bezier Curves

Bezier curves act like a center of mass between points. Each inflection point acts as a gravitational pull on a path from point A to point B.

Let's examine the previous bezier curve path with a little more detail.

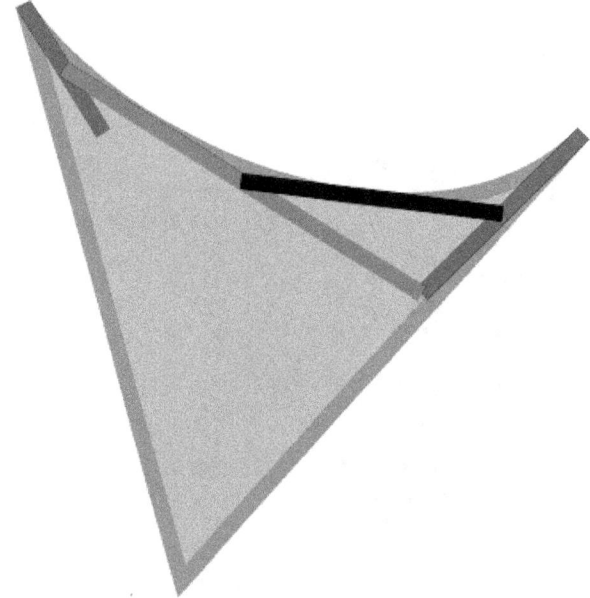

Drawing Bezier Details

The previous screenshot is generated by drawing some additional lines:

1. The blue lines are represent lines from the first point to the first inflection, and from the second point to the second inflection.
2. The green line is drawn from the midpoint of point A and inflection A to inflection B.
3. The black line is drawn from the midpoint of the green line to the midpoint of point B and inflection B.

Here is the code to generate this drawing:

```
function calculateMidpoint(pointA, pointB){
    return [(pointA[0]+pointB[0])/2, (pointA[1]+pointB[1])/2];
}

function demo4(){
    var canvas = document.getElementById('jqueryCanvas');
    var context = canvas.getContext('2d');

    var pointA = [50,20];
    var inflectionA = [100,100];
    var inflectionB = [300,200];
    var pointB = [400,100];
    var pointC = [150, 380];
```

```javascript
            var midpointA = calculateMidpoint(pointA, inflectionA);
            var midpointB = calculateMidpoint(midpointA, inflectionB);
            var midpointC = calculateMidpoint(pointB, inflectionB);

            context.lineWidth = 10;

            //--> draw the "triangle"
            context.beginPath();
            context.fillStyle = 'salmon';
            context.strokeStyle = 'red';
            context.moveTo(pointA[0],pointA[1]);
            context.bezierCurveTo(
                    inflectionA[0], inflectionA[1],
                    inflectionB[0], inflectionB[1],
                    pointB[0], pointB[1]
            );
            context.lineTo(pointC[0], pointC[1]);
            context.closePath();
            context.fill();
            context.stroke();

            //--> draw the inflection lines
            context.beginPath();
            context.fillStyle = '';
            context.strokeStyle = 'blue';
            context.moveTo(pointA[0], pointA[1]);
            context.lineTo(inflectionA[0], inflectionA[1]);
            context.stroke();

            context.beginPath();
            context.fillStyle = '';
            context.strokeStyle = 'blue';
            context.moveTo(pointB[0], pointB[1]);
            context.lineTo(inflectionB[0], inflectionB[1]);
            context.stroke();

            //--> draw the first midpoint line
            context.beginPath();
            context.fillStyle = '';
            context.strokeStyle = 'green';
            context.moveTo(midpointA[0], midpointA[1]);
```

```
56          context.lineTo(inflectionB[0], inflectionB[1]);
57          context.stroke();
58
59          //--> draw the second midpoint line
60          context.beginPath();
61          context.fillStyle = '';
62          context.strokeStyle = 'black';
63          context.moveTo(midpointB[0], midpointB[1]);
64          context.lineTo(midpointC[0], midpointC[1]);
65          context.stroke();
66      }
67
68      demo4();
```

In this code, we have a few seperated sections which draw each path. The biggest detail is in the calculation of the points. Notice that there are three points, and then a calculation of the line endpoints based on the results of the calls to `calculateMidpoint()`.

The Coordinate System

Let's have just a quick word on X and Y coordinates. One might notice that the directions for the X and Y axis are flipped over the Y-axis. This is commonplace in computer graphics, where the origin (0,0) is at the top-left corner of the screen.

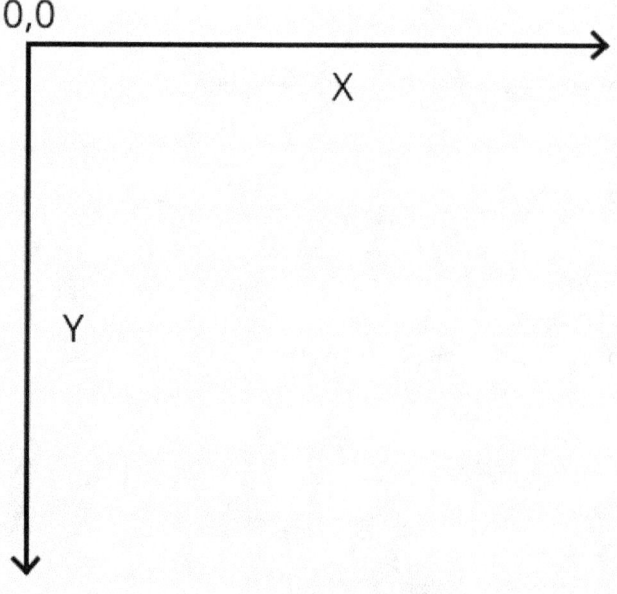

The Coordinate System

Images

Canvas can also draw images. We can draw an image directly to a `<canvas>` object, or even scale, stretch, and slice it.

```
context.drawImage(img, 0,0); //normal drawing
context.drawImage(img, //draw stretched
    0,0,img_width,img_height, //source (x,y,w,h)
    0,0,img_width*2,img_height*2//destination (x,y,w,h)
);
context.drawImage(img, //draw a slice
    img_width/2,img_height/2,img_width,img_height, //source coords (x,y,w,h)
    0,0,img_width*2,img_height*2//destination coords (x,y,w,h)
);
```

The previous code is pretty simple, and commented inline.

Text

We can draw text in `<canvas>` objects as well. Moreover, we can set the font style with CSS font attributes, too.

```
function demo5(){
        var canvas = document.getElementById('jqueryCanvas');
        var context = canvas.getContext('2d');

        context.fillStyle = "#444";
        context.font = "32px Times New Roman";
        context.fillText("jQuery and HTML5!", 20,150);
}

demo5();
```

Note that the Y coordinate for the `fillText()` function is the baseline of the text, not the top or middle.

The previous code produces the following screenshot:

jQuery and HTML5!

Text

Gradients

We can also use Canvas to fill in gradients, instead of plain colors.

The Italian Flag

To create gradients, we simply use similar drawing code as before, only the `context.fillStyle()` argument becomes a `gradient` object:

```
 1  function demo6(){
 2          var canvas = document.getElementById('jqueryCanvas');
 3          var context = canvas.getContext('2d');
 4
 5          var gradient = context.createLinearGradient(0,0,400,0);
 6          gradient.addColorStop(0.33, "green");
 7          gradient.addColorStop(0.33, "white");
 8          gradient.addColorStop(0.66, "white");
 9          gradient.addColorStop(0.66, "red");
10
11          context.fillStyle = gradient;
12          context.fillRect(0,0,400,300);
13  }
14
15  demo6();
```

Notice that the gradient.addColorStop() takes two arguments:

1. A number
2. A CSS color string

The number represents a percent of the gradient's width, thus gradient.addColorStop(0.33, "green"); paints a green color, which is weighted at 33% of the width of the gradient.

The context.createLinearGradient(0,0,400,0); is the real kicker. As we have seen as a paradigm before, each pair of arguments represents an (X,Y) coordinate, where the first pair is the starting point of the gradient, and the second pair is the endpoint of the gradient. The fourth input determines the Y-coordinate that the gradient moves towards. Thus,

1. var gradient = context.createLinearGradient(0,0,400,0); creates a horizontal gradient
2. var gradient = context.createLinearGradient(0,0,400,400); creates a diagonal gardient
3. and var gradient = context.createLinearGradient(0,0,0,400); creates a vertical gradient

Horizontal, diagonal, and vertical gradients

An important thing to notice here is that gradient is painted in the coordinate system that the shape is drawn in, not the internal coordinates of the shape. That is to say, the points specified with `context.createLinearGradient()` are not relative to the shape, rather they are relative to the `<canvas>` object. In the previous screenshot, the first flag is drawn at `(0,0)`, the second at `(110,0)`, and the third at `(220,0)`.

Here is the code that produced the previous screenshot:

```
function demo7(){
        var canvas = document.getElementById('jqueryCanvas');
        var context = canvas.getContext('2d');

        var gradient1 = context.createLinearGradient(0,0,100,0);
        gradient1.addColorStop(0.33, "green");
        gradient1.addColorStop(0.33, "white");
        gradient1.addColorStop(0.66, "white");
        gradient1.addColorStop(0.66, "red");
        context.fillStyle = gradient1;
        context.fillRect(0,0,100,75);

        var gradient2 = context.createLinearGradient(110,0,210,75);
        gradient2.addColorStop(0.33, "green");
        gradient2.addColorStop(0.33, "white");
        gradient2.addColorStop(0.66, "white");
        gradient2.addColorStop(0.66, "red");
        context.fillStyle = gradient2;
        context.fillRect(110,0,100,75);

        var gradient3 = context.createLinearGradient(220,0,220,75);
        gradient3.addColorStop(0.33, "green");
        gradient3.addColorStop(0.33, "white");
        gradient3.addColorStop(0.66, "white");
        gradient3.addColorStop(0.66, "red");

        context.fillStyle = gradient3;
        context.fillRect(220,0,100,75);
}
demo7();
```

If we changed the shape of the flags to be `context.fillRect(…, …, 50, 200);` the gradients will not align because they are drawn to the coordinates specified with `context.createLinearGradient()`.

```js
function demo8(){
        var canvas = document.getElementById('jqueryCanvas');
        var context = canvas.getContext('2d');

        var gradient1 = context.createLinearGradient(0,0,100,0);
        gradient1.addColorStop(0.33, "green");
        gradient1.addColorStop(0.33, "white");
        gradient1.addColorStop(0.66, "white");
        gradient1.addColorStop(0.66, "red");
        context.fillStyle = gradient1;
        context.fillRect(0,0,50,200); //--> changed

        var gradient2 = context.createLinearGradient(110,0,210,75);
        gradient2.addColorStop(0.33, "green");
        gradient2.addColorStop(0.33, "white");
        gradient2.addColorStop(0.66, "white");
        gradient2.addColorStop(0.66, "red");
        context.fillStyle = gradient2;
        context.fillRect(110,0,50,200); //--> changed

        var gradient3 = context.createLinearGradient(220,0,220,75);
        gradient3.addColorStop(0.33, "green");
        gradient3.addColorStop(0.33, "white");
        gradient3.addColorStop(0.66, "white");
        gradient3.addColorStop(0.66, "red");
        context.fillStyle = gradient3;
        context.fillRect(220,0,50,200); //--> changed
}

demo8();
```

When we change just the context.fillRect() arguments to match this, but leave the context.createLinearGra arguments alone, a revealing fact about fill styles is given to us.

The following screenshot shows this change:

Testing Gradient Options

Thus, if a gradient shows as only one color, make sure to check the gradient's coordinates!

Mixing With jQuery

So far, we have addressed how to draw with Canvas. However, there is another half to this book that we have yet to add to this chapter: jQuery! Ideally, we want to make modular and reusable systems so that we create a "tackle-once-apply-everywhere" type of project.

Let's start with the lowest-hanging fruit: getting the `<canvas>`'s 2d context.

```
$.getCanvasContext = function(selector){
    var canvas = $(selector);
    var context = canvas.get(0).getContext('2d');
    return context;
}

function demo9(){
    var context = $.getCanvasContext("#jqueryCanvas");
}

$(demo9);
```

The previous code uses `$.getCanvasContext()` to grab our canvas from the page. However, we can still simplify this a little more, as we may not always want to specify the `id` or `class` for the canvas to be selected:

```
1   $.getCanvasContext = function(selector){
2       var canvas = $(selector || "canvas");
3       var context = (canvas.length > 0 && canvas.first().is('canvas'))
4           ? canvas.get(0).getContext('2d')
5           : null;
6       return context;
7   }
8
9   function demo9(){
10      var context = $.getCanvasContext();
11  }
12
13  $(demo9);
```

There! Now as we work with `$.getCanvasContext()`, we don't need to worry about the input string, and we will receive `null` if no `<canvas>` objects are found.

Next, there are some typical drawing routines we might be aware of. One such routine might be from previous examples:

1. Styling and filling of rectangles and paths.
2. Drawing bezier curves with detailed information about the inflection points.
3. Drawing shapes and paths, and automatically resizing the gradient fill to fit the dimensions.

Each of these routines might combine to make a larger, modular system. One particularly usefuly application is drawing graphs. Graphs are fantastic for communicating a significant amount of data and relations between datum. In fact, you may have seen some of these graphing libraries in the past:

1. Raphaël (http://raphaeljs.com/)[3] and gRaphaël (http://g.raphaeljs.com/)[4]
2. D3.js (http://d3js.org/)[5]
3. Goo.js (http://www.storminthecastle.com/projects/goo.js/)[6]

Graphing, while seemingly simple to deliver, will still need some "nice-to-have" features. Most importantly, the graph should be able to fit into different screen sizes well, so that this graph can be utilized in mutliple devices and presentational formats.

Let's get started with creating a `<canvas>` element that dynamically fits its container. We can do this by reading in the `width()` and `height()` properties of its container, and listening to `resize` events.

---

[3]http://raphaeljs.com/
[4]http://g.raphaeljs.com/
[5]http://d3js.org/
[6]http://www.storminthecastle.com/projects/goo.js/

```javascript
$.graphDefaults = {
        data: null,
        canvas: null
}

$.fn.graph = function(options){
        options = $.extend({}, $.graphDefaults, options);

        var canvas = this.filter(function(i, el){
                return el.tagName==='CANVAS';
        });

        var self = this,
                width = this.width(),
                height = this.height();

        if(canvas.length === 0){
                canvas = $('<canvas></canvas>').attr({width:width, height:height});
                $('body').append(canvas);
        } else {
                canvas = canvas.get(0);
        }

        var context = $.getCanvasContext(canvas);

        context.fillStyle = "#efefef";
        context.fillRect(0,0,width,height);

        $(window).on('resize', function(){
                var width = self.width(),
                        height = self.height();
                canvas.attr({width:width, height:height});
        });
}

function demo10(){
        var context = $.getCanvasContext();
        $('body').graph();
}

$(demo10);
```

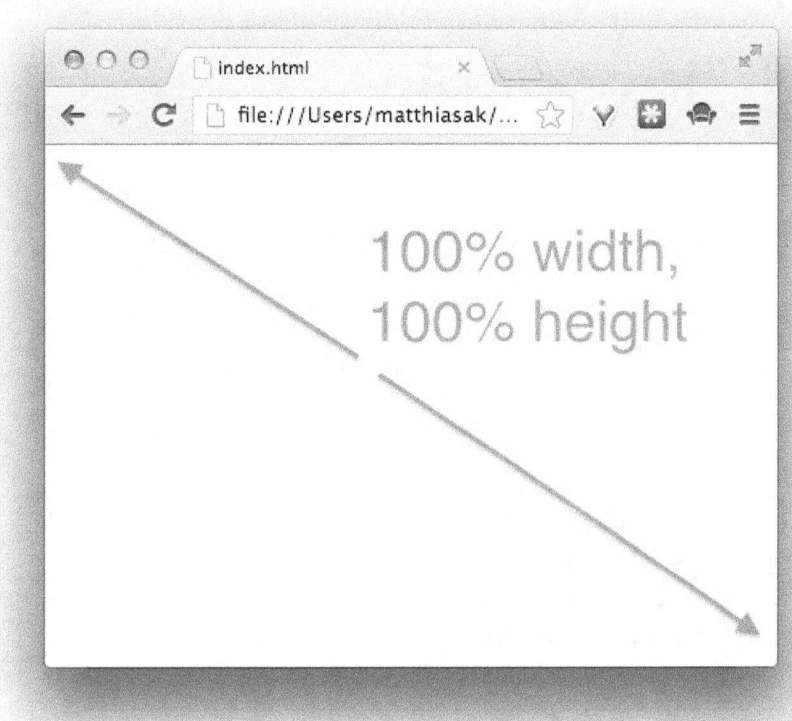

Scaling the canvas.

This creates a fullscreen canvas object. The catch is that `<canvas>` can have two different contexts for the `width` and `height` properties:

1. The layout focused properties which define the size the `<canvas>` in the DOM (e.g. `800px` or `100%`)
2. The Canvas 2d context properties which defines the dimensions of the paint area within the `<canvas>`

If we were to create a `<canvas>` with CSS based properties at `100%` (full height and width to fill the parent), but set the paint dimensions to be 300x300, then the `<canvas>` would scale to the size of the container, however the drawing itself would be pixelated. If we skip setting any layout properties for the `<canvas>`, then the `width` and `height` layout values will default to the same properties as the `width` and `height` paint canvas properties.

Now that we have a `<canvas>` that scales, we need:

1. Data to interpret, for use with a graph
2. Functions to draw graph data on our blank `<canvas>`

First, let's set up some data to present. As a random example, let's graph the number of cups of coffee that we consumed over the past seven days:

```
1  function demo11(){
2      var cupsOfCoffeeDrank = [10, 5, 3, 1, 8, 3, 2];
3      var context = $.getCanvasContext();
4      $('body').graph({data: cupsOfCoffeeDrank});
5  }
```

This will be our jumping-off point to interpreting data in the jQuery plugin:

```
1   $.fn.graph = function(options){
2       options = $.extend({}, $.graphDefaults, options);
3
4       ...
5
6       $(window).on('resize', function(){
7           width = self.width();
8           height = self.height();
9           canvas.attr({width:width, height:height});
10          draw();
11      });
12
13      function draw(){
14          // draw background
15          context.fillStyle = "#efefef";
16          context.fillRect(0,0,width,height);
17
18          //draw data
19          context.fillStyle = "red";
20          for(var i=0; i<options.data.length; i++) {
21              var cupsOfCoffee = options.data[i];
22              context.fillRect(25 + i*100, 30, 50, cupsOfCoffee*5);
23          }
24      }
25
26      draw();
27  }
```

The previous code produces the following screenshot:

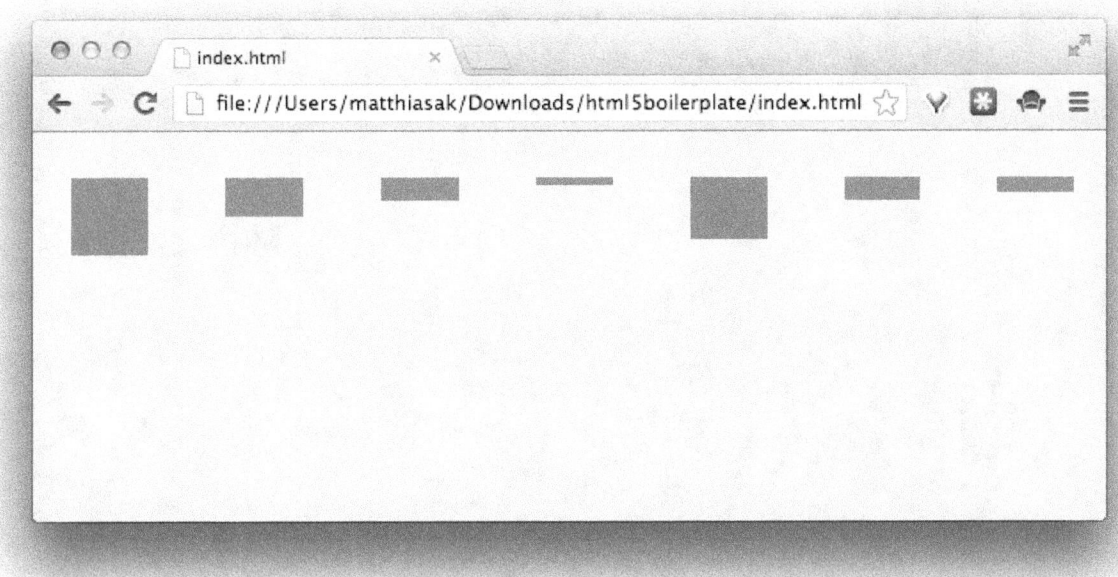

Upside down graph.

Unfortunately, if we resize the window to a smaller size, the graph doesn't fit!

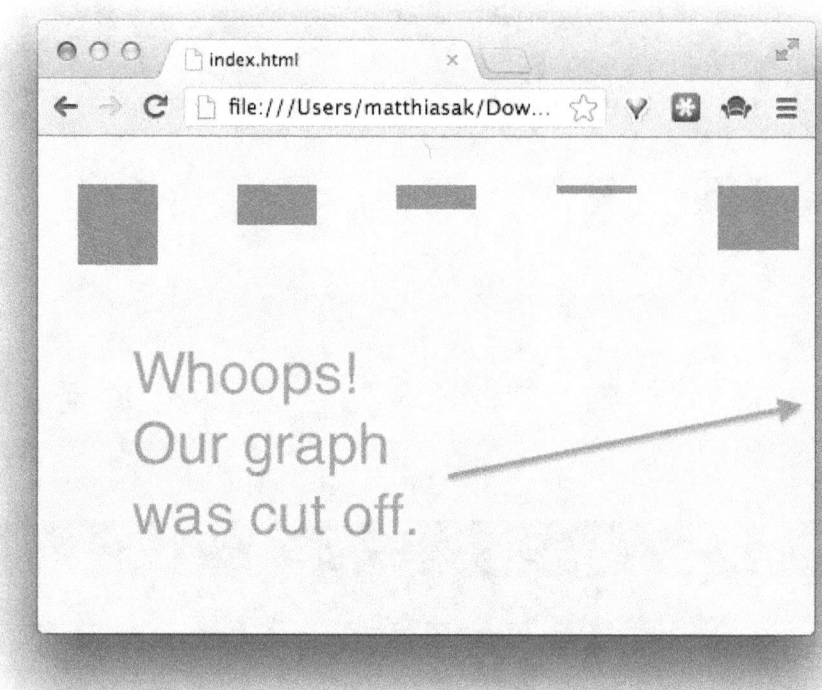

Upside down graph which doesn't scale with the browser.

The next step is to make the bar graph more aware of the width of the <canvas>. We can modify the draw function to set the widths and heights of the bar graph columns relative to those of the Canvas drawing dimensions.

```
function draw(){
    // draw background
    context.fillStyle = "#efefef";
    context.fillRect(0,0,width,height);

    var vertical_padding = height*.1,
        horizontal_padding = width*.1,
        vertical_px = height*(1-(.1)*2),
        horizontal_px = width*(1-(.1)*2),
        maxCupsOfCoffee = 0,
        cups = options.data;

    for(var i = 0; i < cups.length; i++){
        maxCupsOfCoffee = maxCupsOfCoffee > cups[i] ? maxCupsOfCoffee : cups[i];
    }

```

```
17          var vertical_steps = vertical_px / maxCupsOfCoffee;
18          var horizontal_steps = horizontal_px / cups.length;
19
20          //draw data
21          context.fillStyle = "red";
22          for(var i=0; i<options.data.length; i++) {
23                  var cupsOfCoffee = options.data[i];
24                  context.fillRect(
25                          horizontal_padding + i*horizontal_steps,
26                          vertical_padding,
27                          horizontal_padding,
28                          cupsOfCoffee*vertical_steps
29                  );
30          }
31  }
```

The previous code produces the following screenshots (at different browser window sizes).

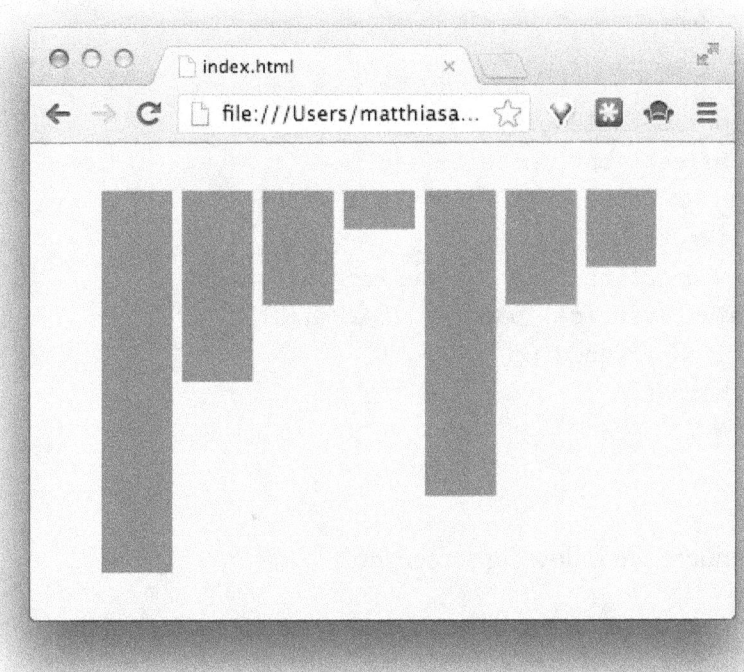

Now, since we have built a scaling graph, it might make sense to get the graph to properly show the data in the graphy by drawing the bars as increasing towards the top of the screen, instead of the bottom.

We can do this by setting each bar's Y offset equal to the difference of the drawable area' height and the height of the bar itself.

```
for(var i=0; i<options.data.length; i++) {
        var cupsOfCoffee = options.data[i];
        var barHeight = cupsOfCoffee*vertical_steps;
        context.fillRect(
                horizontal_padding + i*horizontal_steps,
                (height-vertical_padding)-barHeight,
                horizontal_padding,
                barHeight
        );
}
```

The previous code produces the following screenshot.

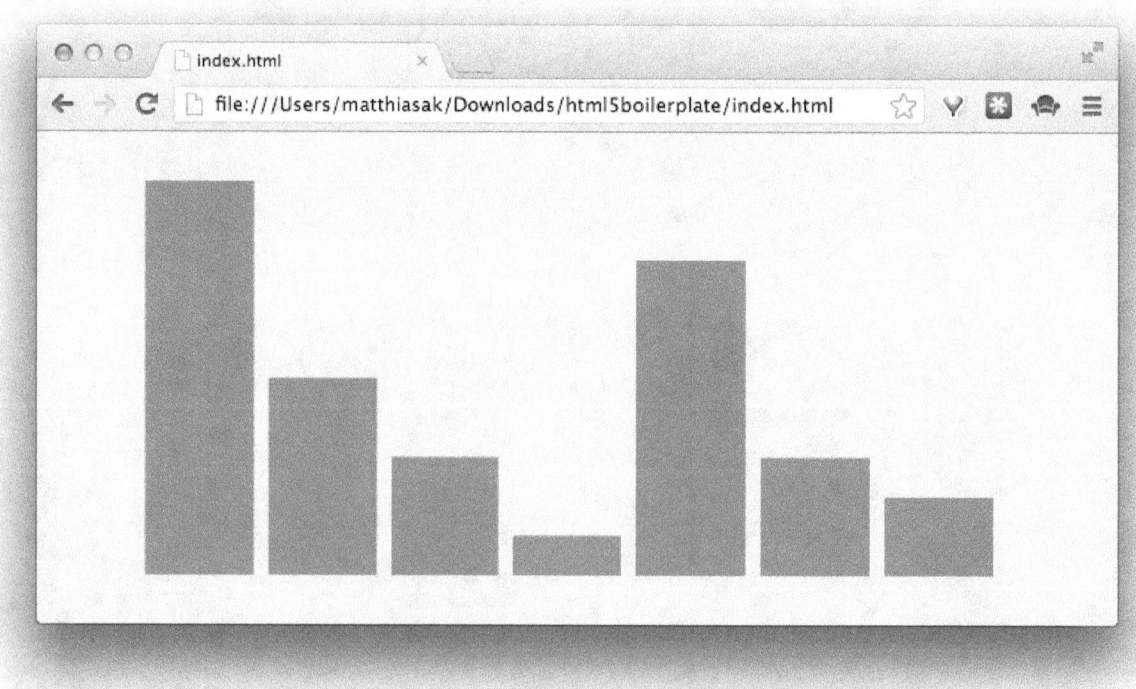

A right-side-up graph that scales!

Unfortunately, without real explanation of the data we can't really understand what is going on with this graph. Thus, the next step is to add some axis lines and information that helps us interpret the data being displayed.

So, let's first draw our axis lines.

```
 1  var padding = 10
 2        , topY = vertical_padding - padding
 3        , leftX = horizontal_padding - padding
 4        , bottomY = (height-vertical_padding)+padding
 5        , rightX = (width-horizontal_padding)+padding;
 6  
 7  context.fillStyle = "black";
 8  context.lineWidth = 2.0;
 9  context.beginPath();
10  context.moveTo(leftX, topY);
11  context.lineTo(leftX, bottomY);
12  context.lineTo(rightX, bottomY);
13  context.stroke();
```

The previous code produces the following screenshot – a nicely padded graph with the axis bars.

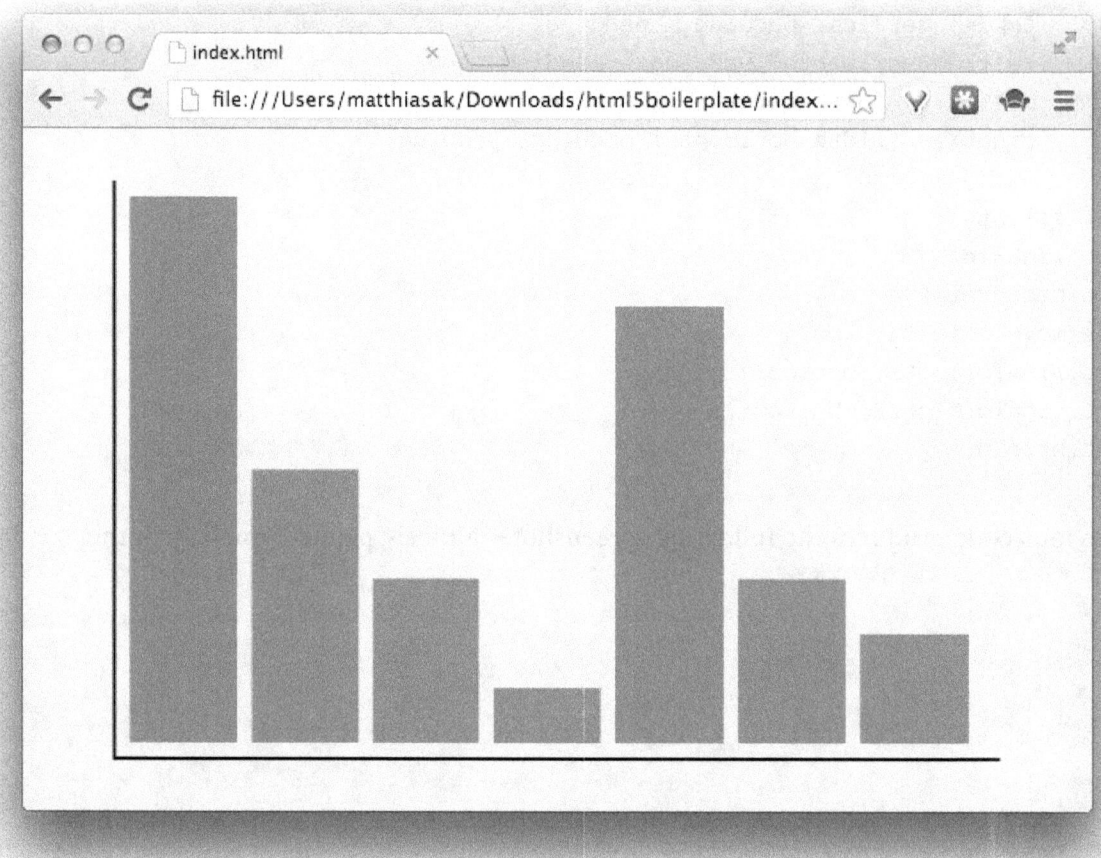

This graph has the X and Y axis drawn.

Next, we should add some text and lines at each interval to understand what the height of the bars actually mean.

```
context.textAlign = 'right';
for(var i = 0; i < maxCupsOfCoffee; i++) {
    context.fillText( (maxCupsOfCoffee - i) + "", leftX-12, i*vertical_steps + ve\
rtical_padding + 3);
    context.beginPath();
    context.moveTo(horizontal_padding-20,i*vertical_steps + vertical_padding);
    context.lineTo(horizontal_padding-10,i*vertical_steps + vertical_padding);
    context.stroke();
}
```

The previous code produces the following screenshot.

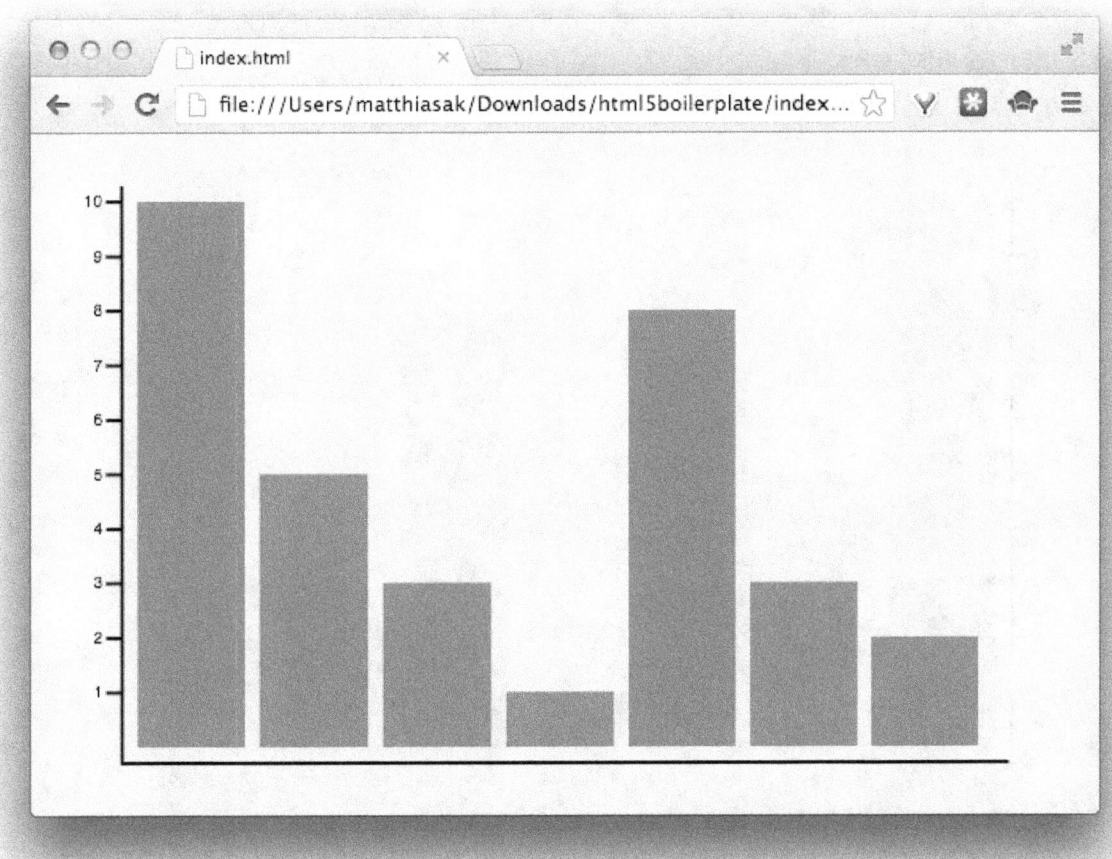

The graph now has ticks along the Y axis.

The graphing functionality is nearly complete. Next, let's finish by adding some labels to each bar, so that we can understand what each bar represents.

```
context.textAlign = 'center';
var labels = ["1 day ago","2 days ago","3 days ago","4 days ago","5 days ago","6 \
days ago","7 days ago"];
for(var i=0; i<labels.length; i++) {
        context.fillText(labels[i], horizontal_padding + i*horizontal_steps + horizontal\
_padding/2, bottomY+12);
}
```

Now that we have more contextual data in the graph, a fresh pair of eyes can interpret the data more meaningfully.

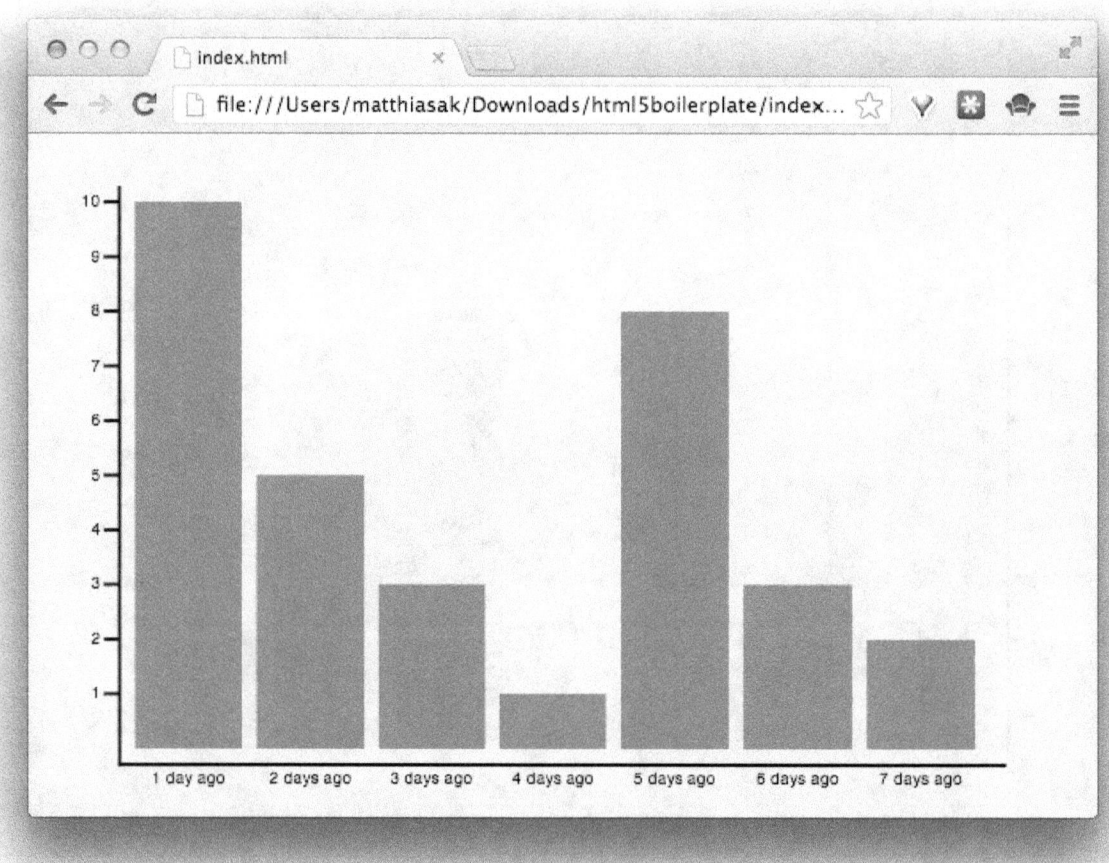

The graph now has labels along the X axis.

Summary

In this chapter, we conquered the HTML5 Canvas API, learned about drawing basics, the coordinate system, the "statefulness" of the Canvas 2d Context, how to draw paths and gradients, the uses of bezier curves, and how to integrate jQuery and Canvas.

We also learnt how to scale `<canvas>` objects and calculate offsets and scaling for variable sized screens.

We also built a jQuery plugin that can interpret arbitrary data, print a graph, and scale the graph to fit the container that is provided within on an HTML page.

Furthermore, we covered some outlandish Canvas code which interprets arbitrary data as input and creates a graph from it, and immersed ourselves in the minutiae of drawing a visually pleasing and elegant graph in detail.

In the next chapter, we will step into the foray of graphically-intensive three-dimensional web applications by introducing ourselves to WebGL. So grab some coffee and your time machine, because we're headed to the future!

10 WebGL

In Chapter 9 - HTML5 Canvas - we wrote a sample graphing application API which could take arbitrary data and draw it on a two-dimensional bar graph. In our particular case, we handled the paths, vertices, and fill colors of Canvas in our own code.

Much in the same light, the Web Graphics Library (WebGL) contains browser-optimized code which draws series of points and paths to the screen. More importantly, WebGL provides us with GPU accelerated functions which can be used in process-intensive calculations such as physics equations, image processing and effects, compositing, shading, and three-dimensional projections.

Moreover, WebGL is not a separate presentation layer. The API is simply meant to provide a "graphics highway" between the javascript APIs we have already discussed in this book and the GPU of a user's computer.

WebGL began as a three-dimensional demo to be used with HTML5 Canvas, and after it became widely adopted, new renderers were created for Canvas, SVG, and a WebGL-specific context. This means that we, as developers, have our choice of front-end rendering technologies, and that WebGL has an opportunity to reach a wider audience on a greater number of platforms.

> Want to run the example code for this chapter? Grab and install the latest version of Node.js[1]. After installing, you can run a simple web server by opening the Chapter 10 code directory and using node to run the server:
>
> `node my/directory/wrinklefree-jquery/ch10/server.js`
>
> Afterwards, simply open a browser to `localhost:8888`.

Examples

All examples for this chapter can be reached on the book's website. A simple HTTP web server is provided as a Node.js script to allow the reader to:

1. Not need to write his or her own server
2. Serve files in a Same Origin Policy-compliant manner
3. Allow jumping back and forth between examples easily

---

[1] http://nodejs.org

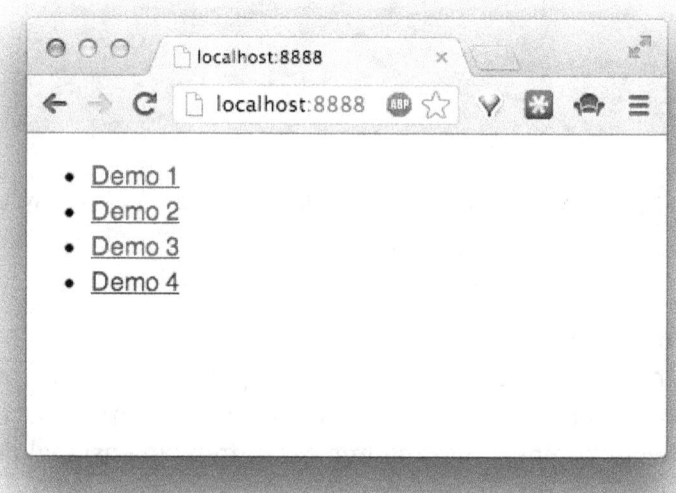

The index of demos for this chapter.

Some other top examples of use of WebGL can be found at these demo sites and project libraries:

1. Three.js (http://threejs.org/)[2]

    The most powerful and popular WebGL library to date - THREE.js - provides a gigantic library of examples and uses for both 3D and 2D WebGL examples.

---
[2]http://threejs.org/

Three.js Example

Three.js Example 2

2. Oz The Great and Powerful (http://www.findyourwaytooz.com/)[3]

    The latest Google Chrome Experiment came about with collaboration from Disney's latest movie. This fantastic and very graphically-demanding application builds on THREE.js.

---
[3]http://www.findyourwaytooz.com/

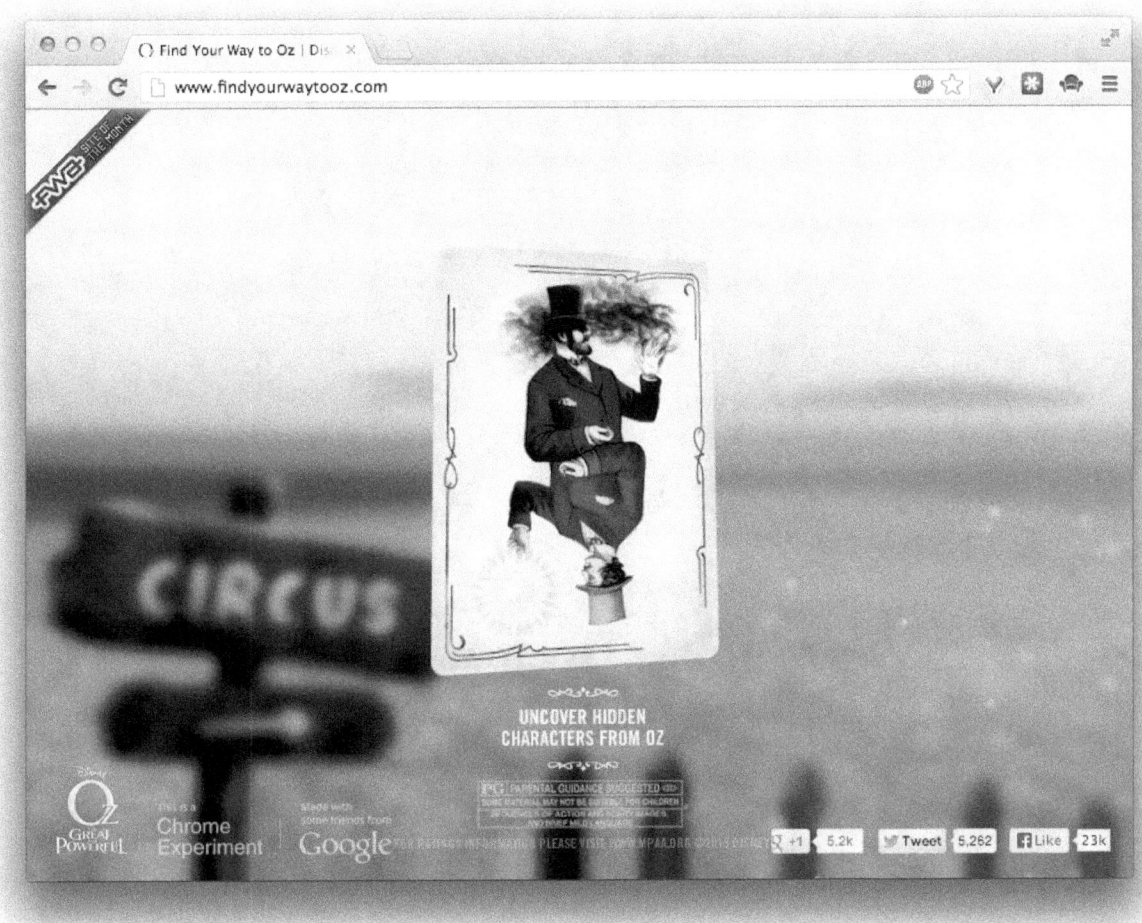

Oz The Great And Powerful

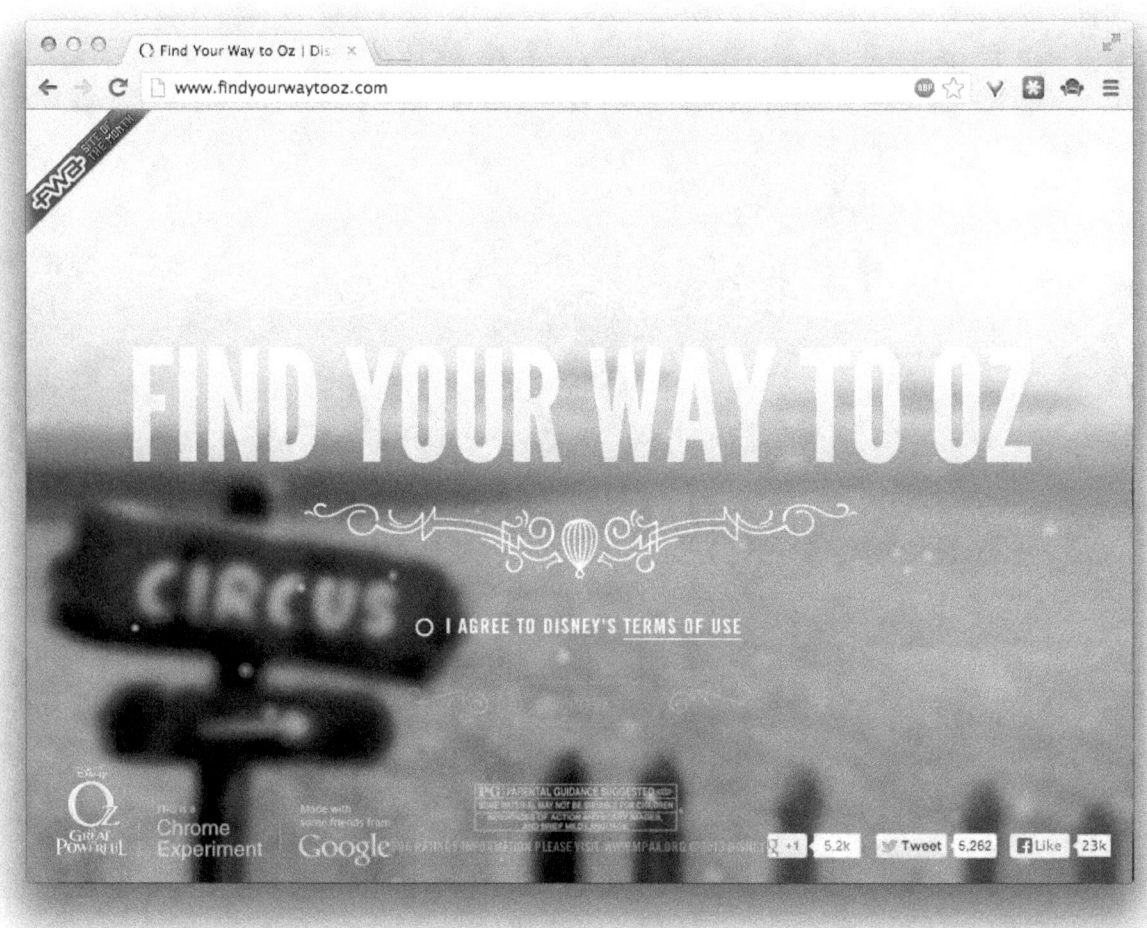

Oz The Great And Powerful 2

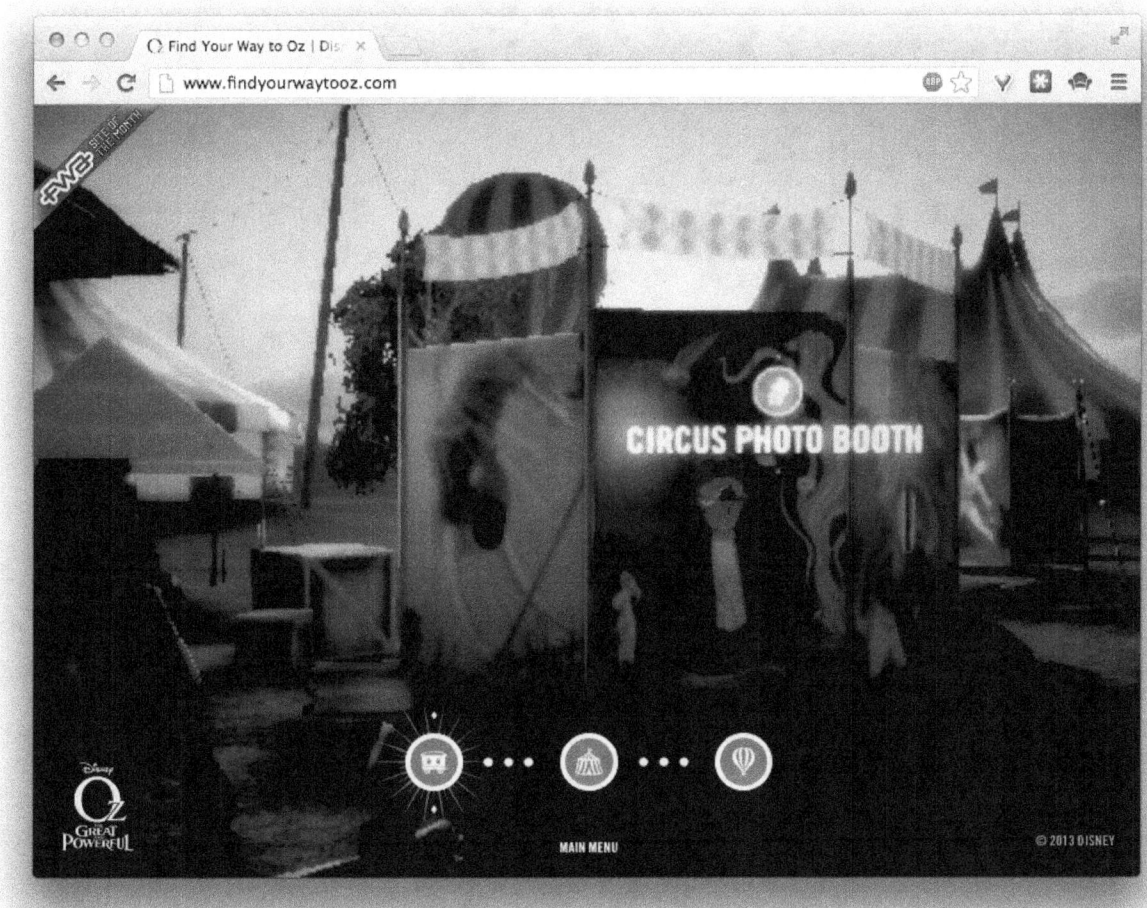

Oz The Great And Powerful 3

3. Voodoo.js (http://www.voodoojs.com/)[4]

    Voodoo.js takes a different approach to using WebGL, and even provides some new approaches to incorporating 2D HTML displays and 3D WebGL presentations where WebGL canvases and standard DOM elements can be mixed.

---

[4]http://www.voodoojs.com/

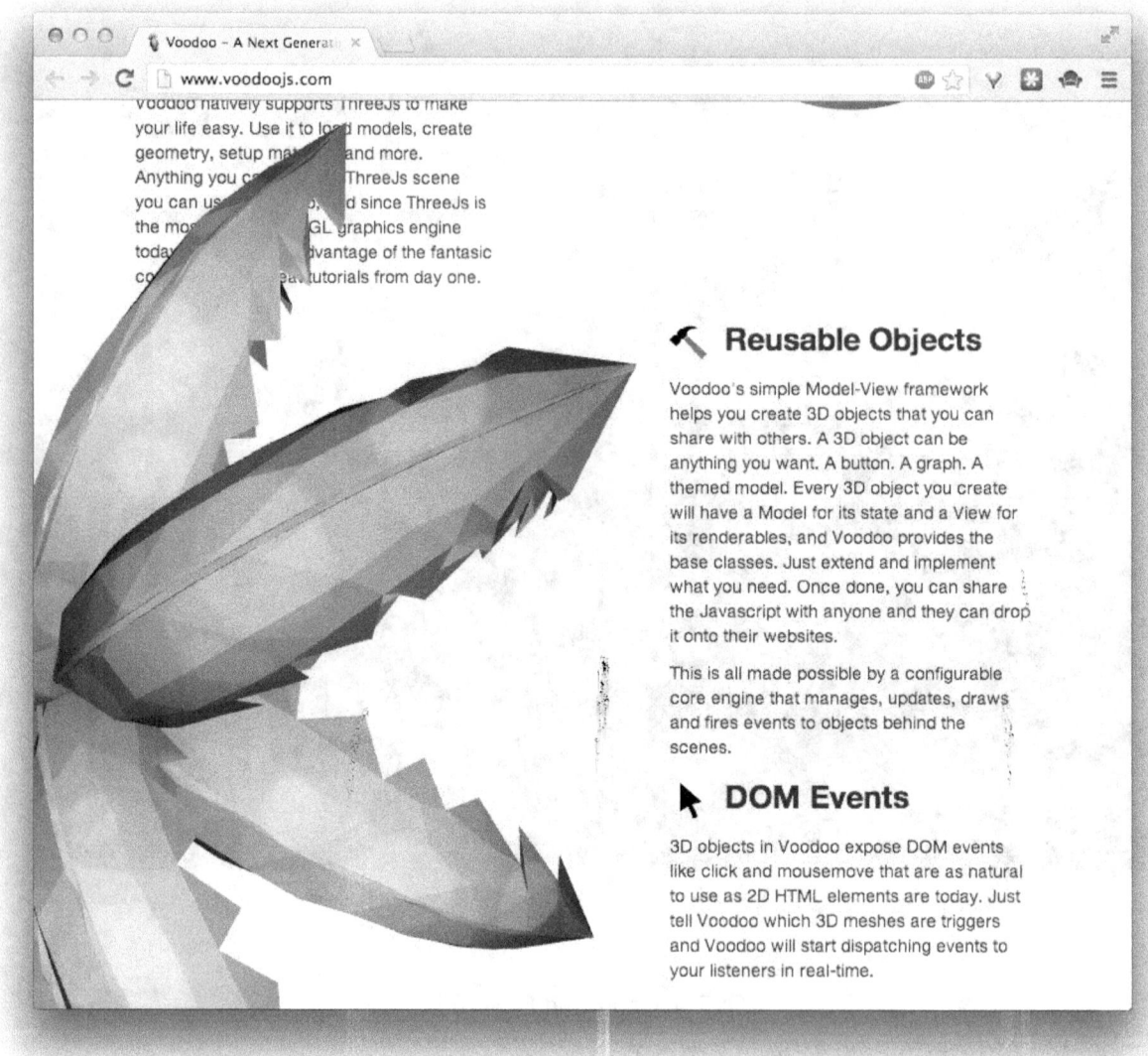

Voodoo.js Example

Which Browsers Currently Support WebGL?

WebGL is supported by these browsers:

1. Internet Explorer 11+
2. Firefox 21+
3. Chrome 26+
4. Safari 5.1+
5. Opera 15+

6. Opera Mobile 12.0+
7. Blackberry Browser 10+
8. Firefox for Android 22+

Get more details at http://caniuse.com/#feat=webgl[5]

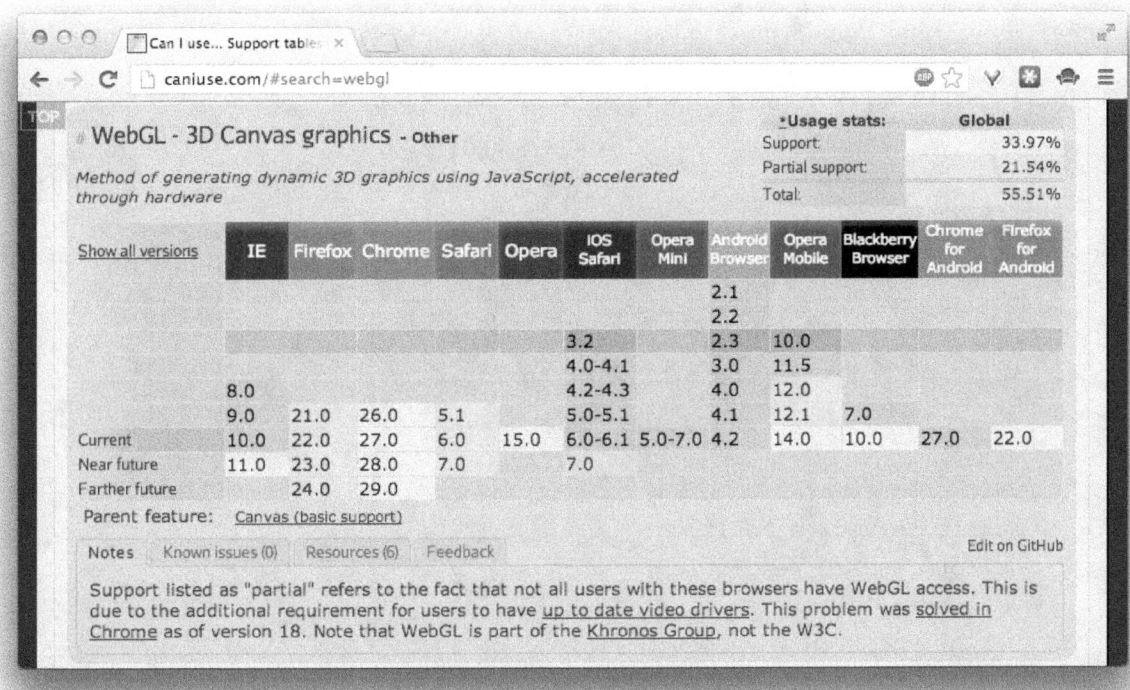

Browser Support for WebGL

WebGL - The Basics

WebGL makes it possible to display amazing realtime 3D graphics in your browser. What many web developers don't realize, however, is that WebGL is a 2D API, and not a 3D API. WebGL only cares about two things:

1. 2D coordinates
2. and colors

Once you provide those two items, WebGL can take care of the rest. To provide 2D coordinates, we supply a vertex shader. To provide colors, we supply a fragment shader.

We will go over these in detail.

---

[5]http://caniuse.com/#feat=webgl

Vanilla WebGL with jQuery and HTML5 Canvas

We mentioned that WebGL started as a 3D layer for HTML5 Canvas. Because of this, we can make use of <canvas> as our first renderer. Here is a simple webpage with a vertex and a fragment shader.

```html
<!DOCTYPE html>
<html>
    <head>
        <meta charset="utf-8">
        <meta http-equiv="X-UA-Compatible" content="IE=edge,chrome=1">
        <meta name="viewport" content="width=device-width">

        <link rel="stylesheet" href="css/normalize.css">
        <link rel="stylesheet" href="css/main.css">

        <script src="../js/webgl-utils.js"></script>
        <script src="../js/jquery.min.js"></script>
    </head>
    <body>
        <script id="2d-vertex-shader" type="x-shader/x-vertex">
            attribute vec2 a_position;
            uniform vec2 u_resolution;
            void main() {
                gl_Position = vec4(a_position, 0, 1);
            }
        </script>

        <script id="2d-fragment-shader" type="x-shader/x-fragment">
            void main() {
                gl_FragColor = vec4(1, .2, .4, 1);
            }
        </script>

        <script src="./ch10.js"></script>
    </body>
</html>
```

Before we discuss the ./ch10.js JavaScript (the basic renderer code), let's take note of a few things from this page.

First, we are loading ../js/webgl-utils.js, which provides us with some basic JavaScript functions, one in particular which will provide us with some code to load the shader scripts. Feel free to browse that code and have a look, as it gives us a lot of code that we won't have to implement ourselves (just as jQuery does).

Notice the `x-shader/x-vertex` script? This creates a vertex shader, which encapsulates some OpenGL Shading Language code (or GLSL for short). In a nutshell, WebGL will pass this vertex shader each of our vertices (2D coordinates), which will then be passed to the GPU and manipulated. It is up to the vertex shader's developer what the shader does with each vertex received. Every vertex shader, however, must fulfill one requirement, which is setting `gl_Position` (a 4D float vector) to represent a 2D position on the screen. We will cover the library `Three.js` later, which will help us translate 3D coordinates to 2D coordinates.

Next, we have the `x-shader/x-fragment` script, which represents a fragment shader. When we have an object with each of its vertices, the vertex shader will position those vertices for us on the 2D screen coordinate grid. After this, these pixels are passed to the fragment shader, which manipulates the colors, lighting, and textures that are dean to the screen. Moreover, just like the vertex shader has a single requirement, so does the fragment shader. The fragment shader must set the `gl_FragColor` to a 4D float vector, which represents the final color of a fragment. So what is a fragment? A fragment happens to be the data provided by a group of vertices for the purpose of drawing each pixel in that group. These will make more sense as we get into the example code.

What Does `x-shader/x-vertex` and `x-shader/x-fragment` Mean?

By default, `<script>` tags under HTML5 automatically parse and execute as JavaScript files. Putting any of these `<script>` types, the browser will parse that tag as JavaScript:

1. `<script>`
2. `<script type="javascript">`
3. `<script type="text/javascript">`

Anything other than these will be ignored by the browser. Thus, by setting a script type for vertex and fragment shaders, we can make sure that the encapsulated GLSL does not get interpreted as JavaScript. Moreover, we use this to store shaders in script tags.

In our case, we will use a function provided called `createShaderFromScriptElement()`, which will find a script with the specified `id` and then looks at the type attribute of that script to determine what type of shader to initialize it as.

Reusing jQuery from Chapter 9

Remember how we created some jQuery plugins to provide us with a 2D Canvas context in Chapter 9? The 2D context renderer is provided by the browser to provide us with a drawing API that can interpret and draw 2D coordinates. This time, however, we want to use a WebGL renderer that is granted access from supported browsers to the GPU. Let's repurpose that code to provide us with the shiny new WebGL context instead.

```
1  $.getCanvasWebGLContext = function(selector){
2      var canvas = $(selector || "canvas");
3      var context = (canvas.length > 0 && canvas.first().is('canvas'))
4              ? canvas.get(0).getContext('experimental-webgl')
5              : null;
6      return context;
7  }
```

The first thing we should notice is that we still are using HTML5 Canvas. Hopefully by now we are feeling more confident with this technology after working with Chapter 9 on the 2D Canvas drawing examples.

In Chapter 9 we also created a jQuery plugin that can monitor and resize our <canvas> to fit its container element. Let's modify that to make use of WebGL instead.

```
1  $.webglDefaults = {
2      draw: function(){}
3      , init: function(){}
4  };
5
6  $.fn.webgl = function(options){
7      options = $.extend({}, $.webglDefaults, options);
8
9      var canvas = this.filter(function(i, el){
10         return el.tagName==='CANVAS';
11     });
12
13     var self = this,
14         width = this.width(),
15         height = this.height();
16
17     if(canvas.length === 0){
18         canvas = $('<canvas></canvas>').attr({width:width, height:height});
19         $('body').append(canvas);
20     } else {
21         canvas = canvas.get(0);
22     }
23
24     var context = $.getCanvasWebGLContext(canvas);
25
26     $(window).on('resize', function(){
27         width = self.width();
28         height = self.height();
```

```
29                canvas.attr({width:width, height:height});
30                options.draw(context, positionLocation);
31            });
32
33            var positionLocation = options.init(context);
34            options.draw(context, positionLocation);
35    }
```

This format should look familiar. We created some defaults with `$.webglDefaults`, and then make use of `$.getCanvasWebGLContext()` to find or create a `<canvas>` element in the HTML. Afterwards, we have two primary functions that will be redefined in our examples: `init()` and `draw()`.

1. `init()` will be used to setup the staging environment and some of the prerequisites for using WebGL.
2. `draw()` will act like it did in Chapter 9, where the staging environment will pass the `context` and a `positionLocation` variable to be used in drawing the scene to the screen.

Now let's quit being so chatty and get something drawn. Here's a basic screenshot of our first WebGL drawing.

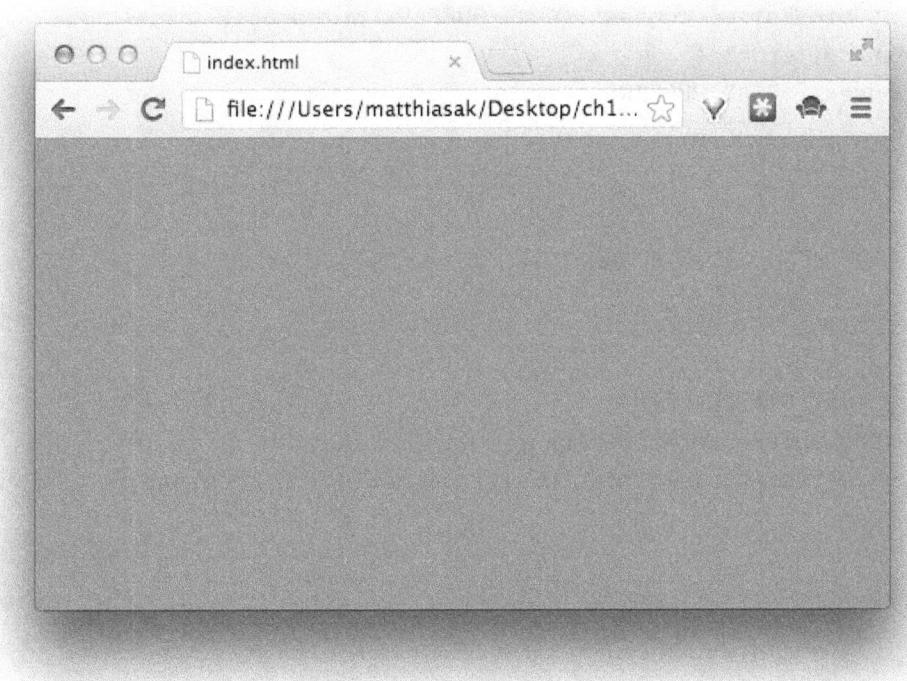

WebGL draws a pink screen.

The previous screenshot was created by the following code. First, we supply the `init()` function.

```javascript
function init(context){
    // setup a GLSL program
    var vertexShader = createShaderFromScriptElement(context, "2d-vertex-shader");
    var fragmentShader = createShaderFromScriptElement(context, "2d-fragment-shader"\
);
    var program = createProgram(context, [vertexShader, fragmentShader]);
    context.useProgram(program);

    // look up where the vertex data needs to go.
    var positionLocation = context.getAttribLocation(program, "a_position");

    return positionLocation;
}
```

Then, we define the `draw()` function.

```javascript
function draw(context, positionLocation){
    // Create a buffer and put a single clipspace rectangle in
    // it (2 triangles)
    var buffer = context.createBuffer();
    context.bindBuffer(context.ARRAY_BUFFER, buffer);
    context.bufferData(
        context.ARRAY_BUFFER,
        new Float32Array([
            -1.0, -1.0,
             1.0, -1.0,
            -1.0,  1.0,
            -1.0,  1.0,
             1.0, -1.0,
             1.0,  1.0]),
        context.STATIC_DRAW);
    context.enableVertexAttribArray(positionLocation);
    context.vertexAttribPointer(positionLocation, 2, context.FLOAT, false, 0, 0);

    // draw
    context.drawArrays(context.TRIANGLES, 0, 6);
}
```

Finally, we pass both the `init()` and `draw()` functions as options to our `$.webgl()` jQuery plugin.

```
1   function demo1(){
2       var options = {
3               init: init
4               , draw: draw
5       }
6
7       $('body').webgl(options);
8   }
9
10  $(demo1);
```

Details

In the `init()` function, we created:

1. The `vertexShader`
2. The `fragmentShader`
3. The `program`

The `program` variable is a product of the WebGL context which manages the shaders and other data, providing access to the GPU pipeline.

The `init()` function also creates `positionLocation`, which acts as a pointer to the information stored under `a_position` in the vertex shader.

When we `draw()` the scene, the context creates a `buffer`, which in this case is an array of 32-bit floating point numbers. These 2D points represent a series of two triangles.

Notice that the coordinates only span from -1.0 to +1.0. This is because the 2D coordinate space in WebGL spans from -1 to +1, no matter what size the rendering context is.

After creating `buffer`, notice that there are only three calls afterwards:

1. `context.enableVertexAttribArray(positionLocation)` - By default, all client-side capabilities under WebGL are disabled, including all generic vertex attribute arrays. If enabled, the values in the generic vertex attribute array will be accessed and used for rendering when calls are made to vertex array commands, such as the drawing function we use: `drawArrays()`.
2. `context.vertexAttribPointer(positionLocation, 2, context.FLOAT, false, 0, 0)` - Defines an array of generic vertex attribute data, which will now be accessible to the WebGL program. The parameters are as follows:
   1. `index` Specifies the index of the generic vertex attribute to be modified.
   2. `size` Specifies the number of components per generic vertex attribute. Must be 1, 2, 3, or 4. The initial value is 4 (as in a 4D float vector).

3. `type` Specifies the data type of each component in the array. 4. `normalized` Specifies whether fixed-point data values should be normalized or converted directly as fixed-point values when they are accessed.
4. `stride` Specifies the byte offset between consecutive generic vertex attributes. If stride is 0, the generic vertex attributes are understood to be tightly packed in the array. The initial value is 0.
5. `pointer` Specifies a pointer to the first component of the first generic vertex attribute in the array. The initial value is 0.
3. `context.drawArrays(context.TRIANGLES, 0, 6)` - Specifies what kind of primitives to render, which in this case are triangles. We also tell WebGL to render the points from index 0, ending at (but not drawing) index 6.

In the last call, if we were to change the last index from 6 to 3, then only one triangle from our `Float32Array` would be rendered.

The following screenshot reflects this change: `context.drawArrays(context.TRIANGLES, 0, 3)`.

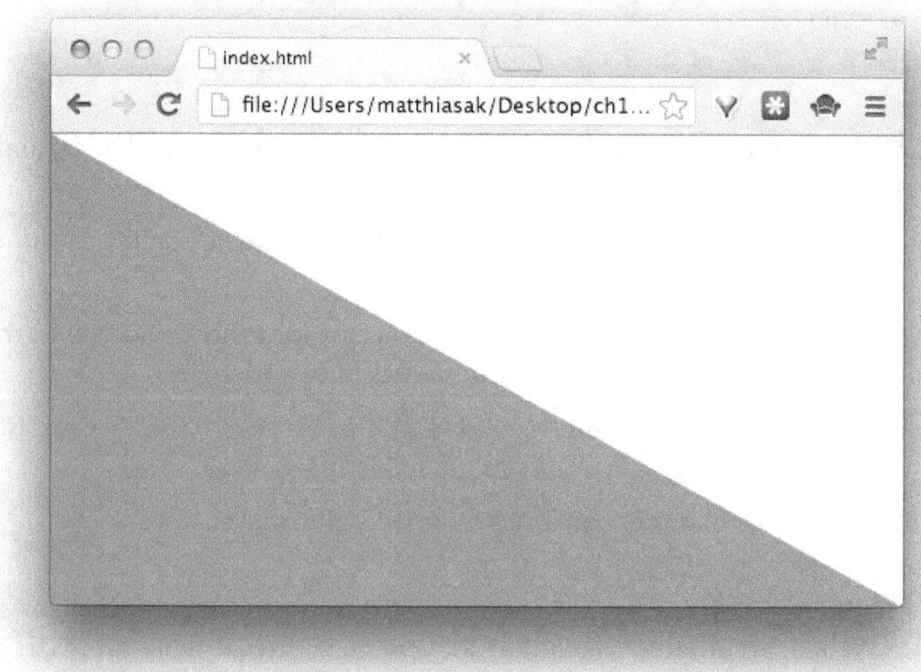

WebGL draws a pink triangle.

Furthermore, notice we are passing in the `Float32Array` as clipspace coordinates, which means that there is no translation from 3D to 2D coordinates. If we want to have some 3D drawings, we need to supply shaders that convert 3D to 2D since WebGL is a 2D API.

Getting out of Clipspace

For 2D drawings, such as the previous example, we may prefer to provide 2D data in terms of pixels, instead of some number between the range of -1.0 to +1.0. We can modify the vertex shader to provide this.

```
<script id="2d-vertex-shader" type="x-shader/x-vertex">
    attribute vec2 a_position;
    uniform vec2 u_resolution;

    void main() {
        // convert the rectangle from pixels to 0.0 to 1.0
        vec2 zeroToOne = a_position / u_resolution;
        // convert from 0->1 to 0->2
        vec2 zeroToTwo = zeroToOne * 2.0;
        // convert from 0->2 to -1->+1 (clipspace)
        vec2 clipSpace = zeroToTwo - 1.0;
        gl_Position = vec4(clipSpace * vec2(1, -1), 0, 1);
    }
</script>
```

This new vertex shader, instead of taking in data from -1.0 to +1.0, will receive data in pixels. We will pass in the u_resolution of the canvas, which will be sized to the browser in pixels.

Unfortunately, the shader still has to provide a vector in clipspace relation. Thus, for each of the vertices we can convert the pixel coordinate (X,Y) provided to the relative percentages of the <canvas> element's width and height:

```
vec2 zeroToOne = a_position / u_resolution;
```

Then, we translate this to a -1.0 to +1.0 scale by scaling the coordinates by 2x in both directions to 0.0 to +2.0 before translating back -1.0 in each direction. Once this is done, we can finish converting the coordinates to -1.0 to +1.0:

```
vec2 zeroToTwo = zeroToOne * 2.0;
vec2 clipSpace = zeroToTwo - 1.0;
```

The final gl_Position looks like:

```
gl_Position = vec4(clipSpace * vec2(1, -1), 0, 1);
```

Here is the screenshot of the above code:

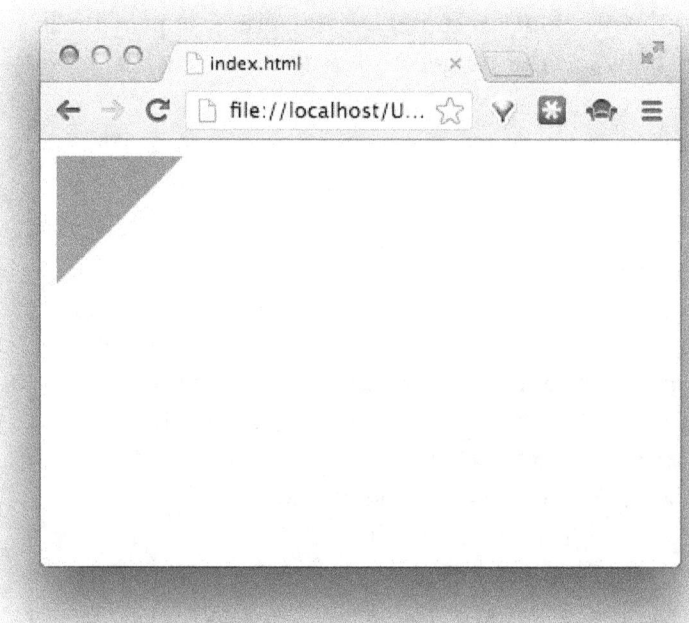

Drawing via coordinates, not clipspace.

One neat thing to note about the WebGL rendering context versus the 2D context discussed in Chapter 9 is that the origin actually starts from the bottom left of the `<canvas>`, instead of the top left.

In the previous line of code, we multiplied the `clipSpace` vec2 by another: `vec2(1, -1)`. This in fact served to flip the coordinates upside down, in order to demonstrate how the coordinates would work in the context of the 2D renderer instead of the WebGL renderer.

By removing the product of `vec2(1, -1)`, we can set the origin of the canvas to start at the bottom-left.

```
1  gl_Position = vec4(clipSpace, 0, 1);
```

This produces the following screenshot.

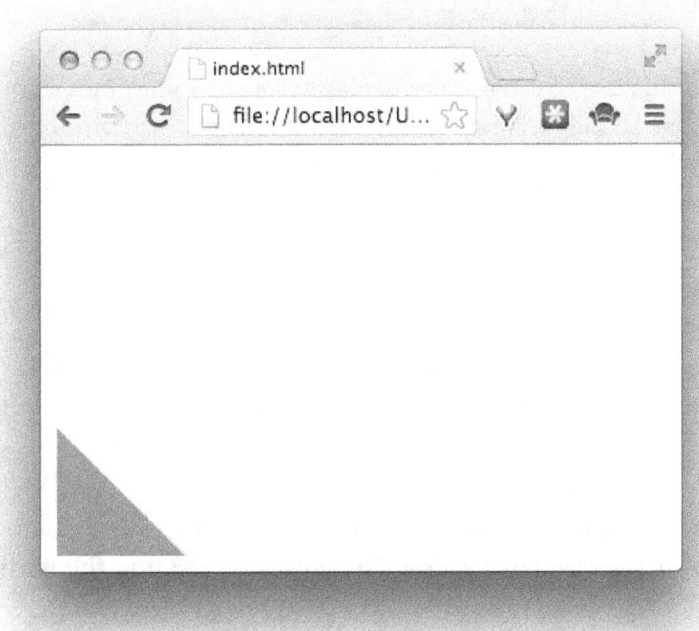

Drawing from the actual origin - the bottom left.

Last but not least, to provide pixels instead of clipspace coordinates, we should probably supply some actual pixels for the data (included in the previous screenshots already) by modifying our draw( ) function:

```
function draw(context, sharedVars){
    var buffer = context.createBuffer();
    context.bindBuffer(context.ARRAY_BUFFER, buffer);
    context.bufferData(
        context.ARRAY_BUFFER
        , new Float32Array([10, 10, 90, 10, 10, 90])
        , context.STATIC_DRAW
    );

    context.enableVertexAttribArray(null);
    context.vertexAttribPointer(null, 2, context.FLOAT, false, 0, 0);

    // draw
    context.drawArrays(context.TRIANGLES, 0, 3);
}
```

This code creates a triangle with points at (10,10), (90,10), and (10,90).

Setting Variables in the Shaders

One might have noticed this use of `uniform` to declare or access variables within the JavaScript that sets up the WebGL, and the shader scripts themselves. These `uniform` variables are shared, accessible variables that can be retrieved and updated from JavaScript. In the previous example code, we wrote a line that sets the `u_resolution` variable as a 2D float vector, and fills it with the width and height of our `<canvas>` element.

```
// set the resolution
var resolutionLocation = context.getUniformLocation(program, "u_resolution");
context.uniform2f(resolutionLocation, $canvasElement.width(), $canvasElement.heig\
ht());
```

This happens once on `init()`. Thus, the resolution itself stays static, even when we resize the browser. This means that no matter the case, the scaling isn't properly scaling the vertices to their correctly translated locations.

We can fix this by (re)calculating the resolution whenever we resize the browser. To carry this out, we can simply move the calculations from `init()` to `draw()`.

The new `init()` and `draw()` functions will look like the following.

```
function init(context, $canvasElement){
        // setup a GLSL program
        var vertexShader = createShaderFromScriptElement(context, "2d-vertex-shader");
        var fragmentShader = createShaderFromScriptElement(context, "2d-fragment-shader"\
);
        var program = createProgram(context, [vertexShader, fragmentShader]);
        context.useProgram(program);

        return {
                program: program
                , canvas: $canvasElement
        };
}

function draw(context, sharedVars){
        // set the resolution
        var resolutionLocation = context.getUniformLocation(sharedVars.program, "u_resol\
ution");
        context.uniform2f(resolutionLocation, sharedVars.canvas.width(), sharedVars.canv\
as.height());

```

```
22          var buffer = context.createBuffer();
23          context.bindBuffer(context.ARRAY_BUFFER, buffer);
24          context.bufferData(
25              context.ARRAY_BUFFER
26              , new Float32Array([10, 10, 90, 10, 10, 90])
27              , context.STATIC_DRAW
28          );
29
30          context.enableVertexAttribArray(null);
31          context.vertexAttribPointer(null, 2, context.FLOAT, false, 0, 0);
32
33          // draw
34          context.drawArrays(context.TRIANGLES, 0, 3);
35      }
```

Now, whenever we resize the browser, the triangle that we draw takes into account u_resolution, which changes for every resize event object:

```
1  context.uniform2f(resolutionLocation, sharedVars.canvas.width(), sharedVars.canva\
2  s.height());
```

The resulting code creates the following screenshots. The first screenshot is when have not yet resized. The second is when we resized the browser.

Before resizing the browser.

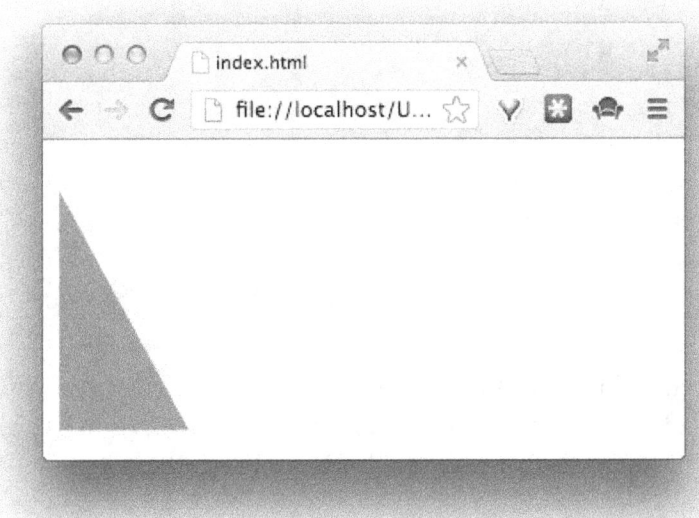

After resizing the browser.

Drawing Images with WebGL

Images in WebGL fall under the blanket term of "textures". Unlike clipspace coordinates, texture coordinates span from 0.0 to +1.0 instead of -1.0 to +1.0.

As in the previous example, we can draw a triangle on the screen. To add a texture, we must specify what coordinates this triangle corresponds to. Remember that the vertex shader handles placement of each vertex on the screen. It's only requirement is to provide a 4D float vector. Furthermore, remember that the fragment shader's only requirement is to return a color in the form of a 4D float vector.

In order to draw the image in the correct location, the place in the texture with which each vertex corresponds to must be supplied. We know this information from the vertex shader. However, the texture is essentially drawn from the fragment shader, not the vertex shader. Thus, we must share the information between the vertex and fragment shaders.

We can share this information with a special type of shader variable called a varying variable. WebGL will then interpolate the values which were supplied in the vertex shader as it draws each pixel using the fragment shader.

Let us add an image to our previous example.

First, we need to modify our jQuery plugin to handle an image's unload event, and call the draw() function afterwards in the callback function. This is because (surprise!) JavaScript is asynchronous.

```
1  $.fn.webgl = function(options){
2      ...
3
4      var sharedVars = options.init(context, canvas, options);
5      sharedVars.image.onload = function(){
6          sharedVars.isReady = true;
7          options.draw(context, sharedVars);
8      };
9  }
```

We can see that the signature of init() has changed, where an extra argument options now exists. This is due to the fact that we may want to specify an image attribute in the options to the jQuery plugin itself. This image attribute will hold the URL to an image file.

```
1  function init(context, $canvasElement, options){
2      // setup a GLSL program
3      var vertexShader = createShaderFromScriptElement(context, "2d-vertex-shader");
4      var fragmentShader = createShaderFromScriptElement(context, "2d-fragment-shader"\
5  );
6      var program = createProgram(context, [vertexShader, fragmentShader]);
7      context.useProgram(program);
8
9      var image = new Image();
10     image.src = options.image;
11
12     return {
13         program: program
14         , canvas: $canvasElement
15         , image: image
16     };
17 }
18
19 ...
20
21 var options = {
22     init: init
23     , draw: draw
24     , image: "../mountains.jpg"
25 }
26
27 $('body').webgl(options);
```

As we can see, the init() function now looks for the options.image, which should represent an image's URL. Note that if this URL does not fit the Same Origin Policy, then some browsers like Google Chrome will throw a security error.

After the init() function is called, the result returned from init() gets passed by the jQuery plugin to the draw() function.

```
function draw(context, sharedVars){
        if(!sharedVars.isReady){ return; }

        // get attributes
        var positionLocation = context.getAttribLocation(sharedVars.program, "a_position\
");
        var textureCoordinatesLocation = context.getAttribLocation(sharedVars.program, "\
a_textureCoordinates");

        // look up where the texture coordinates need to go.
        var textureCoordinatesBuffer = context.createBuffer();
        context.bindBuffer(context.ARRAY_BUFFER, textureCoordinatesBuffer);

        var buffer = context.createBuffer();
        context.bindBuffer(context.ARRAY_BUFFER, buffer);
        context.bufferData(
            context.ARRAY_BUFFER
            , new Float32Array([0, 0, 1, 1, 0, 1])
            , context.STATIC_DRAW
        );
        context.enableVertexAttribArray(textureCoordinatesLocation);
        context.vertexAttribPointer(textureCoordinatesLocation, 2, context.FLOAT, false,\
 0, 0);

        // Create a texture.
        var texture = context.createTexture();
        context.bindTexture(context.TEXTURE_2D, texture);

        // Set the parameters so we can render any size image.
        context.texParameteri(context.TEXTURE_2D, context.TEXTURE_WRAP_S, context.CLAMP_\
TO_EDGE);
        context.texParameteri(context.TEXTURE_2D, context.TEXTURE_WRAP_T, context.CLAMP_\
TO_EDGE);
        context.texParameteri(context.TEXTURE_2D, context.TEXTURE_MIN_FILTER, context.NE\
AREST);
        context.texParameteri(context.TEXTURE_2D, context.TEXTURE_MAG_FILTER, context.NE\
```

```
37          AREST);
38
39          // Upload the image into the texture.
40          context.texImage2D(context.TEXTURE_2D, 0, context.RGBA, context.RGBA, context.UN\
41 SIGNED_BYTE, sharedVars.image);
42
43          // set the resolution
44          var resolutionLocation = context.getUniformLocation(sharedVars.program, "u_resol\
45 ution");
46          context.uniform2f(resolutionLocation, sharedVars.canvas.width(), sharedVars.canv\
47 as.height());
48
49          var buffer = context.createBuffer();
50          context.bindBuffer(context.ARRAY_BUFFER, buffer);
51          context.enableVertexAttribArray(positionLocation);
52          context.vertexAttribPointer(positionLocation, 2, context.FLOAT, false, 0, 0);
53
54          context.bufferData(
55              context.ARRAY_BUFFER
56              , new Float32Array([10, 600, 600, 10, 10, 10])
57              , context.STATIC_DRAW
58          );
59
60          // draw
61          context.drawArrays(context.TRIANGLES, 0, 3);
62      }
```

Due to the fact that we are adding texture data to the screen, there is a lot of new code here. One might first notice the line if(!sharedVars.isReady){ return; }. This code checks for the isReady variable set on the result object returned from the init() function.

Once the image has successfully loaded, then the isReady property will be set to true and the draw function can proceed.

Next, we proceed to get a reference the texture coordinates attribute:

```
1 var textureCoordinatesLocation = context.getAttribLocation(sharedVars.program, "a\
2 _textureCoordinates");
```

Next, we simply need to draw the image as a texture object, and specify the image coordinates. (Which span from 0.0 to +1.0, remember?)

```
1  context.bufferData(
2      context.ARRAY_BUFFER
3      , new Float32Array([0, 0, 1, 1, 0, 1])
4      , context.STATIC_DRAW
5  );
6  ...
7
8  // Create a texture
9  var texture = context.createTexture();
10 context.bindTexture(context.TEXTURE_2D, texture);
11
12 // Set the parameters so we can render any size image.
13 context.texParameteri(context.TEXTURE_2D, context.TEXTURE_WRAP_S, context.CLAMP_T\
14 O_EDGE);
15 context.texParameteri(context.TEXTURE_2D, context.TEXTURE_WRAP_T, context.CLAMP_T\
16 O_EDGE);
17 context.texParameteri(context.TEXTURE_2D, context.TEXTURE_MIN_FILTER, context.NEA\
18 REST);
19 context.texParameteri(context.TEXTURE_2D, context.TEXTURE_MAG_FILTER, context.NEA\
20 REST);
21
22 // Upload the image into the texture.
23 context.texImage2D(context.TEXTURE_2D, 0, context.RGBA, context.RGBA, context.UNS\
24 IGNED_BYTE, sharedVars.image);
```

On the last piece of code here, we manage to apply our image to the texture object, and draw the triangle from the previous example. While this is a lot of steps, there are libraries to help with this. Also, remember again that this is all under two-dimensional coordinates. To have 3D, there are libraries to supply us with simplifying all the work for these graphics.

Our last step is to access the new `varying` and `attribute` variables inside of our shaders.

```
1  <script id="2d-vertex-shader" type="x-shader/x-vertex">
2      attribute vec2 a_position;
3      uniform vec2 u_resolution;
4
5      attribute vec2 a_textureCoordinates;
6      varying vec2 v_textureCoordinates;
7
8      void main() {
9          // convert the rectangle from pixels to 0.0 to 1.0
10         vec2 zeroToOne = a_position / u_resolution;
11         // convert from 0->1 to 0->2
```

```
12                vec2 zeroToTwo = zeroToOne * 2.0;
13                // convert from 0->2 to -1->+1 (clipspace)
14                vec2 clipSpace = zeroToTwo - 1.0;
15                gl_Position = vec4(clipSpace, 0, 1);
16
17                // The GPU will interpolate this value between points behind the scenes
18                // This passes the texture coordinates to the fragment shader
19                v_textureCoordinates = a_textureCoordinates;
20          }
21  </script>
22
23  <script id="2d-fragment-shader" type="x-shader/x-fragment">
24          precision mediump float;
25
26          // our texture
27          uniform sampler2D u_image;
28
29          // the textureCoordinates passed in from the vertex shader
30          varying vec2 v_textureCoordinates;
31
32          void main() {
33                gl_FragColor = texture2D(u_image, v_textureCoordinates);
34          }
35  </script>
```

With these shaders in place, we can print the image to the screen, fit to our triangle (newly resized so that we can see the details).

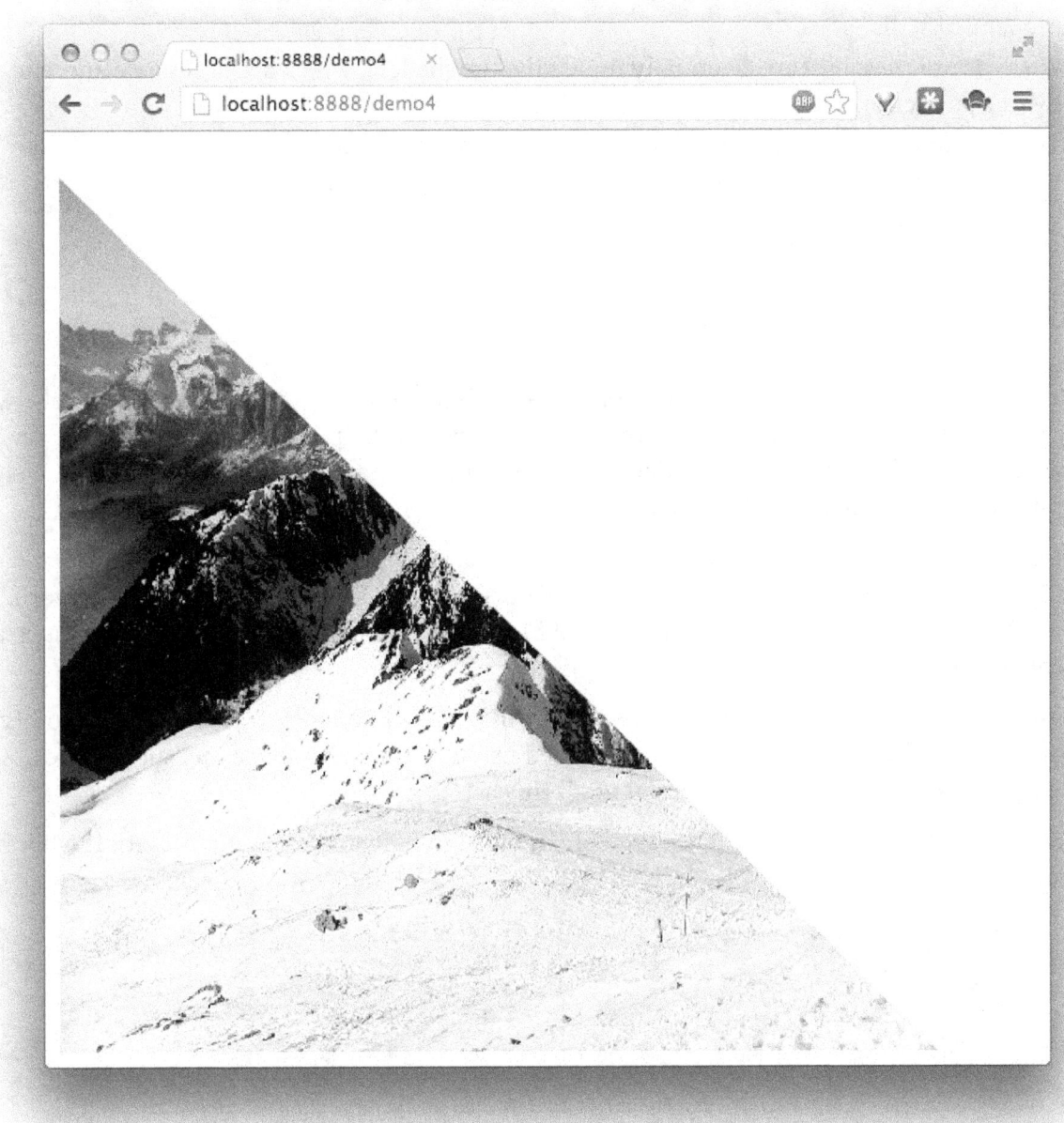

Drawing texture with WebGL

A Final Word on the Variable Types in Shaders

By now, we've seen `attribute`, `uniform`, and `varying` types in our vertex and fragment shaders. What do these variables mean?

1. The `attribute` variables are provided to the shaders by buffers, and in the example code are prepended with `_a`.
2. The `uniform` variables are essentially inputs the the shaders, which are accessible and mutable by our javascript. They are prepended with `u_`.
3. The `varying` variables are values passed from a vertex shader to a fragment shader. They are varied (or interpolated) between the vertices for each pixel drawn. These are prepended with `v_`.

Summary

Unfortunately, there is so much content for WebGL that there are many books that help with this further for the interested developer. This chapter serves to help broaden horizons and general understanding, and finally leave the reader with the position to start working with the basic WebGL API, and even dive further into the details.

In this chapter, we covered what WebGL is, what it is not, the technologies behind it and the general protocol that runs the entire `program`. We also covered details on the types of variables accessible/usable in shaders, some basics of GLSL, and the basic requirements for vertex and fragment shaders.

Furthermore, we looked at lower level detail of drawing, and adding a texture, as well as modifying our jQuery plugin from Chapter 9 - which provided us with some reusable code, such as the ability to scale a `<canvas>` element to fit its parent at all times.

Take this chance to dive further into the WebGL knowledge-base and experiment with the libraries and project out there.

Happy coding!

www.ingramcontent.com/pod-product-compliance
Lightning Source LLC
Chambersburg PA
CBHW080907170526
45158CB00008B/2020